Puerto Rico

Ginger Adams Otis

KT-162-419

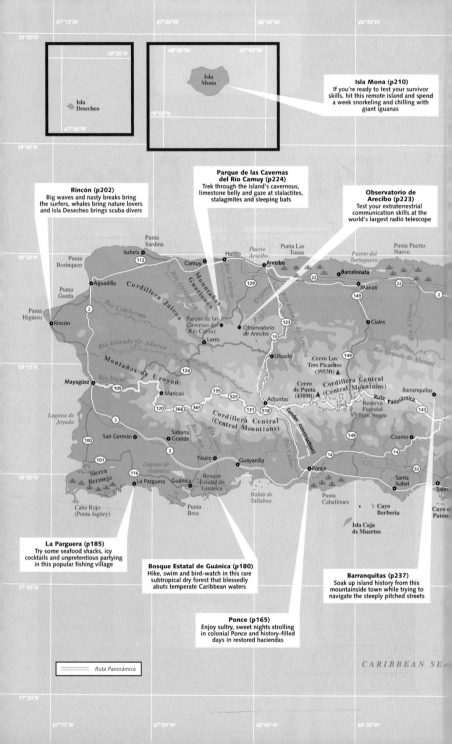

Isla Mona (p210)
If you're ready to test your survivor skills, hit this remote island and spend a week snorkeling and chilling with giant iguanas

Rincón (p202)
Big waves and nasty breaks bring the surfers, whales bring nature lovers and Isla Desecheo brings scuba divers

Parque de las Cavernas del Río Camuy (p224)
Trek through the island's cavernous, limestone belly and gaze at stalactites, stalagmites and sleeping bats

Observatorio de Arecibo (p223)
Test your extraterrestrial communication skills at the world's largest radio telescope

La Parguera (p185)
Try some seafood shacks, icy cocktails and unpretentious partying in this popular fishing village

Bosque Estatal de Guánica (p180)
Hike, swim and bird-watch in this rare subtropical dry forest that blessedly abuts temperate Caribbean waters

Ponce (p165)
Enjoy sultry, sweet nights strolling in colonial Ponce and history-filled days in restored haciendas

Barranquitas (p237)
Soak up island history from this mountainside town while trying to navigate the steeply pitched streets

Ruta Panorámica

CARIBBEAN SEA

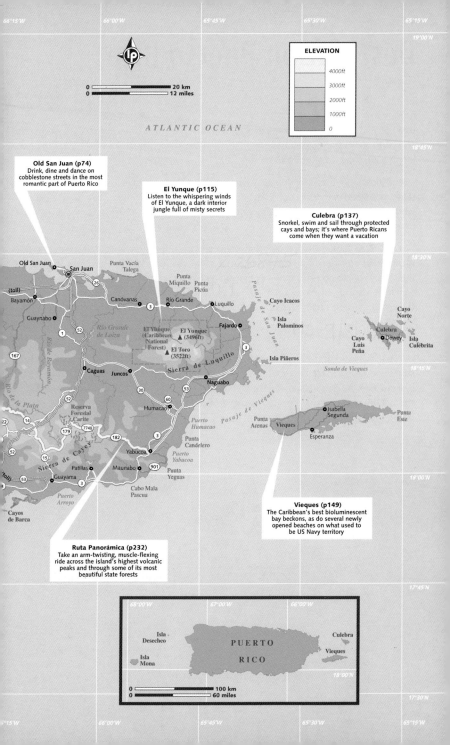

Old San Juan (p74)
Drink, dine and dance on cobblestone streets in the most romantic part of Puerto Rico

El Yunque (p115)
Listen to the whispering winds of El Yunque, a dark interior jungle full of misty secrets

Culebra (p137)
Snorkel, swim and sail through protected cays and bays; it's where Puerto Ricans come when they want a vacation

Vieques (p149)
The Caribbean's best bioluminescent bay beckons, as do several newly opened beaches on what used to be US Navy territory

Ruta Panorámica (p232)
Take an arm-twisting, muscle-flexing ride across the island's highest volcanic peaks and through some of its most beautiful state forests

ELEVATION

4000ft
3000ft
2000ft
1000ft
0

ATLANTIC OCEAN

0   20 km
0   12 miles

Old San Juan
San Juan
Bayamón
(toll)
26
Guaynabo
Canóvanas
3
Río Grande
Luquillo
52
1
Río Grande de Loíza
167
Caguas
Juncos
52
Reserva Forestal Carite
30
60
53
179
7740
Humacao
14
182
22
52
15
Yabucoa
3
Patillas
Maunabo
901
Guayama
53
3
Puerto Arroyo
Cayos de Barca
Cabo Mala Pascua

Punta Vacía Talega
Punta Miquillo
Punta Picúa
El Yunque (Caribbean National Forest)
El Yunque (3496ft)
El Toro (3522ft)
Fajardo
3
Sierra de Luquillo
Naguabo
Puerto Humacao
Punta Candelero
Puerto Yabucoa
Punta Yeguas

Pasaje de San Juan
Cayo Icacos
Isla Palominos
Isla Piñeros
Sonda de Vieques
Pasaje de Vieques
Punta Arenas
Vieques
Esperanza
Isabella Segunda
Punta Este

Cayo Norte
Culebra
Dewey
Isla Culebrita
Cayo Luis Peña

Sierra de Cayey

PUERTO RICO

Isla Desecheo
Isla Mona
Culebra
Vieques

0   100 km
0   60 miles

Destination Puerto Rico

First you feel the heat: searing and densely humid, it presses in on even your lightest clothes. Then the sounds start to penetrate: *bomba*, *plena*, salsa and….are those West African rhythms looping over the beat? You can be sure of it.

And how about that language? A curious hybrid of Caribbean Spanish and American slang, peppered with long-ago words from Yoruba and Taíno cultures, two diverse peoples who mixed intimately when slavery forced them into the sugar fields and gold mines of Latin America.

It's hard to fathom that all of this vibrant energy and history is contained on one tiny island that's small enough to traverse (twice!) in a day. Consider Puerto Rico's myriad options: beachcombing and casino-hopping along Isla Verde, soaking up art and culture in Old San Juan, strolling in Ponce's romantic plaza. For a change of pace, head for the hills and the world's largest radio telescope at Arecibo, or explore Río Camuy's underground caves. There's hiking in nine protected reserves, kayaking in luminescent bays, and world-class diving and snorkeling on Vieques, Culebra and along the western coast.

You'll also quickly see why Puerto Rico is known as America's 51st state: strip malls, chain stores and fast-food restaurants, as well as drug stores, highways and efficient national park systems abound. But if you can take the infrastructure for what it is and look beyond it to the island's great natural beauty – a blend of tangled dark jungle, flat dry plains, steeply curving mountains dropping down to azure seas – you're in for a fabulous time.

Fiesta Time

Variations are endless, but the main ingredient of the Puerto Rican cocktail (p64) is home-grown rum

Elaborate *vejigantes* perform during Carnaval (p171), Ponce

The irresistible beat of Afro-Caribbean fusion (p43) will lighten the heaviest of hearts

Step into the world of *plena* dancing (p45) in San Juan

Life's a Beach

GREG JOHNSTON

Soak up San Juan's sun at
Isla Verde (p85)

OTHER HIGHLIGHTS

- Not as famous as Rincón, but Playa
  Jobos (p219) is the purists' choice for
  fine surf.
- Experience the amazing clarity of Isla
  Desecheo's (p205) underwater
  wonderland at one of the world's best,
  and most little-visited, dive sites.

Opposite page A hedonist's dream
destination: beautiful Boquerón (p193)
PHOTO: GREG JOHNSTON

With the military's departure, the whole of Vieques
(p149) is now open for adventure

STEVE SIMONSEN

For a spot of snorkeling, you can't beat Isla Culebrita (p140), part of the
Culebra National Wildlife Refuge

STEVE SIMONSEN

Old San Juan

ALFREDO MAIQUEZ

Walk the ramparts of El Morro (p74), the New World's oldest Spanish fort

Tropical exuberance on display in Old San Juan (p74)

JERRY ALEXANE

The colorful tones of Old San Juan (p74) reflect its upbeat reincarnation

JOHN NEUBAUER

OTHER HIGHLIGHTS

- Feast on the epicurean delights of SoFo (p82), Old San Juan's vibrant and jam-packed restaurant district.
- Explore the massive Museo de Arte de Puerto Rico (p84), and then cool down in its peaceful sculpture garden.
- Whether it's for a drink, a fine meal or an overnight stay don't miss the elegant Gran Hotel el Convento (p95).

Catch a cooling breeze on the promenade, the Paseo de la Princesa (p78)

JERRY ALEXANDER

ALFREDO MAIQUEZ

The lovingly restored
Catedral de San Juan (p80)

Explore Old San Juan via the city wall (p91)

JOHN ELK III

The red Puerta de San Juan (p75) is one of five orginal gates to the city

JOHN ELK III

Natural Wonders

Culebra is host to some of Puerto Rico's most amazing diving locations (p143)

The lush, rolling hills of the Central Mountains are Puerto Rico's lungs (p231)

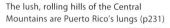

OTHER HIGHLIGHTS

- One of the best examples of rare sub-tropical dry forest is found at Bosque Estatal de Guánica (p180).
- Experience the natural brillance of phosphorescence at Bahía Mosquito (p155) in Vieques.

Take time to rejuvenate amid the lush splendors of El Yunque (p115)

Activities

Vieques boasts some outstanding diving spots (p155)

The most popular of El Yunque's 27 miles of pathways is the Big Tree Trail (p120)

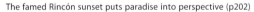

The famed Rincón sunset puts paradise into perspective (p202)

Cultural Gems

JOHN ELK III

Ponce's unique wooden firehouse museum,
Parque de Bombas (p168)

JOHN ELK III

San Juan's austere Fuerte San Cristóbal
(p75), which began construction in 1634

Centro Ceremonial Indígena de Tibes
(p174), an archaeological site near Ponce

JOHN ELK III

Catedral Nuestra Señora de Guadalupe (p168), Ponce
GREG JOHNS

Contents

The Author	**15**
Getting Started	**16**
Itineraries	**19**
Snapshot	**23**
History	**24**
The Culture	**35**
Music & Dance	**43**
Environment	**49**
Puerto Rico Outdoors	**57**
Food & Drink	**62**

San Juan — **69**

History	70
Climate	70
Orientation	70
Information	71
Dangers & Annoyances	74
Sights	74
Beaches	88
Activities	88
Walking Tour	90
San Juan for Children	92
Tours	93
Festivals & Events	93
Sleeping	94
Eating	98
Entertainment	102
Shopping	105
Getting There & Away	106
Getting Around	107
AROUND SAN JUAN	**108**

Piñones	108
Loíza Aldea	110
Cataño & Bayamón	111

East Coast — **113**

El Yunque	115
Luquillo & Around	122
Fajardo & Around	124
Playa Naguabo & Around	131
Yabucoa & Around	133

Culebra & Vieques — **135**

History	136
Climate	136
Dangers & Annoyances	137
Getting There & Away	137
CULEBRA	**137**
History	138
Orientation	139
Information	139
Dangers & Annoyances	140
Sights	140
Beaches	140
Activities	143
Sleeping	144
Eating	146
Entertainment	147
Shopping	147
Getting There & Away	147
Getting Around	148
VIEQUES	**149**
History	149
Orientation	150
Information	150
Sights	151
Beaches	153
Activities	155
Sleeping	156
Eating	159
Entertainment	160
Shopping	161
Getting There & Away	161
Getting Around	161

Ponce & the South Coast — **163**

Ponce	165
Centro Ceremonial Indígena de Tibes	174

Arroyo	175
Guayama	176
Bahía de Jobos	177
Playa Salinas	178
Coamo	179
Bosque Estatal de Guánica	180
Guánica	183
La Parguera	185

West Coast 189

Cabo Rojo	190
El Combate	191
Boquerón	193
Puerto Real	195
Playa de Joyuda	195
San Germán	196
Mayagüez	200
Rincón	202
Isla Mona	210

North Coast 215

Aguadilla	216
Isabela & Around	219
Bosque Estatal de Guajataca	221
Lago Guajataca	222
Arecibo & Around	222
Around Manatí	227
Dorado	229

Central Mountains 231

Reserva Forestal Carite	232
Aibonito & Around	234
Barranquitas	237
Reserva Forestal Toro Negro	238
Adjuntas	241
Bosque Estatal de Guilarte	241
Maricao	242

Directory 244

Transportation 257

Health 264

Language 270

Glossary 277

Behind the Scenes 279

World Time Zones 281

Index 286

Map Legend 292

Regional Map Contents

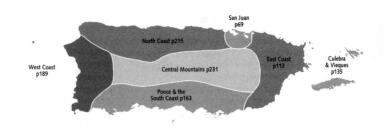

The Author

GINGER ADAMS OTIS

Ginger Adams Otis has reported on Latin American and Caribbean issues since the early 1990s. She covered the 500-year anniversary of Columbus' 'discovery' of the Americas from Old San Juan in 1992, and went to Vieques for the first time in 1999 to report on growing unrest over naval occupation. She returned many times until 2003, when the military pulled out. Ginger is a print and radio reporter, and files for the *Village Voice, Newsday, In These Times*, the BBC, WNYC, Pacifica and other outlets. She is fluent in Spanish, conversational in French and Portuguese, and lives in New York City. She frequently writes about environmental and political issues.

My Puerto Rico

An early morning trip over angry seas brought me to Culebra (p137), where I happily paddled around Playa Brava (p142). Back on the mainland, I got a local fisherman to zip me over to Cayo Santiago (p131) for a little one-on-one with the monkeys. In the distance Ponce (p165) hovered; I arrived just as the local jazz band was warming up in Plaza Las Delicias (p167). A two-hour hike through Guánica (p180) forest left me nearly desiccated, but Rincón's (p202) pristine beaches were only 35 minutes away. To wrap up, inimitable Old San Juan (p74): I ate along Calle Fortaleza (p82), drank along Calle San Sebastián (p103) and doffed my baseball cap to El Pirata Cofresí (p192) on the windy ramparts of El Morro (p74).

CONTRIBUTING AUTHORS

Mario A. Murillo wrote the History chapter. He is an Associate Professor in the School of Communication at Hofstra University in New York, and a veteran journalist and broadcaster. He has reported on Latin America and the Caribbean for a number of media outlets, and his books include *Islands of Resistance: Puerto Rico, Vieques and US Policy*, and *Colombia and the United States: War, Unrest and Destabilization*. He is the host and producer of a morning-drive news and talk show on WBAI 99.5FM, the Pacifica Radio Network's New York City affiliate.

David Goldberg MD wrote the Health chapter. Dr Goldberg completed his training in internal medicine and infectious diseases at Columbia-Presbyterian Medical Center in New York City, where he has also served as voluntary faculty. At present, he is an infectious diseases specialist in Scarsdale NY and the editor-in-chief of the website MDTravelHealth.com.

LONELY PLANET AUTHORS

Why is our travel information the best in the world? It's simple: our authors are independent, dedicated travellers. They don't research using just the Internet or phone, and they don't take freebies in exchange for positive coverage. They travel widely, to all the popular spots and off the beaten track. They personally visit thousands of hotels, restaurants, cafés, bars, galleries, palaces, museums and more – and they take pride in getting all the details right, and telling it how it is. For more, see the authors section on www.lonelyplanet.com.

Getting Started

Whether you want a quick beach getaway or an off-the-beaten track immersion that lasts several weeks, Puerto Rico's got the goods. The beaches of San Juan, Culebra and Vieques are probably the most visited – they are the best known and most easily accessed. You should definitely make reservations in advance if you're planning to visit any of these places during high season, from mid-December through April.

The lack of a real public bus system outside of San Juan makes it hard for budget travelers to get around the island. For anyone who really wants to explore (going into the mountains and around to harder-to-reach areas on the west coast), a rental car is definitely in order. And although culturally speaking Puerto Rico is most assuredly Latin, it's definitely adopted a North American pricing structure – accommodations for people on a truly shoestring budget are practically nonexistent. Puerto Ricans with fewer resources stay with family, while plenty of midrange motels, high-end boutique hotels and chain resorts cater to locals and visitors with deeper pockets.

WHEN TO GO

The Puerto Rican Tourism Company likes to say that temperatures rarely go below 79°F or above 85°F – that's more or less true, but varying degrees of humidity can drastically change how things feel. By mid-May, the heat begins to feel oppressively damp. By July, the hurricane season is moving in.

Hurricane warnings and massive thunderstorms frequently lash the island through the latter summer months. September and October are generally considered the most dangerous time on the island. Roads often wash out, particularly in the mountains, and the ferry service between Vieques and Culebra is often suspended. English-language radio station WOSO San Juan, at 1030AM, will broadcast warnings.

High season runs from early to mid-December through April, while the low season spans June to November. The mountains can be much cooler than the beaches, and nighttime temperatures sometimes dip below 50°F at the higher elevations.

DON'T LEAVE HOME WITHOUT....

Puerto Rico's status as a US commonwealth means travelers will find plenty of well-known stores selling familiar medicines, food and clothing – you could just buy what you need on the island to keep luggage to a minimum. But these essentials should come from home:

- Valid driver's license for Americans or Canadians traveling without a passport and anyone planning to rent a car (p262).
- Proof of citizenship for travelers from Europe, Australia, New Zealand and other countries participating in the Visa Waiver Program (p256).
- Any prescription medicines you need (p268).
- Some kind of bug spray to ward off dengue-carrying mosquitoes (p269).
- An updated tetanus vaccination never hurts (p264).
- Birth control – in some places condoms are hard to find, and getting emergency contraception (the morning-after pill) is impossible without a doctor's prescription (p256).

TOP TENS

Festivals & Events

Puerto Rico celebrates all of the US national holidays in addition to nine of its own. Each town also has a patron saint festival that can last up to 10 days. Mostly Catholic in nature, these festivals often incorporate African and indigenous elements left over from the days when Taíno and Yoruba slaves wove their native rituals into colonial culture.

- Festival San Sebastián, January 20, San Juan (p93)
- Coffee Harvest Festival, February, Maricao (p250)
- Carnaval, February, Ponce (p171)
- José de Diego Day, April 16, nationwide (p250)
- Fiesta Nacional de la Danza, May, Ponce (p171)
- Fiesta de San Juan Bautista Day, June 24, San Juan (p251)
- Festival de Flores, June, Aibonito (p251)
- Fiesta de Santiago, July, Loíza Aldea (p111)
- Hatillo Mask Festival, December 28, Hatillo (p251)
- Festival Casals, dates vary, San Juan (p93)

Must-See Movies

Lots of Hollywood movies use Puerto Rico as a backdrop, but only a few movies have been made that focus on island life specifically. These films will give you a taste of life in Puerto Rico and the immigrant experience.

- *Lo que le pasó a Santiago* (1989) directed by Jacobo Morales (p40)
- *The Blue Diner* (2001) directed by Natatcha Estebanez and Jan Egelson (p40)
- *Piñero* (2001) directed by Leon Ichaso (p40)
- *West Side Story* (1961) directed by Jerome Robbins and Robert Wise (p41)
- *Almost a Woman* (2001) directed by Betty Kaplan (p37)
- *Boricua Béisbol: The Passion of Puerto Rico* (2003; p38)
- *La Guagua Aérea* (1993) directed by Luis Molina (p40)
- *The Puerto Rican Mambo* (1993) directed by Ben Model (p35)
- *Sudor Amargo* (2003) directed by Sonia Valentin (p37)
- *Piñero* (2001) directed by Leon Ichaso (p40)

Top Reads

The following offer great insight into Puerto Rican culture and history.

- *When I Was Puerto Rican* by Esmeralda Santiago (p40)
- *Sataniada* by Alejandro Tapia y Rivera (p39)
- *Puerto Rico, Island in the Sun* by Roger La Brucherie (p42)
- *La llamarada* by Dr Enrique Laguerre (p39)
- *Song of the Simple Truth: The Complete Poems of Julia De Burgos* (p39)
- *Spiks* by Pedro Juan Soto (p40)
- *Puerto Rican Obituary* by Pedro Pietri (p36)
- *The Benevolent Masters* by Enrique A Laguerre (p39)
- *El Gíbaro* by Manuel Alonso (p39)
- *Puerto Rico Mio: Four Decades of Change* by Jack Delano (p42)

COSTS & MONEY

HOW MUCH?

Airport taxi to Old San Juan $20

Average price for day of diving $60

Rental car cost $45

A night in San Juan's best boutique hotel $300

Round-trip ferry to Spanish Virgin Islands $4

Some of the best deals on the island come in a glass during happy hour, when mixed drinks can go as low as $2. Even during normal hours drinks rarely jump above $4 (outside of the pricier places in San Juan, of course). Breakfast and lunch will rarely set you back more than $5 if you eat like the locals – in small bakeries, tavernas and at the *friquitines* (roadside kiosks), which sell salty, deep-fried snacks. Restaurant dinners can range from $8 to $30 and up.

Families will find good bargains at lunchtime – specials range from $5 to $12 (if your children refuse to eat anything but 'familiar' food, there are literally hundreds of fast-food franchises to choose from). In San Juan many museums have discounted rates for children, so always double-check before paying full price for admission.

Inexpensive accommodations are hard to come by. Anything under $75 is in the budget range. In the midrange prices ($80 to $185) you'll find well-recognized chains, government-run paradors and elegant boutique guesthouses, many of which are quite a good deal for the price. For $200 or more a night you can stay in any number of beautiful scenic resorts or designer hotels spread out around the island.

TRAVEL LITERATURE

Lonely Planet's *Diving & Snorkeling Puerto Rico* by Steve Simonsen gives an easy-to-follow overview of the best dive spots to be found all over the island.

Stories from Puerto Rico by Robert L Muckley and Adela Martinez-Santiago will fill you in on how the natives discovered the Spaniards weren't Gods, and other local legends.

Puerto Rico Mio: Four Decades of Change is a sizable picture book. The author, Jack Delano, has been photographing Puerto Rico since 1941.

Boricuas: Influential Puerto Rican Writings – An Anthology by Roberto Santiago showcases the very best Puerto Rican writers from modern to colonial times.

Divided Borders: Essays on Puerto Rican Identity by Juan Flores dissects in greater detail the Puerto Rican struggle to define and maintain indigenous identities as the island becomes more homogeneous. Flores also wrote *From Bomba to Hip-Hop*, a wide-ranging series of essays.

Stan Steiner's *The Islands: The Worlds of the Puerto Ricans* stands out for its vivid evocation of islanders and their anecdotal histories. *The Other Puerto Rico*, by Kathryn Robinson, depicts the island through the eyes of a keen naturalist.

INTERNET RESOURCES

LonelyPlanet.com (www.lonelyplanet.com) There's no better place to start your Web explorations.

Puerto Rico Tourism Company (www.gotopuertorico.com) Run by the island's tourism company, this site contains loads of useful information and 'travel planner' features to help you sketch out itineraries.

Escape to Puerto Rico (http://escape.topuertorico.com) A detailed overview of island life, plus links to other informative sources.

Welcome to Puerto Rico (http://welcome.topuertorico.org/index.shtml) A travel guide plus information on the people of Puerto Rico and some great criollo recipes.

World Factbook (www.cia.gov/cia/publications/factbook) All the latest information from the CIA about safe travel in Puerto Rico and some background material too.

Puerto Rico Wow (www.puertoricowow.com) This for-profit site has good information in between the ads for cars, restaurants and other island products.

Itineraries

CLASSIC ROUTES

PUERTO RICO IN A FLASH
One Week / San Juan to San Juan

Since time is limited, fly to **San Juan** (p69) and make it your home base. With only seven days to spend in Puerto Rico, get right on the beach: **Isla Verde** (p85), **Condado** (p83) or **Ocean Park** (p83). Spend the next day weaving your way through **Old San Juan** (p74), being sure to stop by **El Morro** (p74), **Fuerte San Cristóbal** (p75) and **Calle Fortaleza** (p82). If you're up for some nightlife, stay right there.

The next few days require a rental car. With another early start, you can be the first in line to go inside the caves at **Parque de las Cavernas del Río Camuy** (p224). You'll have plenty of time in the afternoon for a drive up the winding mountain road to the **Observatorio de Arecibo** (p223) and the world's largest radio telescope.

Don't linger too long, though, because you want to get through the mountains to **Parque Ceremonial Indígena Caguana** (p224). Continue on to **Hacienda Gripiñas** (p238) for a restful night on this restored plantation. The next day, follow part of the Ruta Panorámica to Yabucoa, and then up to famed **Playa Luquillo** (p122), settling into the famed white, sandy crescent to care for your tan; sleep at a nearby **ecoresort** (p121).

For a dramatically different next day, explore the cool, green interior of **El Yunque** (p115) and spend the night in **Fajardo** (p129). Sign up for a kayak ride through **Laguna Grande** (p127), the bioluminescent bay. Then it's back to San Juan via **Loíza Aldea** (p110), where you can pick up a *vejigante* mask and get in a little snorkeling or surfing off the wild and lovely beaches. Test your luck at the gaming tables that night at any of the **Isla Verde** and **Condado** hot spots (p105).

This trip covers about 45 miles, hits all the major highlights and still fits in plenty of beach time.

THE BEST OF THE ISLAND   Two Weeks / San Juan to North Coast

Spend five days in **San Juan** (p69) and surrounding areas, making sure to see **Old San Juan** (p74), the **Observatorio de Arecibo** (p223) and the terrific **beaches** (p226). Rent a car and drive east to **El Yunque** (p115) for a day of hiking. That night you can take the bioluminescent bay tour in **Fajardo** (p124) or wait until the next day when you go to **Vieques** (p149) on the ferry.

If you arrive early enough, you can zip right over to **Esperanza** (p152). (Just make sure to rent a scooter or car in advance.) Once there, hit the beautiful **beaches** (p153). Spend that night and the next day in Esperanza, then return to **Isabella Segunda** (p151); check out **Fortín Conde de Mirasol** (p151) and assess the nightlife at **Mar Azul** (p160). Don't stay out until too late, though, because at 6am the next morning you'll be on a ferry to **Culebra** (p137). More fabulous beaches await, and great snorkeling, diving and glass-bottomed boat trips, too.

This trip gives you plenty of time to explore the major island attractions, as well as the Spanish Virgin Islands. Including ferry rides, the whole jaunt covers about 100 miles.

Now that you are nice and relaxed it's time to return to Fajardo, but only long enough to pick up your car and hit the road for **Ponce** (p165). Spend a few days exploring the colonial city's sights, such as **Hacienda Buena Vista** (p175), **Paseo Tablado La Guancha** (p170), **Museo Castillo Serailles** (p170) and the **Centro Ceremonial Indígena de Tibes** (p174).

Definitely allow one day (preferably with an early morning start so you can be done by midafternoon when the sun's at its hottest) for **Bosque Estatal de Guánica** (p180). After hiking, drive scenic Rte 333 along the south coast and stop to swim wherever you wish.

The next morning, the San Juan-Ponce Autopista will get you back to the north coast in less than two hours.

ROADS LESS TRAVELED

RUTA PANORÁMICA   Three Days / San Juan to Isla Desecheo

Head south from **San Juan** (p69) to **Reserva Forestal Carite** (p232) on Hwy 184 for a morning of beautiful hiking and swimming in cold water pools (in nonholiday weeks Carite is almost empty). On your way out in early afternoon grab lunch from one of the *lechonerias* (suckling pig restaurants) that line the highway. Head to **Aibonito** (p234) and check out the views from **Cañón de San Cristóbal** (p235) and **Mirador La Piedra Degetau** (p236); take a stroll around Aibonito's little plaza if you need to stretch your legs. Before it gets too dark, head to **La Casitas Hotel** (p237) and tuck in for the night.

The next day is all about **Barranquitas** (p237) and the numerous museums dedicated to la Familia Muñoz (the Muñoz Family, the closest thing Puerto Rico had to a political dynasty). **Hacienda Margarita** (p238), outside of town, is a great place to sleep. Next on the agenda is **Reserva Forestal Toro Negro** (p238). Bring food, water and sturdy boots for some great all-day hiking (camping, too, if you like).

Continue to romantic **Maricao** (p242). From this point you can easily jump off to **Bosque Estatal de Guánica** (p180), the **Parque de las Cavernas del Río Camuy** (p224) and **Observatorio de Arecibo** (p223) or **Centro Ceremonial Indígena de Tibes** (p174). Or, continue westward and drive through **Mayagüez** (p200) before heading north to the famous surfing center of **Rincón** (p202). Unwind from the cliff-hanging mountain trip by lying on the beach, or arrange for a scuba dive off **Isla Desecheo** (p205).

Ideally this route takes three days, but it's easy to do smaller chunks if you prefer. The entire east–west trip, which includes some mountainous roads, covers 165 miles.

TAILORED TRIPS

FOR NATURE LOVERS

Start with what many believe to be the crown jewel of Puerto Rico's nature reserves, **El Yunque** (p115). Soak up the cool jungle interiors of this unique tropical ecosystem before heading for **Las Cabezas de San Juan Reserva Natural 'El Faro'** (p126), near Fajardo. From there you can ferry to Culebra and the **National Wildlife Refuge** (p140), which includes the coastline as well as more than 20 offshore cays. **Vieques National Wildlife Refuge** (p137) is also a fabulous place to cycle, hike, snorkel and swim on newly opened beaches and pristine land – you can visit one or both, as you wish.

Back on the mainland, head for **Reserva Forestal Carite** (p232) at the mouth of the Ruta Panorámica. That road leads to the **Reserva Forestal Toro Negro** (p238), a remarkable forest with lush, flowery vegetation very unlike what you'll find at nearby **Bosque Estatal de Guánica** (p180), which is short on greenery but long on bird-watching and stunning ocean views. For the truly adventurous, a trip to **Isla Mona** (p210) is imperative – you'll really feel like an out-of-place guest in this animal kingdom.

Bosque Estatal de Guajataca (p221) is next, followed by **Lago dos Bocas** (p224), **Bosque Estatal de Río Abajo** (p225) and **Bosque Estatal de Cambalache** (p227).

MOST EXCITING BEACHES

If getting wet and wild is your idea of fun, then you need to follow the north coast into **Isabela** (p219), where surfers can get some intense action along the rocky cliffs of Playa Jobos (p219). Playa Crash Boat (p217), Surfer's Beach, Table Top and Gas Chambers (all p219) are other favorites.

Rounding the northwestern tip brings you to **Rincón** (p202), a mecca for surfers. Playa Shacks (p219) has good snorkeling, but the best deal for scuba diving is Isla Desecheo (p205). Surfers and snorkelers love Sandy Beach, Domes, Antonio's, the Point, Maria's and Little Malibu (all p206).

Next up is **La Parguera** (p185), known for a phenomenal dive called 'The Wall.' It's a 20-mile coral reef that starts at 60ft and drops to 150ft. **Isla Caja de Muertos** (p170), off the coast of Ponce, can't really compete with that, but offers much gentler snorkeling delights. Scuba divers and snorkelers will thrive on the numerous sites around **Fajardo** (p128) – Palominos and Palominitos, Cayo Diablo and Cayo Lobos – as well excellent dives off **Culebra** (p143) and **Vieques** (p155). Surfers hang 10 from **Luquillo** (p121) westward at La Selva, La Pared, Aviones, Chatarra, Stop 8 (La Ocho) and Los Tubos in San Juan.

Snapshot

You've got to hand it to Puerto Ricans – they know how to have a good time. It seems nothing is discussed with more fervor than *la buena comida, la buena musica y la familia* (good food, good music and family), until the conversation takes a political turn. For a tiny island that could easily fit inside Delaware (the US' second-smallest state), Puerto Ricans muster up an impressive voter turnout at every election – more than 90%. These passionately political people have argued the same issue for around 100 years now: whether to be an independent country, keep the 'status quo' commonwealth or officially become America's 51st state.

Any casual conversation you have with islanders is likely to include at least some mention of certain topics: sports, music and politics. So to hold your own, remember that Puerto Ricans, like most other Caribbean dwellers, adore *béisbol* (baseball) not *fútbol* (soccer), and regardless of who invented the musical stylings of salsa, Puerto Rican Tito Puente put it on the world map. Finally, know that there are as many opinions and variations on the statehood vs independence vs commonwealth argument as there are types of wild orchids in El Yunque.

The debate shows no sign of ending soon, especially as the island struggles to maintain its economic equilibrium. Until 2003 the US Navy kept a base at Roosevelt Roads on the mainland and on the offshore island of Vieques, where it practiced bombardment techniques. After years of burgeoning rebellion from local residents – that peaked after a local man died in a shelling incident – the navy pulled out of Vieques, but also shut (some feel out of spite) its base at Roosevelt Roads, despite protests from then-governor Sila Maria Calderón, who feared the economic fallout. Roosevelt Roads had been one of the island's largest employers, and almost overnight more than 3000 Puerto Ricans lost their jobs. The ripple effect spread all the way to the west coast, and despite some newly opened pharmaceutical factories that have created jobs, the island has still not fully recovered.

Puerto Ricans have accepted US involvement with varying degrees of anger, indifference and satisfaction for about a century – but the strong *'independentista'* movement that wanted to cut all ties with the US in the 1950s has mostly receded to the background. In the November 2004 gubernatorial elections, which were hotly contested for months and involved several hand recounts, Aníbal Acevedo Vilá, a 'status quo' candidate from Partido Popular Democrático (PPD; Popular Democratic Party), won with 48.4% of the vote. He only just squeaked past Pedro Rossello, the statehood candidate from the Partido Nuevo Progresista (PNP; New Progressive Party), who got 48.2%. Puerto Rico will remain a commonwealth at least until 2008 – but beyond that, it's anybody's guess.

FAST FACTS

Population: 4 million

Gross domestic product: $47.01 billion

Gross domestic product (per capita): $11,068.28

Inflation rate: 5%

Unemployment rate: 12%

Major League Baseball players of Latin descent: 200

Major League Baseball players who are Puerto Rican: 38

Percentage of rum consumed in the US that comes from Puerto Rico: 80%

History Mario A. Murillo

Mario A. Murillo is an Associate Professor in the School of Communication at Hofstra University in New York, and a veteran journalist and broadcaster. He is the author of *Islands of Resistance: Puerto Rico, Vieques and US Policy.*

For many observers of Puerto Rico, the island's contemporary history began on July 25, 1898 when the United States invaded during the height of the Spanish-American War. This was the sounding bell that began more than 100 years of US control over Puerto Rico's political, economic and military affairs. Prior to this, however, Puerto Rico had already experienced 400 years of Spanish colonialism. The rich traditions of today's Puerto Rican culture have been created by a mix of traditions stemming from these colonizers combined with the people who resisted their control or who were corralled against their will: the original Taíno inhabitants and the African slaves brought to the island during the colonial period.

As countless writers have noted, Puerto Rico is flavored with contrast and contradiction, a blending of cultures and nations that to this day is not so easily pigeonholed. It's considered a commonwealth of the US, but many feel it should be a state, or even an independent nation. Is it African, indigenous or European? Is it part of Latin America, the Caribbean or the US? Puerto Rico's history demonstrates these contrasts in a dramatic fashion.

PRE-COLUMBIAN TIMES

Knowledge of the people who inhabited the islands prior to the arrival of the Spanish is based on chronicles left by the Spanish conquerors, as well as on archaeological excavations of the remaining settlements and burial grounds. In recent years there has been a growing interest in reaffirming the role and the presence of these original indigenous communities, who were, for the most part, decimated by the middle of the 16th century.

When Columbus arrived on November 13, 1493, Borinquen – the native word for 'the land of the noble lord' – was inhabited primarily by Taínos, who were the third wave of indigenous people on the island.

Ronald Fernandez' *The Disenchanted Island: Puerto Rico and the United States in the 20th Century* explores the complicated relationship between the island and the US.

The first wave, descended from the Archaic people of the West Indies, came to the Caribbean region roughly 1700 years earlier.

In between were the Igneris, or Saladoids, originally from Venezuela's Orinoco Valley, who skillfully navigated their way through the region before settling in Puerto Rico. Remains found in the Loíza river basin in northeastern Puerto Rico date the arrival of the Igneris to approximately AD 120. These remains were discovered in 1948 by Puerto Rican archaeologist Ricardo Alegria in a cave known as Cueva Maria de la Cruz. Although little is known about the Igneris' social organization, they did produce pottery, using exotic designs. These communities settled on Puerto Rico until roughly AD 600, although the archaeological record is divided as to what happened to them. One theory says the Igneris gradually evolved into what became known as the Ostionoid culture, while another train of thought says they were conquered by a different wave of migration from South America.

By AD 1000, the Ostionoids had developed a more complex social and material organization, slowly evolving into what we now know as

TIMELINE

AD 120	1000
Puerto Rico's earliest-known inhabitants, the Igneris, migrate to the island	Taíno Indians establish settlements

the Taínos. Taínos spread throughout the Greater Antilles, but reached their height in Hispaniola and Puerto Rico between the 13th and 15th centuries, numbering about 30,000 when Columbus arrived in 1493. They shared a common language with other Caribbean groups, had a strong grasp of agriculture and organized their settlements into chiefdoms – *cacigazgos* – that were set up into a confederation. In Taíno culture, the chief could be either a man or a woman.

At Tibes near Ponce in the south, and at Caguana near Utuadu in the north, archaeologists have discovered and preserved impressive ball courts marked by rows of massive stone blocks. Here, native rituals were practiced – tribal events that brought the communities together and kept the collective spiritual and social memory alive. Drums made from hollow trunks, as well as *maracas* and *güiros*, provided the percussive accompaniment – instruments that still fill the sounds of Puerto Rican traditional and popular music today.

For a fascinating peek into the lives of Puerto Rico's first inhabitants, check out *Puerto Rico: An Interpretive History* from Pre-Columbian times to 1900 by Olga Jimenez de Wagenheim.

According to the Spanish conquerors, the Taínos were friendly, sedentary people. Nevertheless, by the end of the 15th century, the Taínos began to develop an increasingly defensive posture. New weapons such as the bow and arrow, the *macana* (wooden club) and the stone ax were developed, as well as a deadly poison extracted from the yucca plant. By the time the Spanish arrived, the Taínos' hold on Borinquen was being challenged by the belligerent Caribs, a new migratory tribe from South America that was winding its way northward through the Caribbean. According to chronicles from the time of conquest, the Caribs practiced ceremonial cannibalism on their victims and raided the island for women to take with them to the Lesser Antilles. The Caribs posed a direct threat to the Taínos, but eventually they joined forces to challenge the Spanish colonization of the island.

CONQUEST & COLONIZATION

Several years were to pass after Columbus' arrival before the Spanish attempted to colonize the island he called San Juan Bautista. It was in 1508, when Juan Ponce de León led a group of settlers from Hispaniola to the town of Caparra, that the process began in earnest. The recognized leader of the Taínos at the time was the elderly chieftain Agueybaná, the *cacique* (chief) of the southern settlement of Guainia. While the Taínos were perceived to be welcoming, there was resistance to the Spanish – especially in 1511, when a rebellion of Taíno and Carib Indians confronted the Spanish settlers, who were enslaving the locals into a new labor force. Ultimately, their stone axes and rudimentary weapons were no match for the firearms of the Europeans, and the rebellion was quashed. The Indians were forced to either flee or surrender.

The Taínos: Rise and Decline of the People Who Greeted Columbus by Irving Rouse is an excellent description of Boricua life before the Europeans arrived. It uses maps and drawings to great effect.

By 1521, Borinquen had become a fortified settlement in Spain's ever-expanding empire. Its name had been changed once again, from San Juan to Puerto Rico. At this point, it was considered to be Spain's most important strategic outpost in the Western hemisphere, necessary to defend its interests from other imperial rivals and potential enemies throughout the region.

The Taínos and their culture, meanwhile, were for the most part annihilated by this European colonization and conquest. Historians and

1493	1508
Invading Carib Indians reach Puerto Rico's shores; Christopher Columbus claims the island for Spain	Juan Ponce de León leads Spanish colonists to Puerto Rico in search of gold

The Four Voyages of Christopher Columbus by JM Cohen is an engaging compilation of excerpts from Christopher Columbus' log book, letters and the very mixed opinions that crew members had about the 'Admiral of the Sea.'

archaeologists estimate that by 1550, only 60 Taínos remained alive. By then intermixing had taken place, both with the Spanish colonizers and with the African slaves brought to the island from 1513 when the Spanish government began authorizing the entry of slaves through a system of licenses. Despite losing their ethnic cohesion as Taínos, the peasantry of this period clearly inherited their rich legacy. Many of the indigenous names have remained with islanders to this day, such as Humacao, Caguas and Mayagüez. Throughout the Spanish period, *bohios* (round-houses), *hamacas* (hammocks), maracas and guiros remained, along with many other traditions, and they continue to play an important role in Puerto Rican culture.

FORTIFICATION OF THE SPANISH EMPIRE

Spain consolidated its grip on Puerto Rico, its greatest threat came not from indigenous communities but from other European powers, including the French, the British and the Dutch. These nations recognized the strategic importance of the island and took exception to Papal bulls that declared Spain the rightful owner. Today's most recognizable tourist icons – among them El Morro fort, La Fortaleza (currently the Governor's mansion), El Boquerón and the entire walled structure that runs along the coastal perimeter of Old San Juan – are the clearest manifestations of the centuries of battles waged for control of Puerto Rico. Between 1532 and 1540, La Fortaleza was built close to the bay of San Juan and, in 1540, construction began on El Morro, a project that took a century to complete, all the while withstanding almost constant attack from foreign forces. Puerto Rico was invaded twice by the British in the 1590s and once by the Dutch in the 1620s.

The ultimate failure of these invasions stemmed from a combination of factors. These included the defensive strategy employed by Spanish forces mobilized in fortified San Juan; the epidemics that almost immediately struck the British and Dutch forces after they temporarily gained a foothold on the island; and a wave of resistance from islanders living in the interior, both native-born Puerto Ricans and Spanish.

Puerto Rico: The Four Storeyed Country and Other Essays by José Luis González (translated by Gerald Guinness) is a compelling treatise on the importance of African and mestizo peoples in the development of Puerto Rican culture.

Throughout the first two centuries of Spanish colonialism, the island's population did not grow noticeably. This is a reflection of the limited growth of the island's sugar economy, as well as the lack of the large mineral deposits that existed in other parts of Spain's large empire, specifically in Peru, Mexico and Colombia. Puerto Rico was seen more as a strategic asset than an economic one, and by the end of the 17th century the population had barely reached 6000 inhabitants.

THE SLAVE TRADE & PUERTO RICO'S AFRICAN PRESENCE

As it was throughout the Caribbean, slavery was employed to develop the Puerto Rican economy, primarily in the late 18th and early 19th centuries. The two types of slaves that were brought to the island – *ladinos*, born and acculturated in Spain, and *bozales*, brought from Africa – were first used to mine the limited gold and silver deposits. Once these deposits were depleted, the slaves were used primarily in the sugarcane industry and other areas of agriculture, predominantly in the coastal areas of the island. While the rest of the population experienced normal growth due to reproduction and voluntary migration, the slave population rose much faster throughout the late 18th century, with census figures in 1765 showing 12.6% of the population as slaves. By 1830, the slave population had increased to more than 31,000, mainly due to the introduction of new slaves directly from Africa and other parts of the Caribbean. However, despite these increases, by 1795 the majority (more than 60%) of black and mulatto people living in Puerto Rico were free. This trend, unusual for the Caribbean at the time, is often attributed to the island's asylum policy, which granted freedom to fugitive slaves from throughout the region.

There is considerable historic debate as to how slaves were actually treated on the large sugar estates. Some accounts claim conditions were better in Puerto Rico than in other colonies due to Spain's relatively strict slave code, which provided more protections and benefits than elsewhere. Other studies discount this argument, pointing to evidence of runaway slaves who preferred living as fugitives to living on a plantation. Regardless, by the late 1830s, as it became increasingly apparent that slavery was not going to be justifiable for much longer, plantation owners began enacting measures guaranteeing cheap access to other laborers – *jornaleros*. The landed sugar elite utilized both low-wage *jornaleros* and slaves to generate wealth for themselves and grow the island's economy. In both cases, the exploitation by European whites of African- and island-born blacks and mulattos led to the perpetuation of racial myths that allowed for the continuation of social inequities and racism.

Many slave uprisings occurred on the island, some larger than others. Later, this resistance by the black population ran parallel with a political movement for emancipation led by Julio Vizcarrondo, a Puerto Rican abolitionist living in Spain, as well as island-based political leaders such as Segundo Ruiz Belvis, Roman Baldorioty de Castro and Ramón Emeterio Betances. After years of struggle, the Spanish National Assembly abolished slavery on March 22, 1873.

Today, the African presence in Puerto Rican culture is striking, described by the late Puerto Rican cultural and social writer Jose Luis Gonzalez as *el primer piso*, or 'the first floor' of Puerto Rican culture. In its music, art and religious icons, African traditions are powerfully felt. And despite the racial stereotypes and inequalities that continue to exist on the island and within the Puerto Rican diaspora, Puerto Rico will always be considered an Afro-Indigenous-Caribbean experience.

RESISTANCE TO THE EMPIRE

By the 1820s, growing numbers of islanders, specifically elites from the Creole population, began demanding that Spain grant Puerto Rico more autonomy, if not outright independence. In the previous three decades, a sense of nationalism had started to emerge, reflecting a deep love of their homeland, as well as a sense of privilege given their growing influence and role in internal affairs. This sentiment really began to emerge after islanders successfully repelled the last British attempt to conquer the island in 1797.

As other parts of Latin America started winning their independence from the Spanish crown, the breakaway movement on the island gained momentum. It was brutally repressed at every turn, despite many instances

The Puerto Rican 'nation' is a new kind of translocal entity related more to culture than place, at least according to Jorge Duany in *The Puerto Rican Nation on the Move: Identities on the Island and in the United States*, an engaging and well-written book.

Mi Puerto Rico, directed by Sharon Simon, contains revelatory stories by poets, abolitionists, revolutionaries and politicians in a fabulous documentary touching on the island's African, Taíno and European ancestry.

1798–1810	1850–67
Sugar, rum and coffee trade between Puerto Rico and the fledgling US burgeons	Puerto Rican liberation movement gathers strength under Ramón Emeterio Betances

Guillermo A Baralt's
*Buena Vista: Life and
Work on a Puerto Rican
Hacienda from 1833–1904*
is a stirring account of
hacienda life. Read it, and
then visit the working
museum at Hacienda
Buena Vista (p175).

of solidarity and cooperation by the recently independent states of the region. Ironically, while the young government of the US warned Spain not to attempt to retake some of the territory it had lost in the Americas, Washington supported keeping Puerto Rico, as well as Cuba, firmly within Spanish control. This enabled Spain to maintain its grip on both islands until later in the 19th century.

One of the most important acts of resistance to Spanish power came on September 23, 1868 when hundreds of rebels mobilized to protest the lack of social and economic development on the island. Known as el Grito de Lares, or 'the shout of Lares,' this rebellion was carried out by the *jornaleros*, farmers and former slaves who declared an independent Puerto Rican nation. It was spearheaded initially by Ramón Emeterio Betances, who a year earlier had issued *los diez mandamientos de hombres libres* – the ten commandments of free men – which called for, among other things, the abolition of slavery, the right to determine taxes and the right of citizens to elect their own leaders. While the rebels in the central-west town of Lares made progress in their revolt, similar uprisings in other parts of the island did not ensue. Without the masses stepping in to back them up, Spain successfully repressed the independence movement, jailing and killing dozens of nationalists. Nevertheless, to this day, el Grito de Lares serves as a symbol of Puerto Rico's constant struggle in the face of foreign meddling, and is one of the few national holidays that is celebrated by islanders of all political persuasions.

THE SPANISH-AMERICAN WAR

It was not until the last decade of the 19th century that Spain's 400-year domination of Puerto Rico would finally come to an end.

Hunter College's Centro
de Estudios Puertor-
riqueños has an excellent
website focusing on the
history and culture of
Puerto Ricans on the
island and in the United
States. Check it out at
www.centropr.org.

Like the Spanish of the 16th century, the US had for years viewed both Puerto Rico and Cuba as key strategic components of its growing empire. Washington was wary of any European involvement in its 'own backyard,' and deemed such meddling as a direct threat to national security. Cuba was the main target of US expansionism. The US government and its allies in the yellow newspapers of the time, particularly Hearst's *New York Journal*, carefully orchestrated tensions with Spain in an effort to win the hearts and minds of the public and get them ready for war. This was taking place within the backdrop of ongoing negotiations between President William McKinley and the Spanish government, ostensibly to resolve the autonomy issue with regard to Cuba.

Tensions increased between Spain and the US just as Cuba and Puerto Rico were being set up for limited autonomy. Despite the signing of the Autonomic Charters for Cuba and Puerto Rico on November 25, 1897, the US sent the battleship *Maine* to Havana, ostensibly to protect the lives of American citizens and property. On February 15, 1898, the *Maine* exploded in Havana Bay, killing 260 crew members and wounding dozens of others. Almost immediately, US newspapers began pressing the slogan 'Remember the *Maine*.' Despite little evidence linking Spain to the explosion, it provided the justification to get the US into a war with Spain.

When US General Miles and his 3000 men landed in the southern port of Guanica on July 25, 1898, the outcome of the war had already been decided. Miles knew there would be very little resistance to US forces, as

1868	1873
Revolutionaries take the town of Lares and declare a Puerto Rican republic, but the uprising fails	Slavery is abolished

islanders saw them as an ally in their struggle to win independence from Spain. Indeed, his arrival was embraced by many Puerto Ricans as the first major step towards the island's inevitable independence. On August 12, 1898, the Treaty of Paris officially ceded Puerto Rico to the US, while Cuba gained its independence.

UNCLE SAM MOVES IN

Within 18 months, after officials in Washington failed to act on petitions from prominent Puerto Ricans demanding an end to the military government, the US Congress passed the Foraker Act (1900), making Puerto Rico the first unincorporated territory of the US. Unlike other territories that had been annexed by the US, Puerto Rico was never given a stated promise that it would eventually become a state of the Union. The Foraker Act – known as the First Organic Act of Puerto Rico – established the key institutions that would run the colony, including the Executive Council and the elected House of Delegates. The act tried to legitimize US colonial rule over the island by declaring the dollar the official currency, making the Supreme Court the final arbiter of the island's judicial system, and recognizing Puerto Ricans as citizens of Puerto Rico, not of the US. Puerto Ricans were left without any true representation in the US Congress, with only a nonvoting delegate.

Resistance to the new arrangement was spearheaded by Puerto Rico's Partido Unión de Puerto Rico (Union Party), which for years had been calling for a resolution to their lack of fundamental democratic rights. The Union Party was led by Luis Muñoz Rivera, one of the most important political figures in the history of Puerto Rico. Despite being remembered as someone willing to compromise with the US, Muñoz Rivera was the first to call for a plebiscite to allow Puerto Ricans to vote on their future, specifically whether or not they wanted to be granted US citizenship. Like a majority of his compatriots, Muñoz Rivera was adamantly opposed to US citizenship for Puerto Rico.

In 1917, President Woodrow Wilson signed the Jones Act, which made Puerto Ricans on the island US citizens and established a bicameral legislature in Puerto Rico whose decisions could be vetoed at will by the President of the US. No Puerto Ricans were involved in the debate over citizenship.

NATIONALISM & THE STATUS ISSUE

But US citizenship for Puerto Ricans by no means resolved the status issue. The debate over the future of Puerto Rico's relationship with the US intensified, and has since been at the heart of Puerto Rican politics, both for the main political parties on the island and the millions of Puerto Ricans living in the diaspora. The status issue was at the heart of the political development of two major figures who would emerge in the late 1920s and early '30s on the island, both of whom have had a lasting impact on Puerto Rican history: Pedro Albizu Campos, a leader of the pro-independence Partido Nacionalista (Nationalist Party); and Luis Muñoz Marín, who established the Partido Popular Democrático (PPD; Popular Democratic Party) in 1938.

Luis Muñoz Marín avoided the radical politics of Albizu, taking a more moderate approach to challenging the colonial situation of Puerto

An excellent site, run by a local amateur historian, is www.solboricua.com /history.htm. It's got a complete history section ranging from precolonial to modern times.

Puerto Ricans have fought for the US in every major conflict since WWI, but are not allowed to vote in presidential elections.

1897	1898
Spain charters Puerto Rico as an autonomous state under a Spanish governor	US forces invade Puerto Rico, ending the Spanish-American War; Spain cedes Puerto Rico to the USA

ALBIZU, NATIONALIST HERO

Pedro Albizu Campos was a Harvard-educated lawyer who spent years studying in the US, and was even drafted to serve in the armed forces in 1918. A Puerto Rican of African descent, Albizu became agitated by the policies of racial segregation he experienced while in the US. He could not help but make the connection between this racism and the colonial status of his homeland. For Albizu, the struggle for Puerto Rico's independence was of primary concern, and he felt there should be no compromise with the US.

Founded in 1933, the Partido Nacionalista (Nationalist Party) under Albizu was most active between 1930 and the mid-1950s. They demanded independence, and did not recognize the right of the US to control the internal affairs of the island. They used the US Constitution and the Declaration of Independence as justification for their struggle, and at first carried out their campaign through legal, political means.

But much like the Spanish rulers of the previous century, US officials provided independence leaders little room for open campaigning, and when they did, things had a way of going tragically wrong (see The Ponce Massacre, p169). The Nationalists gradually adopted a campaign of political attacks and violent confrontations against the US in their effort to overthrow the colonial government. As a result, Albizu and his supporters were directly targeted by US federal authorities. Albizu was convicted of seditious conspiracy in 1936 and sentenced to over ten years in US prisons, where he was subjected to various forms of physical and psychological torture. Albizu never denied his role in wanting to overthrow the US government, and remains to this day a symbol of Puerto Rican patriotism and resistance, even among those who do not advocate independence.

The Nationalists carried out their boldest actions against the US in the 1950s, including an islandwide insurrection in the fall of 1950 and an attack on the US House of Representatives on March 1, 1954. For some, the Nationalist Party was seen as an extremist organization that was out of step with the Puerto Rican people, while for others they represented a long line of political parties and social movements that to this day are demanding independence as the only viable option for the future of the island.

A special cask of high-grade rum was set aside by a brewer 1942 with orders that it be opened only when Puerto Rico becomes an independent nation. When (or if) that happens, free drinks for everyone!

Rico. As the US Congress avoided resolving the status question, Muñoz Marín's PPD pressed for a plebiscite that would allow Puerto Ricans to choose between statehood and independence as their final options. In the late 1930s and early 1940s, the majority of the PPD favored independence. However, neither President Franklin D Roosevelt nor the Congress were seriously considering independence as an option, and laws were enacted to criminalize independence activities such as those waged by the Nationalists.

This led Muñoz Marín to adopt a strategy that incorporated the status issue with other issues affecting the Puerto Rican people, such as the dire economic and social effects of the Great Depression. He declared his support for a new political status granted by Congress in 1948, what is referred to today as Estado Libre Associado, or ELA, the Free Associated State. This approach was meant to give the island more political autonomy, yet maintain and even embrace the very close relationship between the US and Puerto Rico.

In 1952, this status description was approved by a referendum held on the island. The voters also approved a Constitution that for the first time in Puerto Rico's history was written by islanders. Muñoz Marín

1900	1917
US Congress passes the Foraker Act, granting a US-run civil government to Puerto Rico; island population exceeds one million	The Jones Act unilaterally grants islanders US citizenship regardless of islanders' objections

became the first governor of Puerto Rico to be elected by Puerto Ricans. Nevertheless, despite claims by Muñoz Marín and his supporters that the status question was finally resolved with ELA, for all intents and purposes, nothing changed: the Congress still had plenary powers over Puerto Rico. Although islanders were now exempt from paying federal income taxes, they still had no representation in Congress (apart from a nonvoting delegate), could not vote in US national elections, and were still being drafted into the US Armed Forces to fight alongside young Americans in foreign wars.

Over the years a number of referenda and plebiscites have been held, ostensibly to allow the Puerto Rican people to decide the future of the island's status. Two official plebiscites, in 1967 and 1993, resulted in victories for 'commonwealth' status, that is, the ELA. Other votes have been held, with the status options, as well as the approach to self-determination, defined in different ways. All of these popular votes have been shaped by the ruling party at the time of the vote, either the pro-ELA PPD, or the pro-statehood Partido Nuevo Progresista (PNP; New

In an attempt to forward the cause of independence, two Puerto Rican nationals tried to assassinate US President Harry Truman in 1950.

POLITICAL PARTIES & THE STATUS QUESTION

For generations, the question of Puerto Rico's status has been one of the defining components of the island's major political parties, despite ongoing differences – albeit subtle at times – on other key issues, such as economic development, education policies and strategies for fighting crime. The two most powerful political forces are the Partido Popular Democrático (PPD; Popular Democratic Party) founded in 1938 by Luis Muñoz Marín, and the Partido Nuevo Progresista (PNP; New Progressive Party), founded in 1967.

The PPD advocates that 'commonwealth' should remain the permanent status of the island, while constantly demanding from Washington that the administrative powers granted under this status be increased in order to strengthen the island's autonomy. Indeed, in recent campaigns, the PPD has tried to make status almost a nonissue, preferring to focus its attention on the problems facing Puerto Ricans on a daily basis, including unemployment, inadequate healthcare and poor housing. This approach is consistent with the PPD's earliest campaigns, where they tried to argue that a vote for them should not reflect any status preference, but rather a vote for or against the present economic situation. The current governor, Aníbal Acevedo Vilá, and his predecessor, Sila Maria Calderón, are both from the PPD.

The PNP, as reflected in its Declaration of Principles, advocates statehood as the only viable option to lift the Puerto Rican people from the 'political inferiority to which we have been submitted for a space of five centuries.' Unlike the PPD, they describe the current status as a colonial relationship that must be terminated. Since 1968, when the PNP elected Luis Ferré as the first statehood governor of Puerto Rico, the party has been the other major political force on the island, regularly garnering between 43% and 48% of the vote. Its most visible contemporary leader is Pedro Roselló, who won two terms in the governor's mansion from 1992 to 2000, and just barely lost the election in 2004.

While the pro-independence movement has seen various manifestations over the past century, ranging from the Nationalist Party of Albizu Campos to the Socialist Party, the Partido Independentista Puertorriqueño (PIP; Puerto Rican Independence Party) is the one party that has consistently worked within the political system set up by the colonial establishment. Led by Rubén Berríos Martínez, the PIP is committed to making Puerto Rico an independent nation, citing its distinct nationality, language and cultural identity.

1937	1947
Student *independentistas* (independence advocates) clash with police on Palm Sunday; 19 people die in the 'Masacre de Ponce'	With US Congressional approval, Puerto Ricans craft their own constitution and elect their first governor, Luis Muñoz Marín

Progressive Party). None of the plebiscites held over the years have been binding for the US Congress.

In 1998, as the island was getting ready to mark the 100th anniversary of US control, another attempt to address the issue came in the form of a bill introduced by Alaskan Republican Don Young. For the first time, Congress acknowledged that the current status was no longer viable. The Young Bill called for a plebiscite on the island where Puerto Ricans would vote on only two status options: either statehood or independence. It did not provide ELA or any other form of 'enhanced commonwealth' as an option, angering members of the PPD. Ultimately, the Young Bill went nowhere. While it was approved in the House by a narrow margin, the Senate never seriously considered it.

THE US NAVY'S DEFEAT IN VIEQUES

One of the most pressing issues framing the status debate in Puerto Rico over the years has been the presence of the US military. The first US military base in the region was located in San Juan in the early part of the 20th century. As far back as 1902, the small island of Culebra housed Camp Roosevelt, which later became a full naval station designed for landing aircraft.

Among the most important installations constructed during WWII was the Roosevelt Roads naval base in Ceiba, on the eastern end of Puerto Rico. Roosevelt Roads was originally built to house the entire British Navy in the event that the Nazis invaded Great Britain, and up until March 2004 when it closed down, was the largest US military base outside the continental US.

Throughout the more than 100 years of US domination, there have been as many as 14 different military bases and installations scattered throughout the Puerto Rican archipelago, leaving a permanent impact on many communities – politically, economically and, perhaps most of all, culturally. For the most part, this military presence has not been well known outside the island. However, a year after the failure of the Young Bill, one incident on Vieques island brought the issue to the forefront of the relationship between Puerto Rico and Washington.

On April 19, 1999, 35-year-old Vieques resident David Sanes Rodriguez, a civilian security guard on the naval base, was killed by what was described by the Pentagon as an errant 500lb bomb dropped by navy planes, which missed its target on their practice range. His death sparked massive protests not only in Vieques, which had been expropriated by the US Navy in 1941, but throughout Puerto Rico and in the US. It led to more than a full year of civil disobedience on Vieques, where protesters crossed into the navy's bombing range and camped out on the beach to prevent more tests. The protesters' actions were instrumental in stopping the tests for more than a year, and after considerable lobbying pressure in Washington, President George W Bush signed an order closing the base in May 2003, ending more than 60 years of operation. Along with pulling out of Vieques, the navy closed down the Roosevelt Roads naval base in Ceiba.

These developments were a rare case where groups organized across party lines to confront US' authorities. Pro-statehooders argued the lack of

Military Power and Popular Protest: The US Navy in Vieques, Puerto Rico, by Katherine T McCaffrey, is the perfect resource for someone who wants to know every detail of the civil disobedience that drove the navy off Vieques.

If you want the short, unadorned version of Puerto Rican history, www.geocities.com /TheTropics/3684/history .html can't be beaten.

1952	1967
Puerto Rico becomes a Estado Libre Associado (Free Associated State)	Puerto Rico holds its first plebiscite on the issue of Puerto Rico becoming a US state (it fails)

THE PUERTO RICAN DIASPORA

The wave of Puerto Rican migration to the US began in the early 1940s, but really began to pick up steam between 1950 and 1960, when more than one million people left the island. Despite the many factories that had opened in Puerto Rico under Muñoz Marín's 'Operation Bootstrap,' which was designed to promote investment by using low wages and tax concessions, the island's economy was still in a terrible state, prompting people to migrate in search of better opportunities. The US, on the other hand, was undergoing a boom due to the Korean War, and needed the labor.

Most Puerto Ricans came to New York City, settling in El Barrio – 'Spanish Harlem' – on Manhattan's Upper East Side. The area became a vibrant cultural center: although salsa music had its origins on the island (and in Cuba), it came into its own in New York; and Nuyoricans have also been at the forefront of visual arts and literary movements, particularly spoken word.

Today there are nearly as many Puerto Ricans in the US as on the island. Many retain close cultural and political ties to the island, visiting often and increasingly returning to Puerto Rico upon retirement. Like those who remained on the island, US-based Puerto Ricans span the spectrum on the status question, but no matter what their political affiliation, they are passionate about and committed to the future of the homeland.

Not surprisingly, New York City's annual **Puerto Rican Day Parade** (www.nationalpuertorican dayparade.org) is a major event. Held in June, it features floats, music, dancing, 100,000 marchers and three million spectators.

---

accountability of the navy in Vieques would not have happened if Puerto Rico was fully integrated into the Union, while independence activists decried it as another act of colonial arrogance. Meanwhile, supporters of the current status took the middle road, denouncing the ongoing use of Vieques for bombing exercises as an affront to Puerto Rican autonomy and wellbeing, while embracing the US military as a natural reflection of Puerto Rico's unique relationship with the US and its role in defending its national security.

Today Vieques residents, no longer forced to withstand the bombing tests of the past, are embracing the renewed interest of tourists in its pristine beaches, its archaeological sites and its famous museum, housed on a hilltop in the Fortín Conde de Mirasol (p151). But, more importantly, they are also continuing their struggle to make sure that the navy cleans up the environmental mess it left after decades of military maneuvers.

The Puerto Rican diaspora is the subject of Boricuas in Gotham: Puerto Ricans in the Making of Modern New York City, edited by Gabriel Haslip-Viera, Angelo Falcon and Felix Matos Rodriguez.

CURRENT POLITICS

Puerto Rico's status continues to be a major point of contention for its political leaders and often overshadows discussions about how to resolve other issues affecting the island, such as economic development, unemployment, education and crime. In the 1990s, politics were dominated by pro-statehood Governor Pedro Roselló, who, when re-elected to a second term in 1996, received more votes than any other governor before him. However, his obsession with the status issue and his almost fanatical desire to convince Washington to make Puerto Rico a state overwhelmed his administration, especially in his second term, when he campaigned tirelessly for the Young Bill and other status-related measures.

1999	2000
Major protests break out on Vieques against the US Navy, following the killing of an islander during target practice	Puerto Ricans elect Sila Maria Calderón, the first woman governor of the commonwealth

In *Puerto Rico: The Trials of the Oldest Colony in the World*, Jose Trias Monge provides an excellent introduction to the issues around the status question.

In the end, charges of corruption in his administration left him somewhat discredited as he left office in 2001, turning over the reigns of the governor's mansion to the first woman ever elected into the office, Sila Maria Calderón, the standard-bearer of the PPD.

Calderón was committed to bringing back integrity to the governorship, and, not surprisingly, pushed the status issue off the agenda during her four years in office. She took a very vocal position against the navy and lobbied regularly to make certain that Washington would stick to its commitment to close down the Vieques bombing range and remove its forces from the island, despite opposition from certain elements within the Pentagon and more hawkish members of the US Congress. However, she did not run for reelection, instead passing the baton to Aníbal Acevedo Vilá, the young former resident commissioner for Puerto Rico (nonvoting delegate to the Congress).

Ironically, Acevedo's primary opponent in the November 2004 election was Pedro Roselló. Once again, the voters were split almost precisely down the middle, with Acevedo narrowly beating the former governor by 3566 votes, a result that was immediately challenged by Roselló. In yet the latest example of the contradictions in Puerto Rican politics and its relations with federal authorities, the ultimate winner was not officially declared until the first US Circuit Court of Appeals in Boston ruled in late December that a federal court in Puerto Rico did not have jurisdiction in the recount dispute involving the November 2 gubernatorial election. Once again, a non–Puerto Rican entity, in this case a US court, had the final word in determining who was to be the next governor of the island.

In January 2005, Acevedo was sworn in as the island's eighth democratically elected governor. Simultaneously, the pro-statehood leader Luis Fortuño was sworn in as Puerto Rico's resident commissioner in Washington, making it the first time in history that these two key elected positions were held by opposing parties. As for Roselló, he ended up in the Puerto Rican Senate, refusing to recognize the results of the 2004 elections.

In the past 500-plus years, Puerto Rico's had 17 months of autonomous rule – from November 1897 until April 25, 1898, the day the US declared war on Spain.

2003	2005
The US Navy pulls out of Vieques	Aníbal Acevedo Vilá of the Partido Popular Democrático (PPD) is declared winner of the November 2004 election

The Culture

THE NATIONAL PSYCHE

If you're a non-native Spanish speaker who likes to *habla* with the locals, you may feel slightly rebuffed when Puerto Ricans immediately answer you in English – even if you speak with relative fluency. It's hard not to feel a bit shut down when that happens, but it's not personal. You've just encountered a little psychological tic that many islanders share: they're not backward bumpkins, and they want you to know it.

Which is not to say that Puerto Ricans carry great, big chips on their shoulders – they are, if anything, overly generous and solicitous of friends and neighbors. And most will bend over backwards for a visitor who is in trouble or needs some assistance.

However, for three or four generations now, many Puerto Ricans have grown up bouncing back and forth between mainland US cities and their beloved island. And even those who stay put assimilate a great deal by proxy. The full scope of their bilingual and bicultural existence can take a long time for outsiders to comprehend. Lots of Puerto Ricans are perfectly comfortable striding down Manhattan's Fifth Ave during the week for a little shopping, then passing the weekend eating with family at *friquitines* (street vendors) along Playa Luquillo. You simply never know who you're interacting with.

The Instituto de Cultura Puertorriqueña has a great site (www.icp .gobierno.pr) on its organization in San Juan and general information about Puerto Rican culture, but it's all in Spanish.

Once that little bump in the road gets out of the way, Puerto Ricans are incredibly friendly and open; they like nothing better than to show off their beloved Borinquen (Puerto Rican Spanish). You'll note that despite their obsession with cars – just like mainland Americans – they are much more into experiences than things. A favorite island pastime is to wade into warm beach waters just before sunset – beer in hand and more in the cooler – to shoot the breeze with whoever else is out enjoying the glorious changing skies. Bank executive, schoolteacher, fisherman – it doesn't matter who you are, as long as you share an appreciation for how good life is in Puerto Rico.

LIFESTYLE

About 60% of the island still lives in what the US defines as poverty, but the remaining 40% is doing quite well – they are the managers of the ever-present pharmaceutical factories, the beneficiaries of the burgeoning tourism business or bankers or business owners in Hato Rey. San Juan is the only city that has much of a middle class – people who do administrative and clerical work in restaurants, hotels, tourism businesses and so on. Many were born in Puerto Rico and raised in the US, and returned to the island after college to find work. This return migration is a boon for the island businesses, which need skilled workers, but has made it harder for Puerto Ricans with high-school diplomas to fill those spots.

The Puerto Rican Mambo (Not a Musical) is based on Luis Caballero's stand-up comedy. This 1993 film (definitely not a musical) takes a satirical look at daily life, the media, movies, prejudice and more.

With an unemployment rate of 12% and average salaries around $12,000, many Puerto Ricans can't afford to pay the real-estate taxes the government has been levying of late, and consequently are losing their traditional homes – old farms that have been handed down for generations. Those who left Puerto Rico in their youth and return to live off an American pension find that their dollars don't stretch like they used to.

Still, this is the strongest economy in the Caribbean, and you'll see that almost every household owns at least one car. Puerto Rico hasn't quite gotten to the point of having 'two countries' living on the island, but the economic disparities are growing more apparent. Tons of fast-food outlets and strip malls cater to the working-class families, while trendy eateries doing fancy *comida criolla* (traditional cooking) pull in not just tourists but a newly created yuppie class of American-educated thirty-somethings enjoying their relative prosperity.

POPULATION

Puerto Rico – with nearly four million inhabitants – is one of the most densely populated islands in the world. According to US census figures, there are about 1000 people per square mile, a ratio higher than that of many American states. But the figures are misleading: approximately one-third of the population is concentrated in the San Juan–Carolina–Bayamón metropolitan area. Other large cities, such as Caguas, Hatillo, Arecibo and Adjuntas, are attracting new residents every day, with manufacturing and agro-businesses providing jobs. In comparison, the coastal sections along the west and south coast, and much of the lush interior mountain territory, are practically desolate. You can drive for miles and see absolutely nothing but a few slow-moving iguanas and maybe a wild horse or two. Avoid the *tapones* (traffic jams) that blight the major highways and you'll simply have no idea at all that you are close to any urban sprawl.

No better homage to the turbulent, creative frustration Puerto Ricans sometimes feel in their dual roles as Latins and Americans exists than *Puerto Rican Obituary* by Pedro Pietri, a lovely, epic book of poems.

MULTICULTURALISM

Like most Caribbean cultures, Puerto Ricans are an ethnic mix of Native American, European and African genes. About 80% of the island classifies itself as white (meaning of Spanish origin, primarily), 8% as black, 10% as mixed or 'other', and 4% as Indian. You will see Puerto Ricans who look exactly like the 18th-century portraits of Spanish grandees, and others who can't be placed anywhere. Along the coast of Loíza Aldea, where the African heritage is most prominent, distinct features from the Yoruba people abound, and in the mountains, where the few surviving Taíno are said to have fled, you'll find unique profiles that remind you of faded pictures in high- school history books.

Ed Dubrowski's *The Sights and Sounds of Puerto Rico* is a beautifully filmed video that highlights the geographical and demographic diversity of the island.

Puerto Ricans will tell you that ethnic discrimination doesn't exist on their island, but politically correct Spanish speakers may be aghast at some of the names Puerto Ricans use to refer to each other – words like *trigueño* (wheat-colored) and *jabao* (not quite white). It may sound derogatory (and sometimes it is), but it can also simply be a less-than-thoughtful way of identifying someone by a visible physical characteristic, a habit found in much of Latin America. You'll also hear terms like *la blanquita,* for a lighter-skinned woman, or *el gordo* to describe a husky man.

Identifying which terms are racial slurs, rather than descriptive facts, will be a hard distinction for nonislanders to make, and it's wisest to steer clear of all such vernacular. Compared to much of the Caribbean, Puerto Rico is remarkably integrated and even-keeled about race. The island's most important challenge is to correct the historical fact that the poorest islanders – those descended from the slaves and laborers who were kept from owning land until the early 20th century – have been short-changed when it comes to higher education. Cuban refugees arrive with their college diplomas and advanced degrees, while successive waves of immigrants from the Dominican Republic have filled many of the factory and manual-labor jobs. Meanwhile, hundreds of Puerto Ricans, who are desperately trying to find jobs, are dependent on government handouts and public housing.

Arlene Davila's *Sponsored Identities: Cultural Politics in Puerto Rico* provides an overview of Puerto Rican culture.

WOMEN IN PUERTO RICO

Puerto Rican culture is often stigmatized as a 'macho' world where women bear children, cook meals and care for the home. That is superficially true: women generally do all those things and more. Stereotypes paint men as possessive, jealous and prone to wild acts of desperation when in love, and that's also superficially true. Both sexes seem to enjoy the drama that comes along with these intertwined roles – pay close attention to couples twirling on the dance floor to a salsa song or, better yet, a steamy bolero, and you'll see clearly what game they are both happily playing.

None of that has prevented Puerto Rican women from excelling at business, trade and, most importantly, politics. San Juan elected a female mayor decades before a woman won a comparable office in the US, and, in 2000, a woman called Sila Maria Calderón was elected governor of Puerto Rico. She ran on a campaign that promised to end government corruption, and clean house she did.

Abortion is legal in Puerto Rico (although the rest of the Caribbean, outside of Cuba, is completely antichoice) and politicians remain acutely aware of the effects of a high birthrate on family living and quality of life. The facts of life are taught early in the home, but it's worth noting that high-school-aged Puerto Rican girls wait longer to have sex, are better informed about sex, and use condoms more responsibly when they do have sex than their American counterparts – and that's according to the US government's own figures. Puerto Rican culture still has plenty of macho myths that pose a challenge to full empowerment of women, but no more so than any other Western culture.

> Love, jealousy and murder in a failing Puerto Rico fish-processing plant – Sonia Valentín's *Sudor Amargo* (Bitter Sweat; 2003) is low budget, but entertaining as a slice of cinema verité.

RELIGION

Protestantism and Roman Catholicism are the two most widely (or openly) practiced religions on the island – 40% each – but followers of both have been widely influenced by centuries of indigenous and African folkloric traditions. Slaves brought from West Africa between the 16th and 19th centuries carried with them a system of animistic beliefs that they passed on through generations of their descendants.

You can hear it in the cadences of the African drums in traditional music like *bomba* and, more recently, in salsa. You also hear Africa in dance names like rumba and in variations on 'Changó,' the name of the Yoruba god of fire and war, like *machango, changuero, changuería* and *changuear* (all are island words that relate people, things and behavior to Changó).

The little wooden *santos* figurines that have been staple products of Puerto Rican artists for centuries descend to some degree from Santería beliefs in the powers of the saints (although many Puerto Ricans may not be aware of the sources of this worship). Many Puerto Ricans keep a collection of their favorite *santos* enshrined in a place of honor in their homes, similar to shrines West Africa's Yoruba keep for their *orishas* like Yemanjá, the goddess of the sea.

Belief in the magical properties of small carved gods also recalls the island's early inhabitants, the Taínos, who worshipped little stone *cemíes* and believed in *jupías,* spirits of the dead who roam the island at night to cause mischief.

Tens of thousands of islanders consult with *curanderos* (healers) when it comes to problems with love, health, employment, finance and revenge. Islanders also spend significant amounts of money in *botánicas,* shops that sell herbs, plants, charms, holy water and books on performing spirit rituals.

> Check out *Almost a Woman*, a PBS Masterpiece Theater production of Esmeralda Santiago's book reliving her childhood in Puerto Rico; it's a sentimental version of a well-written book.

> The techniques used to carve *santos* – small wooden statues of saints – date back to the 1500s.

SPORTS
Baseball

Follow the stories of Major League Baseball stars and discover the Puerto Rican passion for baseball in Thomas E Van Hyning's *The Santurce Crabbers: Sixty Seasons of Puerto Rican Winter League Baseball.*

If Puerto Rico has an official sport, *béisbol* is probably it. The Caribbean boasts a Puerto Rican Winter League, Dominican Winter League and Panamanian Winter League, and, in the off-season, Major Leaguers from the US come down to test their mettle against these up-and-comers. Major League teams also hold spring training camps in Puerto Rico, and regularly use the island's league as a farm team. Early season exhibition games are held every spring, and you can see teams like the Montreal Expos work the winter kinks out at bargain prices.

Cockfighting

No amount of international outcry, it seems, will wean Puerto Ricans off the 'Spectacle of Blood,' *peleas de gallos* (cockfights). The 'sport' of placing specially bred and trained *gallos de pelea* (fighting cocks) in a pit to battle each other for the delight of humans goes back thousands of years to ancient Persia, Greece and Rome.

Long a popular pastime in Puerto Rico and the rest of Latin America, the spectacle was outlawed upon the US occupation of the island in 1898. After almost four decades underground, cockfighting was once again legalized on the island in the 1930s.

Boricua Béisbol: The Passion of Puerto Rico (Wea Corp; 2003) features highlights of great Puerto Rican players, and you will learn about the Montreal Expos 'homestand' in San Juan.

During the 20-minute fight the cocks try to peck and slash each other to pieces with sharpened natural spurs, or with steel or plastic spurs taped or tied to their feet. Feathers fly. Blood splatters. The fight usually ends with one bird mortally wounded or dead. Then the aficionados collect their winnings or plunk down more money – to get even – on the next fight. Betting usually starts at $100 and goes well into the thousands.

Volleyball

Puerto Rico's national volleyball team can hold its own against any challenge – they've stunned teams from Canada and much of Europe at international competitions. Plenty of volleyball fans head to the beaches of Puerto Rico during the last weekend of May and each weekend of June to watch the one-on-two National Beach Volleyball Tournament. During the last weekend of the tournament, teams from around the world participate for the championship. July sees more competition as three-player, pro and amateur teams compete in the Return to Sand

---

HERO FOR THE AGES

Roberto Clemente was born in Carolina on August 18, 1934, the youngest of four children. He first gained the attention of Major League scouts while playing with the Santurce Crabbers in the Puerto Rican Winter League. From Santurce he signed with the Brooklyn Dodgers and was assigned to play for their top affiliate, the Montreal Royals. In 1955 Clemente joined the Pittsburgh Pirates, where he stayed until 1972. He played in two World Series, batting .310 in 1960 and .414 in 1971. He was the National League Batting Champion four times, was awarded twelve Gold Gloves, was selected National League MVP in 1966, and was chosen as the MVP in the 1971 World Series.

Fourteen months after his 1971 World Series victory, Roberto Clemente died in a plane crash on December 31, 1972, while taking food and relief supplies to earthquake-torn Nicaragua. Packed with five men and over 16,000 pounds of supplies, Clemente's little DC-7 plane bobbed, buckled and wheezed asthmatically for air. Moments later, the engines burst into flames, and the plane nose-dived straight into the water off Isla Verde, Puerto Rico. His body was never recovered. Dedicated fans still mark the anniversary of his death on Isla Verde every year.

Volleyball Tournament each weekend of the month. The Caribbean Beach Volleyball Tournament follows in late summer. For times and locations, contact the **Federación Puertorriqueña de Volleyball** (☎ 787-282-7525; www.fpvoleibol.proamvolleyball.com).

ARTS

Abundant creative energy hangs in the air all over Puerto Rico (maybe it has something to do with the Bermuda Triangle), and its effects can be seen in the island's tremendous output of artistic achievement. Puerto Rico has produced renowned poets, novelists, playwrights, orators, historians, journalists, painters, composers and sculptors. While it's known for world-class art in many mediums, music and dance are especially synonymous with the island – so much so that we've given them their own chapter (p43).

A young attorney tries to find his way through island life in *The Benevolent Masters*, by well-known contemporary author Enrique A Laguerre.

Literature

The island began inspiring writers in the earliest years of the Spanish colonial period. In 1535, Spanish friar Gonzalo Fernández de Oviedo wrote the *Historia general y natural de las Indias* (General and Natural History of the Indies), in which he painted a lush portrait of the island Ponce de León and his company found. About 100 years later, two thorough accounts of colonial life on the island came from the pen of the Bishop of Puerto Rico; Fray Damián López de Haro, and that of Diego Torres Vargas.

Puerto Rico was without a printing press until 1807, and Spain's restrictive administrative practices inhibited education and kept literacy rates extremely low on the island during almost 400 years of colonial rule. But an indigenous literature developed nonetheless, particularly in the realms of poetry (which was memorized and declaimed) and drama. The 19th century saw the rise of a number of important writers in these fields. Considered the father of Puerto Rican literature, Alejandro Tapia y Rivera (1826–82) distinguished himself as the author of poems, short stories, essays, novels and plays. His long, allegorical poem, the *Sataniada,* raised islanders' eyebrows with its subtitle, 'A Grandiose Epic Dedicated to the Prince of Darkness.' Tapia y Rivera's play *La cuarterona* (The Quadroon) depicted the struggles of a biracial woman in San Juan.

Run by the Institute of Puerto Rican Art and Culture, iprac.aspira.org has excellent information on cultural events, and features leading artistic figures from the island.

In 1849, Manuel Alonso wrote *El Gíbaro,* a classic collection of prose and poetry vignettes that delineate the cockfights, dancing, weddings, politics, race relations and belief in *espiritismo* (spiritualism) that characterize the island *jíbaro* – an archetypal witty peasant who lives in the mountains. When the US claimed the island as a territory in 1898, scores of island writers responded with protest literature. Out of that activity came Julia de Burgos (1914–53) one of the island's major female poets. Her work came to embody two intertwining elements of Boricua national identity – an intense, lyrical connection to nature and an equally passionate commitment to politics.

Poet Julia de Burgos, the first Puerto Rican woman to wear pants, died impoverished in Harlem and was buried in a nameless grave; her family finally found her and brought her home.

In the 1930s, Puerto Rico's first important novelist, Dr Enrique Laguerre, published *La llamarada* (Blaze of Fire), which takes place on a sugarcane plantation, where a young intellectual wrestles with the destitution of his island in the wake of US corporate exploitation. During this epoch of intellectual foment, the architect of the modern Puerto Rican Commonwealth, Luis Muñoz Marín, was composing poetry and sowing the seeds of his Partido Popular Democrático.

As more islanders migrated to the US in the 1950s, the Puerto Rican 'exiles,' known as 'Nuyoricans,' became grist for fiction writers. One of the most successful authors to take on this subject is Pedro Juan Soto, whose 1956 short-story collection *Spiks* (a racial slur aimed at Nuyoricans) depicts life in the New York barrios with the hard-biting realism that the musical *West Side Story* could only hint at. Luis Piñero, Miguel Algarin and Pedro Pietri started a Latino beatnik movement on Manhattan's Lower East Side, creating the first Nuyorican Café and holding poetry slams long before such things were considered cool. All three became major poets – honored by both English and Spanish readers – although only Algarin is still living today.

More recently, Esmeralda Santiago's 1986 memoir, *Cuando era puertorriqueña* (When I Was Puerto Rican), has become a standard text in many US schools.

Piñero, directed by Leon Ichaso, is a powerful film about Luis Piñero, playwright, poet and convict who co-founded the Nuyorican Café in Manhattan and died aged 40.

Cinema & TV

Movie and TV producers have always known that Puerto Rico's weather, geography, historic architecture and modern infrastructure make it a great place to shoot background scenes. But a home-grown movie industry only started to flourish in the late 1980s, thanks largely to one director, Jacobo Morales. He wrote, directed and starred in *Dios La Cría* (God Created Them). He was no stranger to the big screen at that point, having appeared in Woody Allen films in 1971 and 1972, but *Dios La Cría* was his first turn behind the camera, shooting in his native land. The movie, which offers a critical look at Puerto Rican society, was lauded by both critics and fans. His next movie, *Lo que le pasó a Santiago* (What Happened to Santiago?) won him an academy award nomination in 1990 for best foreign film. *Linda Sara* (Pretty Sara), his follow-up film in 1994, earned him a second Oscar nomination for best foreign film.

An acclaimed bilingual indie flick set in Boston, The Blue Diner, directed by Natatcha Estebanez and Jan Egleson, follows the trajectory of a young Puerto Rican woman trying to care for her mother and herself.

Marcos Zurinaga also made a name for himself in the 1980s, first with *La Gran Fiesta* (The Big Party) in 1986, which focused on the last days of San Juan's biggest casino, where all the hotshots met, and then *Tango Bar* (1988) and the acclaimed *Disappearance of Garcia Lorca* (1997). But the most widely distributed and financially successful Puerto Rican film is probably Luis Molina's 1993 tragic comedy, *La Guagua Aérea* (The Arial Bus), which explored the reasons behind Puerto Ricans' push to emigrate in the 1960s.

Nowadays, Puerto Ricans are making splashes on the big and small screens – Rita Moreno, one of the first Puerto Rican actresses to star on Broadway and in a major American film, is considered a cultural icon, and Jimmy Smits, a popular TV actor, is also a proud Boricua. Of course, for sheer glitz and glamour, nobody can compete with power couple Jennifer Lopez and Marc Anthony, both Nuyoricans with close island ties. Oscar winners Raul Julia – who died in the 1994 – and smoldering Benicio del Toro are considered two of the best actors to come out of Puerto Rico.

Lo que le pasó a Santiago (What Happened to Santiago?), directed by Jacobo Morales, is a poignant film that sketches out the story of Santiago, a man on the brink of retirement who finds love.

Folk Art

Four forms of folk art have held a prominent place in the island's artistic tradition since the early days of the colony. Some of the island's folk art draws upon the artistic traditions of the Taínos, like their 1ft- to 2ft-high statues of minor gods, called *cemíes*. Crafted from stone, wood or even gold, the idols were prized for the power they were believed to bestow on their owners. Visitors can see collections of the simple, primitive-looking *cemíes* at a number of museums on the island, including the Museo del Indio (p79) in Old San Juan.

Shortly after the arrival of the Spaniards in 1508, the Taínos and their civilization were assimilated. But the islanders' affection for magical

---

EL CUATRO

When the first Spaniards arrived on the island bereft of their beloved guitars, for which there had been no room aboard the Spanish galleons, the colonists quickly set about making their own. A number of indigenous variations of this instrument developed on the island, but the most enduring is the *cuatro*. No doubt the original *cuatro* had four strings, but over time it developed into a 10-string instrument played in the mode of a classical Spanish guitar. But the *cuatro* is significantly different from a guitar in construction: its body is hollowed and shaped from a single piece of wood. For contemporary *cuatros*, prices start in the hundreds of dollars and rise into the thousands.

---

statuary did not vanish. Instead, the Indians and their immediate descendants – who were quickly converted to Christianity – found a new outlet for their plastic arts in the colonial Spaniards' attachment to small religious statues called *santos* (saints). Like the *cemíes*, *santos* represent religious figures and are enshrined in homes to bring spiritual blessings to their keepers. Importing the *santos* from Spain was both difficult and expensive, so islanders quickly began making their own.

Puerto Rico is also famous for its *mundillo*, a type of lace made only in Spain and on the island. The tradition came to the island with the early nuns, who practiced the art in order to finance schools and orphanages. Over the 17th, 18th and 19th centuries, the nuns perfected the art in their schools and convents, but the intricate process was almost lost in the face of mass-produced textiles during the 20th century. Renewed interest in island folk arts, generated by the Instituto de Cultura Puertorriqueña, has revived the process.

Máscaras (masks), the frightening and beautiful headpieces traditionally worn at island fiestas, have become popular pieces of decorative folk art in recent years. The tradition of masked processions goes back to the days of the Spanish Inquisition and perhaps earlier, when masqueraders known as *vejigantes* brandished balloonlike objects (called *vejigas*) made of dried, inflated cow's bladders, and roamed the streets of Spanish towns as 'devils' bent on terrifying sinners into returning to the fold of the church.

Spaniards brought their tradition to Puerto Rico, where it merged with masking traditions of the African slaves. Red-and-yellow papier-mâché masks with a multitude of long horns, bulging eyes and menacing teeth are typical of the headpieces created for festivals in Ponce, Loíza and Hatillo.

West Side Story, a musical set in New York and based around two Puerto Rican street gangs, was made into a film in 1961. It garnered 11 Academy Awards, including best supporting actress for Rita Moreno.

The three points of the Bermuda Triangle are Miami, Bermuda and Puerto Rico.

Architecture

The most dramatic architectural achievements of Old San Juan are the fortresses of El Morro (p74) and San Cristóbal (p75), the stone ramparts surrounding the city and the mammoth seaside entry gate – all built from sandstone gathered from the shore and built in the 16th century.

A visit to Puerto Rico's important southern city of Ponce brings visitors to an equally large trove of historical architecture, particularly the Plaza Las Delicias (p167), which holds a 16th-century church and several colonial houses from the 18th century. The Hacienda Buena Vista (p175) is a thoroughly restored estate that includes not only a grand manor house but also a collection of 19th-century farm machinery, including waterwheels, all restored to working condition. Hacienda Esperanza (p227), a sugar plantation west of San Juan in Manatí, is being restored and is partly open under the auspices of the Conservation Trust of Puerto Rico.

Visual Arts

San Juan's Museo de Arte e Historia (p79) is a perfect symbol of Puerto Rico's dedication to the visual arts, which can be traced back to the very early days of Spanish colonization. The first great local artist to emerge was self-taught painter José Campeche (1752–1809), who burst onto the scene. Masterpieces such as *Lady on Horseback* and *Governor Ustauriz* demonstrate Campeche's mastery over the genres of landscape and portraiture, as well as his most frequent subject – the story of Jesus.

Francisco Oller (1833–1917), the next big thing to come out of Puerto Rico, did not gain recognition until the second half of the 19th century. Oller was a very different artist from Campeche; he studied in France under Gustave Courbet and felt the influence of acquaintances such as Paul Cézanne. Like his mentor Courbet, Oller dedicated a large body of his work to the portrayal of scenes from humble, everyday island life. Bayamón, Oller's birthplace, maintains a museum (p112) dedicated to its native son, and many of his works are in San Juan's Museo de Arte. Both Oller and Campeche are honored for starting an art movement that drew inspiration from Puerto Rican nature and life, and helped formulate the idea of a distinct cultural and artistic identity for the island.

When the US gained control of the island, Puerto Rico's artists began to obsess over political declarations of national identity. During this period, the island government funded extensive printmaking, commissioning artists to illustrate pre-existing literary texts. Poems, lines of prose, memorable quotations and political declarations all inspired poster art. Among the best of these practitioners have been Mari Carmen Ramírez and Lorenzo Homar. In Homar's masterworks, such as *Unicomio en la Isla,* a poster becomes a work of art, as it has in the hands of some of his students, including Antonio Martorell and José Rosas.

In the midst of the storm of poster art that covered the island in visual and verbal images during the 1950s and '60s, serious painters such as Julio Rosado de Valle, Francisco Rodón and Myrna Báez – as well as Homar himself – evolved a new aesthetic in Puerto Rican art, one in which the image rebels against the tyranny of political and jingoistic slogans and reigns by itself. Myrna Báez is one of a new generation of female artists, building on Puerto Rico's strong visual traditions to create new and exciting installation art. Her work is exhibited in many San Juan galleries (p93).

Today, one of the island's most famous artists is actually a Nuyorican – Rafael Tufiño, who was born in Brooklyn to Puerto Rican parents. Using vivid colors and big canvases, Turfiño paints scenes of poverty; one of his most well-known works is *La Perla,* named after the picturesque slum that sits right under the nose of El Morro in San Juan. Another celebrated living artist is Tómas Batista, who does three-dimensional art made from wood. Trained in New York and Spain, Batista settled in Luquillo some years ago and has made numerous pieces of public art for the island. Look for Batista statues in plazas in Río Piedras, Luquillo and Ponce.

Jack Delano first photographed Puerto Rico in 1941 and after a 40-year absence came back to see what had changed; the entrancing result is *Puerto Rico Mio: Four Decades of Change,* a heavy picture book.

Puerto Rico, Island in the Sun by Roger La Brucherie is filled with fantastic pictures of all the charms – hidden and otherwise – of La Isla Encantadora from a world-class photographer.

Music & Dance

Salsa is still king in Puerto Rico, but lately its supremacy has been threatened by an upstart musical styling known as reggaeton – an inventive combination of reggae, salsa, merengue and hip-hop, with aggressive drum beats layered over the top. To the chagrin of conservative forces on the island, the music has spread like wildfire through the Caribbean, and is even played on many mainstream rap, hip-hop and salsa radio stations in New York City.

But traditionalists needn't despair. There are plenty of classic sounds in Puerto Rico, from heart-tugging ballads underscored by strumming *cuatro* guitars to the hollowed-out thumps that characterize the percussive *bomba y plena*. Merengue, cha-cha and boleros are also common.

FOLK

The Taíno were skilled at carving wind and percussive instruments out of modest materials. When the Spaniards arrived and introduced the guitar, strings became part of the musical fabric. As a result, there are at least half a dozen string instruments native to the island, such as the *cuatro* (p41). The arrival of West African slaves, who brought with them a long history of drum-based songs, heralded the Afro-Caribbean fusion that within a few centuries would be celebrated the world over.

During Spanish rule, criollos (Spaniards of mixed European and island ancestry) invented the *danza,* a ballroom dance that flourished in elite homes and was later adopted by merchants, laborers and farm hands.

There's plenty of debate as to how *danza* was born, but the most accepted theory maintains that it's rooted in the *contradanza* from Spain, with a flourish of *cachucha* and *rigodon* (South American dances) thrown in. The real backbone of the *danza,* however, appeared in 1840 when new music and dance steps called *habaneras* were exported from Cuba. A freer and less rigid dance, it was quickly embraced by youth, who kept in a few recognizable steps to placate their parents. It didn't take long for island musicians to start putting their own stamp on the Cuban *habanera* music; early composers included Manuel G Tavarez, the 'Father of Danza,' and later, his most famous student, Juan Morel Campos, who wrote more than 300 *danzas* before he died at 38. The Puerto Rico national anthem, 'La Borinqueña,' is a *danza.*

Lanceros, a ballroom dance from Ireland, Paris and Spain, arrived in the second half of the 19th century. In Puerto Rico, the music called for eight to 16 couples in the formation of a quadrille. The ladies were elegantly dressed in ballroom gowns and fans, the men in romantic white tie and tails. A caller led the couples through five formations, leaving plenty of time for over-the-fan flirting.

Probably the most appealing colonial-era music found on the island is the *décima* – the vehicle through which the *jíbaro* (rural mountain resident) expresses joy and sorrow. Puerto Ricans call it the poetry of the island's soul. A *décima* requires multiple instruments – the three-, four- and six-stringed guitars known appropriately enough as the *tres, cuatro* and *seis.* It also has a rhythm section usually comprised of gourd drums.

To sing *décima,* one must be willing to improvise. Often a band will have two lead singers who alternate stanzas and try to outdo each other with sizzling rhymes and political statements – always encouraged by the

Jaime Serrat, a Puerto Rican living in New Jersey, keeps fresh all the information on www .musicofpuertorico.com, a dense and jam-packed site. Detailed explanations of all genres and types of music.

Music and Dance in Puerto Rico from the Age of Columbus to Modern Times by Donald and Annie Thompson is a simple timeline of music and dance in Puerto Rico that has great information on the origins of mambo, son, salsa and more.

enthusiastic crowds, of course. And for a mountain song, there have to be mountain dances: the Bailes de las Montañas typically followed solemn religious ceremonies on weekend afternoons in the 17th, 18th and mid-19th centuries. These lively celebrations lasted long into the night, and always ended with a *Seis Chorreao,* the fastest of all the *seis* rhythms. *Seis* is considered the backbone of *jíbaro* music, and the influence of eight centuries of Moorish domination in Spain can clearly be heard.

Another traditional version was created in the small town of Villalba in the Cordillera Central. If you arrive during a coffee harvest or saint's-day celebration, you may see white-clad locals with red sashes wildly dancing and hitting long, lethal-looking sticks together over their heads. No, it's not village warfare, just the Seis de Los Palitos.

Today, many Puerto Ricans associate *jíbaro* music with Christmas because of *parrandas,* a tradition in which groups of friends stroll from house to house singing joyful *aguinaldos* (Christmas songs set to mountain music) and begging for *pasteles* (tamales) and *coquito* (eggnog). Hosts must provide plenty to eat and drink, and then join the crew as it moves on to the next house.

CLASSICAL

Bernie Williams, a Puerto Rican baseball star and acclaimed jazz musician, was the 2000 US cultural ambassador.

Puerto Rico's opera company takes on ambitious productions every winter, and often sends its stars to New York to compete at the highest levels. Justino Diaz is arguably the most famous opera singer born and raised on the island. In 1957, at the age of 17, he participated in his first show – a local production of Verdi's *La Forza del Destino.* Hooked immediately, he took his deep, dark voice and brooding good looks to the New England Conservatory of Music. In 1963, after winning a radio competition, he signed with the Metropolitan Opera Company in New York, and never looked back. After playing Iago in Franco Zeffirelli's film *Otello* in 1986 it became his signature opera role which he performed in opera houses around the world. He still sings, but only rarely in Puerto Rico.

If your visit doesn't coincide with one from Justino Diaz, check out the Puerto Rico Ballet Company, which does classic and modern productions at the Centro de Bellas Artes (p177), and the Puerto Rican Symphony Orchestra (p104), touted as the best in the Caribbean.

To see the best that the island has to offer – and the whole Caribbean, actually – you can do no better than visit during the Festival Casals (p93), held for two weeks every year.

Pablo Casals – despite being born in Barcelona, Spain – is considered Puerto Rico's most prominent son (his mother was from Mayagüez). Long before WWI, he was already considered the pre-eminent cellist of his era. Avidly political, he left Spain in 1936 to protest the Franco regime and eventually settled in Puerto Rico, where he lived out the rest of his days. In 1957 he founded the Festival Casals, which is attended by music fans from around the world, and went on to form the Puerto Rico Symphony Orchestra and the Puerto Rico Conservatory of Music. By the time he died in 1973 at the age of 97, he considered himself – and was considered by his compatriots – to be Puerto Rican.

POPULAR

There's an old saying in the Caribbean: Puerto Rico and Cuba are two wings of the same bird. As it pertains to music and dance, nothing could be truer. There are so many twists and turns and similarities between *son* and *seis,* so to speak, that historians have made careers arguing which musical beats got started where and when (and by whom).

Bomba y Plena

Bomba y plena refers to two distinct types of music coupled with a dance. Together they are the island's most popular folk music, and they are created out of the fertile marriage of European, Caribbean and African sounds that occurred in Puerto Rico more than 500 years ago.

The *bomba* is purely African, brought over by Yoruba slaves who labored on sugar plantations. Consider it a friendly competition between the drummer and the dancer, where one eggs on the other to create an ever-more frenzied beat. The streets of Loíza Aldea resound with *bomba* throughout the summer, particularly during the festival for St James the Moor Slayer (p111).

Bomba was initially played on goat skin stretched over barrels of rum, creating a unique sound perfect for call-and-respond elements. There are many different beat patterns – the most popular one, used by many orchestras, is called *sica*, and is taken straight from Africa. Other patterns include *yubá, cuembé* and, oddly enough, one called *bomba holandes*. While Loíza Aldea claims to the birthplace of *bomba,* Santurce and Mayagüez also have quite a tradition, with distinct patterns of their own.

Plena, which originated in Ponce, is lighter than *bomba,* but still drum-driven. Locals once referred to it as *'el periodico cantado'* (the sung newspaper), because *plena* songs contain stories about the history and everyday life of the people. It involves several musicians all using a diverse selection of hand-held instruments weaving varying rhythms into a song. This folk music can also be traced back to the early island settlers, but its influences are North African and Arab. *Plena* was brought to Ponce by *cocolocos* – slaves who migrated north from islands south of Puerto Rico. Instrument aficionados will notice that *plena* uses *panderos,* which look like Irish tambourines without the cymbals; however, the resemblance is misleading. Musicologists say *panderos* were brought over by the Spaniards, who had lifted them from their Moorish neighbors. *Plena* music employs a rhythm that is clearly African and very similar to calypso, soca and dancehall music from Trinidad and Jamaica.

MUST-HAVE CDS

- *El Abayarde by Tego Calderon* – a good introduction to reggaeton with Calderon's signature sexually charged lyrics and basso profundo delivery.
- *Feliciano!* – all the greatest hits from the amazing guitarist and vocalist, José Feliciano, including 'Light My Fire.'
- *King of Mambo* – featuring 'Patricia', the unforgettable song used in Fellini's *La Dolce Vita*; this album by Perez Prado will get your fingers popping in no time.
- *100% Azucar: The Best of Celia Cruz & La Sonora Matancera* – the Cuban Songbird as a young woman had a crispness to her voice not soon forgotten.
- *Grandes Exitos* – this is a bargain CD, because you get Willie Colon, a big band and guest singers like Hector Levoe, Celia Cruz, Ruben Blades and José Feliciano.
- *The Best of Tito Puente, Vol 1* – you can choose from a plethora of Puente CDs, but this combines some of Tito's classic hits with infectious dance-driven beats.
- *Serie Platino: 20 Exitos* - the 'Barbaro del Ritmo', Benny More, infused son, bolero and mambo with more tenderness and sex appeal than the island of Cuba could contain.
- *Puerto Rico* – all the island's greatest singers and songs on one impeccably produced CD compiled by Putumayo Records.

Bomba y plena developed side by side on the coastal lowlands, and the island's always-inventive musicians eventually realized the call-and-response of *bomba* would work well with *plena*'s more satirical narrative style of lyrics, which is why the two elements are often played back to back by bands.

Salsa

One of the definitive articles on the origin of the name 'salsa' is found at www.salsaroots.com.

Which came first – Cuban or Puerto Rican salsa? It's an age-old question. Salsa – as we know it today – is a distillation of many Latin and Afro-Caribbean dances and sounds, and each played a large part in its evolution. Before we wade into the controversial topic of salsa's origins, let's run through all the variations that can be heard within this irresistible rhythm.

Start with the Cuban son, which was a relatively foreign music to audiences outside the Caribbean until the *Buena Vista Social Club* got it back on the charts in the 1990s. Son originated in eastern Cuba and mixed Spanish-derived and Afro-Cuban elements. The basic two-part format of the son has remained the same from the 1920s to the present, and many salsa songs (which Cubans would call *guaracha*) also follow this pattern.

Merengue, the national dance of the Dominican Republic, features lots of hip-shaking movements that are fun and easy to learn. Some historians say the merengue beat mimics the movement of slaves who were chained together and forced to drag a leg as they cut sugar to the bang of drums. Others claim that a great hero, wounded in the leg during one of the many revolutions in the Dominican Republic, was welcomed home by a party of villagers, who, out of sympathy, danced while dragging one foot. In Haiti it's called meringue, an apt name for a sugary dance that consists of short, frothy rhythms. Merengue tempos vary a great deal and it's not uncommon for a song that starts out slow, almost like a bolero, to quicken significantly toward the end of the dance.

While all these genres of music and movement indubitably contributed to the creation of 'salsa', the direct parent has to be mambo – a dance that originated in Cuba where there were substantial settlements of Haitians. A 'Mambo' in Haiti is a voodoo priestess and the name was applied to this hypnotic music in the mid-1900s.

Mambo is a fusion of swing, American jazz and Cuban son, and it's a sensational dance. Historians agree that one man is responsible for creating its fascinating combinations – Cuban Perez Prado, who introduced it at La Tropicana nightclub in Havana in 1943. What Perez Prado started in Cuba, Tito Puente (opposite), Tito Rodriguez, Machito and Xavier Cugat carried to the US. Mambo was eagerly embraced by Latino and North American audiences frequenting dance halls in New York City. It reportedly debuted at the Palladium in 1947.

Oscar Hijuelos' graceful and heartbreaking novel, *The Mambo Kings Sing Songs of Love*, is a thinly fictionalized account of the life his musician uncles from Cuba lived in New York in the '60s.

The original mambo dance wasn't easy for beginners to master and it died out on popular dance floors for a time, although a renewed interest in Latin dances has seemingly resurrected it. Those who find it too challenging can try the cha-cha, also known as the cha-cha-cha. This mambo offshoot is danced in slow tempo, and consists of three quick steps (triple step or cha cha cha) and two slower steps on the one beat and two beat.

From mambo and cha-cha, the incessant musical tinkering of Puerto Rican artists on the island and in Borinquen neighborhoods in the US led inexorably to salsa. How that name came about – literally it means 'sauce' – has also been fervently debated. Salsa has many antecedents

---

THE 'BRIDGE' OF TITO PUENTE

Puerto Ricans and Cubans jovially argue over who invented salsa, but the truth is neither island can claim to be the commercial center of salsa success. That honor belongs to the offshore colony known as El Barrio: the Latin Quarter, Spanish Harlem, New York City. In the euphoria following the end of WWII, New York's nightclub scene bloomed as dancers came in droves to the Palladium on 52nd St to bump and grind to the sound of the mambo bands they heard, or dreamed of hearing, in the casinos of Havana, Cuba. At the time, the music carried a basic Latin syncopated beat and relied heavily on a horn section typical of the great swing bands of Stan Kenton and Count Basie.

Then a young Puerto Rican drummer named Tito Puente came into the picture. After serving three years in the US Navy and attending New York's Juilliard School of Music, Puente began playing and composing for Cuban bands in New York City. He quickly became notorious for spicing up the music with a host of rhythms that came from endless combinations of Puerto Rican *bomba*. Soon Puente had formed his own band, the Latin Jazz Ensemble, which was musically going way beyond the old Cuban templates.

When Fania Records came around, Tito Puente was already a star. Celia Cruz, the late Héctor Lavoe, Eddy Palmieri, Gilberto Santa Rosa, El Gran Combo de Puerto Rico and plenty of other *salseros* have made their mark on the world, but none can claim quite the same place as Tito Puente, who – true to his name – bridged cultural divides with his spicy music decades before multiculturalism was even considered a word. Shortly after the legendary *salsero's* death in 2000, at the age of 77, a stretch of road in Harlem – East 112th Street at Lexington Ave – was renamed Tito Puente Way.

---

and many practitioners, but two stand above the rest: Puerto Rican Tito Puente and Cuban Celia Cruz, who both lived and worked in New York City. By the time these two became household names in the 1960s, the Latin/Caribbean-influenced style of big band music, which used congas, bass, cowbells (a Puerto Rican addition), bongos, maracas, a horn section, bass and multiple singers, had firmly taken hold in the northeast.

In 1963 Johnny Pacheco, a visionary producer, created Fania Records, a new record label that began to snap up talented Nuyorican musicians like Willie Colon, and island draws like Ismael Miranda and Hector Lavoe. Their hip-popping, heel-kicking music drew raves from critics and brought crowds to the clubs. All that was lacking was a name to put on this new craze. As the story goes, a 1962 record by Joe Cuba made the first mention of 'salsa' music, and the rest was history. It wasn't long before Charlie Palmieri, another Nuyorican, released 'Salsa Na' Mas', which swept the nation. When Carlos Santana's now-ubiquitous rock song 'Oye Como Va' hit the music stores in 1969, followed shortly thereafter by torrid guitar songs from José Feliciano, 'the genius from Lares,' the craze for all things Latin reached its peak in America.

The salsa torch flickered and almost went out in subsequent decades – it was always played in Puerto Rico, but its almost exclusive grip on main-stream discos in Los Angeles and New York ended abruptly as musical tastes shifted radically in the 1980s.

It took a modern Nuyorican – salsa crooner Marc Anthony, aka Mr Jennifer Lopez – to bring salsa back from the brink, which he did with authority. Long before his wife even conceived of her breakout Latina-influenced pop album *On the 6*, Marc's music packed New York's Madison Square Garden several times over with screaming salsa-loving crowds. As both Lopez and Anthony grew in stature, a native Puerto Rican appeared and briefly eclipsed them both: Ricky Martin's 'La Vida Loca,' which owed much of its success to Martin's slinky salsa moves

The Harlem-born Tito Puente outlines different Latin rhythms in his book, *Tito Puente's Drumming With the Mambo King*, and then performs them on the accompanying CD.

José Feliciano, a six-time Grammy award winner, taught himself to play the guitar despite being born blind.

(if not salsa sounds), created renewed interest in island music. All three artists continue to produce pop music flavored with traditional rhythms. (For purists, Tito Nieves and José Feliciano are still among the top living performers.)

Salsa is still the most widely played music in clubs, discos and bodegas in Puerto Rico, although in certain sectors reggaeton is giving it a run for its money. For those who want to dance salsa, remember this simple tip: salsa is similar to mambo in that both have a pattern of six steps danced over eight counts of music. The dances share many of the same moves, but in salsa turns have become an important feature, so the overall look is different. Mambo moves generally forward and backward, while salsa has more of a side-to-side feel. For suggestions on where to learn salsa in San Juan, see p101.

Reggaeton

The bastard child of reggae, salsa and hip-hop, this rough-and-tumble music came to life on the unpaved streets of Loíza Aldea, and proudly flaunts its blue-collar roots with over-the-top, sexually explicit lyrics. Now that it's been adopted by youth from all walks of life, reggaeton looks set to take over the Caribbean – and possibly some New York dance spots as well.

As the name suggests, it draws heavily on reggae, which first arrived in Latin America with Jamaican laborers who came to help build the Panama Canal in the 1900s. By the time the 1970s rolled around, Panama was producing record after record of the music, and the scene flourished as a local form of reggaeton.

At the same time, Jamaican ragga burst onto the scene in Puerto Rico, and mixed with local Latin beats to create another form of reggaeton, which is now the dominant reggaeton style on the island. It has a much heavier salsa influence than Panamanian reggaeton, and fans amuse themselves by dancing hip-to-hip with the beat. The most popular reggaeton dance – known as *perreo,* or dog dance – leaves little to the imagination.

The driving drum-machine track taken from early Jamaican dancehall rhythms is reggaeton's most notable feature – well, that and the beyond X-rated lyrics. Sometimes hip-hop-styled vocals, an import from the US, are favored by singers. Reggaeton stars like Tego Calderon, Daddy Yankee, Don Omar and Ivy Queen played to thousands of fans at New York's Madison Square Garden in October 2004, highlighting reggaeton's growing international appeal and potential commercial power.

Environment

THE LAND

Cartographers group Puerto Rico with the Caribbean's three largest islands – Cuba, Jamaica and Hispaniola – in the so-called Greater Antilles. But at 100 miles long and 35 miles across, Puerto Rico is quite clearly the little sister, stuck off to the east of Hispaniola at about 18° north latitude, 66° west longitude. With its four principal satellite islands – Mona and Desecheo to the west, Culebra and Vieques to the east – and a host of cays hugging its shores, Puerto Rico claims approximately 3500 sq miles of land, making the commonwealth slightly larger than the Mediterranean island of Corsica.

Like almost all the islands ringing the Caribbean Basin, Puerto Rico owes its existence to a series of volcanic events. These eruptions built up layers of lava and igneous rock and created an island with four distinct geographical zones: the central mountains, karst country, the coastal plain and the coastal dry forest. At the heart of the island, running east to west, stands a spine of steep, wooded mountains called the Cordillera Central. The lower slopes of the cordillera give way to foothills, comprising a region on the island's north coast known as 'karst country.' In this part of the island, erosion has worn away the limestone, leaving a karstic terrain of dramatic sinkholes, hillocks and caves.

Forty-five non-navigable rivers and streams rush from the mountains and through the foothills to carve the coastal valleys, particularly on the east and west ends of Puerto Rico, where sugarcane, coconuts and a variety of fruits are cultivated. The island's longest river is the Río Grande de Loíza, which flows north to the coast. Other substantial rivers include the Río Grande de Añasco, the Río Grande de Arecibo and the Río de la Plata.

Little of the island's virgin forest remains, but second- and third-growth forests totaling 140 sq miles now comprise significant woodland reserves, mostly in the center of the island.

Sikeo, the name the Taíno gave to Desecheo Island, is a news service website full of recent articles, books and press releases on environmental issues in Puerto Rico. Check out http://premium.caribe.net/~fantosva.

WILDLIFE
Animals

Very few of the land mammals that make their home in Puerto Rico are native to the island; most mammal species have been either accidentally or intentionally introduced to the island over the centuries. Among the most distinctive of these is the Paso Fino horse, which is a small-boned,

---

HURRICANES

The word 'hurricane,' denoting fierce cyclonic storms with winds in excess of 75mph, comes to English and Spanish from the Taíno language and their god of malevolence, Jurakán. This fact is warning enough that Puerto Rico lies along one of the most frequently traveled paths of these vicious tropical storms (see p16).

Puerto Rico has been devastated by at least four major storms since 1988. But good, long-range storm predictions, thorough preparation and the practice of building new houses and public and commercial buildings of cement block or reinforced concrete have gone a long way toward reducing casualties and property damage.

Tune in to English-language radio station WOSO San Juan, at 1030AM, for hurricane advisories in the central Caribbean.

easy-gaited variety. The Paso Finos have been raised in Puerto Rico since the time of the Spanish conquest, when they were introduced to the New World to supply the conquistadores on their expeditions throughout Mexico and the rest of the Americas. They now number 8000, and are unique to Puerto Rico. The horses are most dramatic on the island of Vieques, where they roam in wild herds on vast tracts of land.

Not far from Vieques lies the 39-acre Cayo Santiago (p131), where a small colony of rhesus monkeys, introduced for scientific study in 1938, has burgeoned into a community of more than 700 individuals. Puerto Rico is also home to a special boa, which grows to more than 7ft, and 3ft-long giant iguanas on Isla Mona.

Recently, some tour guides at El Yunque have reported that poisonous snakes have been introduced to the forest as a result of people freeing exotic pets into the wild. We cannot confirm this as fact, but given the island's centuries-old tradition of releasing exotic animals such as the wild Paso Fino horses of Vieques and the caimans of Laguna Tortuguero, the snake story has plenty of historical precedent. Hikers and campers should inquire about snake threats with local rangers, brush up on their snake identification skills and be prepared.

The coastal dry forest of Guánica features more than 130 bird species, largely songbirds. Some of these are migratory fowl, such as the prairie warbler and the northern parula. Many are nonmigratory species, including the lizard cuckoo and the endangered Puerto Rican nightjar. One of the joys of winter beachcombing is watching the aerial acrobatics of brown pelicans as they hunt for fish.

The island also has a supply of unusual flying and crawling insects, including a large tropical relative of the firefly called the cucubano, and a centipede measuring more than 6in in length with a sting that can kill.

Plants

Mangrove swamps and coconut groves dominate the north coast, while El Yunque's rainforest, at the east end of the island, supports mahogany

---

CORAL ECOLOGY

A coral is a tiny animal with a great gaping mouth, surrounded by tentacles for gathering food at one end. The polyps, which resemble flowers or cushions upholstered with plush fabric, live protected by external skeletons, the production of which is dependent upon algae that live inside the polyps' tissue. The creatures live in vast colonies that reproduce both asexually by budding and sexually through a synchronous release of spermatozoa that turns the surrounding sea milky. Together they build up huge frameworks – the reefs.

A reef is usually composed of scores of species of coral, each occupying its own niche. However, all corals can flourish only close to the ocean surface, where they are nourished by sunlight in clear, unpolluted waters above 70°F. Each species has a characteristic shape – bulbous cups bunched like biscuits in a baking tray for the star coral; deep, wending valleys for the well-named brain coral. These lacy fans and waving cattails look like plants, but a close perusal shows them to be menacing animal predators that seize smaller creatures, such as plankton.

Coral reefs are the most complex and sensitive of all ecosystems. Taking thousands of years to form, they are divided into life zones gauged by depth, temperature and light. When a coral polyp dies, its skeleton turns to limestone that another polyp may use to cement its own skeleton. The entire reef system is gnawed away by parrotfish and other predators. Careless snorkelers and divers, or sailors who anchor indiscriminately, have begun to damage the easily accessible reefs around Culebra and Vieques. See Responsible Tourism (p53) for advice on how to avoid damaging these fragile areas.

BRIGHT LIGHTS, BLACK WATER

There are seven known regions worldwide that are phosphorescent – meaning they glow in the dark thanks to little microorganisms, known as dynoflagellates, in the water. Puerto Rico has some of the best places to see this phenomenon, including Bahía Mosquito (p155) in Vieques, the south coast's Bahía de Fosforescente (p185) at La Parguera, and the east coast's Laguna Grande (p127) north of Fajardo. There are a number of these organisms in tropical waters, but the most abundant in Puerto Rico's 'phosphorous' bays is *Pirodinium bahamense*. The term 'Pirodinium' comes from 'pyro,' meaning fire, and 'dirium,' meaning rotate.

When any movement disturbs these creatures, a chemical reaction takes place in their little bodies that makes the flash. Scientists speculate about the purpose of the flash; many think that the dynoflagellates have developed this ability to give off a sudden green light as a defense mechanism to ward off predators.

You can see these microorganisms flashing like tiny stars in Atlantic waters as far north as New England in the summer, but never in the brilliant concentrations appearing in Puerto Rico. Enclosed mangrove bays, where narrow canals limit the exchange of water with the open sea, are the places that let the dynoflagellates breed and concentrate. In a sense, the bay is a big trap, and vitamins produced along the shore provide food for the corralled microorganisms.

---

trees and more than 50 varieties of wild orchid. Giant ferns thrive in the rainforest as well as in the foothills of karst country, while cacti, mesquite forest and bunchgrass reign on the dry southwest tip of the island, which has the look of the African savanna.

Exotic shade trees have long been valued in this sunny climate, and most of the island's municipal plazas spread beneath canopies of magnificent ceibas or kapoks (silk-cotton tree), the flamboyán (poinciana) with its flaming red blossoms, and the African tulip tree. Islanders often adorn their dwellings with a profusion of flowers such as orchids, bougainvillea and poinsettias, and tend lovingly to fruit trees that bear papaya, uva caleta (sea grape), carambola (star fruit), panapen (breadfruit) and plátano (plantain). Of course, sugarcane dominates the plantations of the coastal lowlands, while farmers raise coffee on the steep slopes of the Cordillera Central.

Above and below ground, and under water, *Puerto Rico and Virgin Islands Wildlife Viewing* by David W Nellis gives you all the facts on the flora and fauna of Puerto Rico.

PARKS, RESERVES & STATE FORESTS

Puerto Rico has more than a dozen well-developed and protected wilderness areas, which offer an array of exploration and a few camping opportunities. Most of these protected areas are considered *reservas forestales* (forest reserves) or *bosques estatales* (state forests), although these identifiers are often treated interchangeably in government-issued literature and maps.

The best-known of these preserves is the 43-sq-mile El Yunque, officially named the Caribbean National Forest, which dominates the cloudy yet sun-splashed peaks at the east end of the island. A second large tract of forest, the Reserva Forestal Toro Negro, dominates the central section of the cordillera and encompasses the island's highest peak (Cerro de Punta, 4389ft).

Reserva Forestal Carite, Bosque Estatal de Guilarte (p241) and Bosque Estatal de Maricao (p242) are all on the slopes of the cordillera. The Bosque Estatal de Río Abajo covers 5780 acres in karst country near the Observatorio de Arecibo. Bosque Estatal de Guajataca is a slightly smaller preserve near the northwest corner of the island, while Bosque Estatal de Guánica, on the southwest coast, is home to a tropical dry forest ecosystem and a Unesco biosphere forest.

PARKS

Name	Features	Activities	Page
El Yunque (Caribbean National Forest)	lush forests, sun-splashed peaks	hiking, mountain biking	p115
Isla Mona	limestone cliffs, giant iguanas	hiking, spelunking	p210
Reserva Forestal Toro Negro	misty mountain tops	hiking, mountain biking	p238
Culebra National Wildlife Refuge	wild turtles, sleepy iguanas, rolling hills	biking, diving, sailing, hiking, swimming	p140
Reserva Forestal Carite	easy hikes through pristine forest	hiking, kayaking, biking, camping	p232
Bosque Estatal de Río Abajo	karst country formations & limestone caves	biking, hiking, camping	p225
Bosque Estatal de Guajataca	pretty man-made lakes in natural settings	hiking, swimming, biking	p221
Bosque Estatal de Guánica	arid scenery, beautiful birds	hiking, swimming, biking	p180
Las Cabezas de San Juan Reserva Natural 'El Faro'	coastal views & mangrove hikes	hiking, kayaking, swimming	p126
Parque de las Cavernas del Río Camuy	hiking	cave exploration	p224

Another notable coastal preserve is the 316-acre Las Cabezas de San Juan Reserva Natural 'El Faro', at the northeast corner of Puerto Rico, where El Faro (the Lighthouse) stands guard over the offshore cays. Eighteen miles east of here lies the island of Culebra, 7 miles long and 4 miles wide. Much of the island has been designated the Culebra National Wildlife Refuge, under the control of the US Fish & Wildlife Service.

Some 300 acres of wilderness make up the Parque de las Cavernas del Río Camuy, near Lares, in karst country; the park marks the entrance to one of the largest known cave systems in the world and is also the site of one of the world's largest underground rivers.

The most isolated of Puerto Rico's nature sanctuaries, Isla Mona, lies about 50 miles east of Mayagüez, across the often-turbulent waters of Pasaje de la Mona. This tabletop island is sometimes called Puerto Rico's Galápagos or Jurassic Park – because of its isolation and total lack of development, 200ft limestone cliffs, honeycomb of caves and giant iguanas.

Commonwealth or US federal agencies administer most of the natural reserves on the island, and you will find that admission to these areas is generally free. Private conservation groups own and operate a few of the nature preserves, including Las Cabezas de San Juan Reserva Natural 'El Faro'; visitors to these places should expect to pay an entrance fee (which is usually under $5). The best time to visit nearly all of the parks is from November to March; however, Bosque Estatal de Guánica is an inviting destination year-round.

All you need to know about the insects, reptiles, four-legged mammals and greenery that they inhabit is in *The Nature of the Islands: Plants and Animals of the Eastern Caribbean* by Virginia Barlow. Very helpful for campers.

Organizations

The **National Park Service** (NPS; www.nps.gov), part of the US Department of the Interior, oversees several Puerto Rican national parks, including San Juan's El Morro (p74).

The **US Forest Service** (USFS; campground & reservation information ☎ 800-280-2267; www.fs.fed.us) is a part of the Department of Agriculture and manages the use of forests such as El Yunque. National forests are less protected than parks, allowing commercial exploitation in some areas (usually logging or privately owned recreational facilities). Current information about national forests can be obtained from ranger stations. (Ranger station contact information is given in this book.)

Puerto Rico maintains regional **US Fish & Wildlife Service** (FWS; www.fws.gov) offices that can provide information about viewing local wildlife. Their phone numbers appear in the white pages of the local telephone directory under 'US Government, Interior Department,' or you can call the **Federal Information Center** (☎ 800-688-9889; www.pueblo.gsa.gov).

> For birders heading to Puerto Rico or the Caribbean, *A Guide to the Birds of Puerto Rico and the Virgin Islands* by Herbert Raffaele is a must-have. It will help you spy lots of hard-to-find birds in the dense forests of nature reserves.

ENVIRONMENTAL ISSUES

Puerto Rico has long suffered from a number of serious environmental problems, including population growth and rapid urbanization, deforestation, erosion of soil, water pollution and mangrove destruction. While Puerto Ricans still have a long way to go toward undoing generations of environmental damage and preserving their natural resources, the past

---

RESPONSIBLE TOURISM

At the outset of the 21st century, with overpopulation and corollary threats to the global environment leading the list of problems confronting humans, the need to protect the environment should not be news to travelers or island residents. Puerto Rico suffers from many environmental troubles, and visitors must be careful not to contribute to these problems.

Travelers should remember that discarded fishing line, plastic bags and six-pack rings entangle and kill birds and sea creatures. Plastics in particular are a serious threat to marine life. Turtles can mistake plastic for jellyfish and eat it. Avoid buying jewelry made from endangered species such as black coral and sea turtles, which threatens the existence of the remaining animals. Remember, too, that taking plants or animals as souvenirs from a forest reserve is stealing.

When possible, recycle – failure to recycle paper, plastic containers, bottles and aluminum cans destroys global resources just as surely as a logging operation in a rainforest. Boaters must not travel at high speeds over seagrass beds, to avoid hitting or even killing endangered turtles and manatees. Discharge of fuels, oils and cleaning bleaches kill all kinds of marine organisms and the birds that feed on them. Do not use anchors on reefs, and take care not to ground boats on coral. Encourage dive operators and regulatory bodies to establish permanent moorings at popular dive sites.

Avoid touching living marine organisms with your body or dragging equipment across the reef. Polyps can be damaged by even the gentlest contact. Never stand on corals, even if they look solid and robust. If you must hold on to a reef, touch only exposed rock or dead coral. Be conscious of your fins. Even without contact, the surge from heavy fin strokes near the reef can damage delicate organisms. When treading water in shallow reef areas, take care not to kick up clouds of sand. Settling sand can easily smother delicate reef organisms. Divers who descend too fast and collide with a reef can do major damage. Taking turns in underwater caves lessens the chances of damaging contact.

Resist the temptation to feed fish. You may disturb their normal eating habits, encourage aggressive behavior or feed them food that is detrimental to their health. Minimize your disturbance of marine animals. In particular, do not ride on the backs of turtles, as this causes them great anxiety.

few decades have seen a general gradual increase in the level of awareness, resources and action dedicated to conservation efforts.

Without a doubt, population growth and rapid urbanization have long posed the greatest threat to the island's environment. Shortsighted solutions, including locking out blacks and the poor or – later in the 19th century – knocking down the fortress wall marking the eastern edge of Old San Juan, have been among the island's ways of coping with its booming population.

The most recent attempts to isolate elements of the citizenry as a means of reducing population density have included the development of large, low-income federal housing projects called *caserios*. As recently as 15 years ago, sociologists identified the *caserios* as a nightmare vision of the island's future. They saw Puerto Rico's population density approaching that of Singapore and projected that the expansion of metropolitan San Juan would envelope virtually all land within a 20-mile radius of the old city.

All this has come to pass, but the birthrate on the island has fallen from almost four children per mother to two. The current birthrate puts the island on track for zero population growth within the decade

A grassroots group of diverse communities in Puerto Rico have come together to fight air pollution, especially in the Cataño Air Basin. Check out their website at http://home.coqui .net/rosah.

Deforestation & Soil Erosion

During the late 19th and early 20th centuries, massive logging operations denuded much of the island. Consequently, untold acres of rich mountain topsoil have eroded away to clog the mouths of rivers and streams. But in the 1920s and '30s, thoughtful islanders and forward-looking conservationists in the island's US colonial government began to set aside and reforest an extensive network of wilderness reserves, mostly in karst country and the Cordillera Central.

Today these reserves are mature forests, and nearly the entire central part of the island – about one-third of Puerto Rico's landmass – is sheltered by a canopy of trees. While the creation of wilderness reserves and reforestation have retarded Puerto Rico's erosion problems, much damage has been done by clearing hillside land for housing subdivisions in places such as Guaynabo and Trujillo Alto, both suburbs of San Juan. Consequently, when heavy rains and hurricanes strike, mudslides and hillside streets that turn into rivers threaten life and property.

Mi isla y yo (My Island and I) by Alfonso Silva Lee and Alexis Lago is a wonderful book for children on how to explore and protect nature. It entertains youngsters with captivating stories about the kinds of wildlife they're likely to encounter in Puerto Rico.

Water Pollution

Reforestation, the creation of wilderness reserves to preserve mountain watersheds, and generally thoughtful creation of mountain reservoirs have gone a long way toward assuring that the island's freshwater resources remain pollution-free. Nevertheless, streams, rivers and estuaries on the coastal plain have long been polluted by agricultural runoff, industry and inadequate sewer and septic systems. And while a number of environmental groups lobby for the cleanup of these cesspools, little has been accomplished. Visitors should not be tempted to swim in rivers, streams or estuaries near the coast (including Bahía de San Juan) – nor should they eat fish or shellfish from these waters – because of the risk of disease and chemical pollutants.

Mangrove Destruction

As with the island's other environmental problems, mangrove destruction was at its worst decades ago when Operation Bootstrap (p33) and the rush to develop business and housing lots saw the devastation of vast mangrove swamps, particularly along the island's north shore in the vicinity of Bahía de San Juan. Small bays such as Laguna Condado, now lined with hotels, homes and businesses, were rich mangrove estuaries just 60 years ago.

Environmentalists began fighting to preserve the island's remaining mangrove estuaries in the mid-1970s, and the late '90s brought a number of significant victories in this arena. Environmentalists won a court battle in 1998 to preserve as wilderness most of the land at the western end of Laguna de Piñones, long slated for development as resort property. Environmentalists have won a similar battle to protect the mangroves around La Parguera, on the island's southwest shore. The creation of the huge 2883-acre Reserva Nacional de Investigación Estuarina de Bahía de Jobos (p177) assures the preservation of the island's largest mangrove estuary, although one power plant stands on the fringe, and a second may be coming.

> The National Astronomy & Ionosphere Center runs www.naic.edu, a site about the Observatorio de Arecibo that has information for the general public as well as academic types.

Heavy-Metal Pollution

Nobody knows for sure what cumulative damage has been done to the land and sea life around Vieques during the years of persistent naval bombardment. When the US Army pulled out of Culebra decades ago, it left an underwater legacy of unexploded ordnance that divers and boaters still have to be wary of today.

The environmental movement has come a long way since then, and when the US Navy announced its departure from Vieques in 2003, locals immediately began asking who was going to be responsible for the cleanup, and who would be paying for any latent health issues that might appear in the future.

Studies done as far back as the 1980s show that the soil of the eastern end of the island is laced with heavy-metal pollution, and quite a few residents of Vieques have been tested and turned up with dangerous levels of heavy metals in their bodies. The Navy has promised to continue regular testing of residents.

The US government deemed Vieques a Superfund site shortly after the pullout, which made its cleanup a federal responsibility organized and implemented by the Environmental Protection Agency (EPA). Environmental assessors and Navy contractors did visual inspections of Red Beach and Blue Beach, and deemed them safe for public use. The Live Impact Area, which encompassed 900 acres on the tip of the eastern end, was designated a Wilderness Area and closed to public access by an Act of Congress in 2003.

> In 2002 the University of Puerto Rico won an international science contest for an innovatively designed house that had solar-powered electricity and hot water. Many houses use solar power on the island.

Many other areas of the Vieques National Wildlife Refuge are closed to the public until heavy metals, unexploded ordnance and left-over fuels and chemicals can be taken care of. According to the US Fish & Wildlife Service, the cleanup will take quite a few years – possibly even a decade – but it will include underwater sites as well. Progress may be hampered, though, by recent revelations from the US government that the Superfund itself – which raised money through a small tax on the chemical and oil industry – is now bankrupt.

Recycling

Although Puerto Rico has a government recycling campaign, there are very few receptacles in public places for the recycling of aluminum cans or other materials, and recycling appears not to be an ingrained habit. The Solid Waste Management Authority collects cans, glass, paper and plastic on the second Saturday of every month, as if recycling day is simply another religious feast day to observe and forget.

Conservation Groups

To combat the mounting destruction of the island's environment, citizens in many municipalities have formed local environmental action groups. Contact one of these organizations listed if you see or hear of a problem or – even better – want to collaborate with professionals and volunteers to help save the island:

Caribbean Environmental Information (☎ 787-751-0239)
Conservation Trust of Puerto Rico (☎ 787-722-5834)
Natural History Society of Puerto Rico (☎ 787-726-5488; www.naturalhistorypr.org)
Puerto Rican Association of Water Resources (☎ 787-977-5870)
Puerto Rican Conservation Foundation (☎ 787-763-9875)

Puerto Rico Outdoors

There's tremendous diversity on this tiny island – you can hike, swim, kayak, hang glide, surf, scuba dive, horsback ride and more. There's a different type of forest to explore or beach to experience for every mood or activity.

HIKING

Among both tourists and islanders, the most popular hiking area in Puerto Rico is the national rainforest at El Yunque (p115), with about 23 miles of hiking trails, including the steep ascent to El Toro peak (3522ft).

Another favorite is the Reserva Forestal Toro Negro (p238) inland on Hwy 143. Don't expect constant dramatic vistas: clouds often shroud the peaks and keep the trails and flora damp.

All the commonwealth's *reservas forestales* (forest reserves; p51) offer good hikes, as does the dry forest in Guánica (p180).

To make a trek in the company of Puerto Rican hikers with local knowledge, take the Saturday hike through the Cañón de San Cristóbal (p235).

Fondo de Mejoramiento (☎ 787-759-8366) run day hikes covering the entire length of the island from east to west along the Cordillera Central (Central Mountains) in successive weekend day trips. The cost of a guided hike depends on the number in your group, but plan on paying from $10 to $30.

Trails Illustrated's *Caribbean National Forest, Puerto Rico, El Yunque Recreation Area* is a hiking guide with illustrated information and topographical maps, as well as backcountry information.

DIVING & SNORKELING

You will find good snorkeling reefs off the coasts of Vieques, Culebra, Fajardo and the small cays east of Fajardo, such as Palominos and Icacos. The cays off the south and east coasts – including Isla Caja de Muertos, Cayo Cardona and Cayo Santiago – also have good shallow reefs. Although the waters off the north and east coasts are often rough, on calm days you can snorkel the fringe reefs off Condado and Isla Verde, as well as Rincón's Little Malibu.

Dive operators run day trips out of the major ports and resort hotels around the island (see the regional chapters for more details). If you are in the San Juan area, consider a dive trip to the caves and overhangs at Horseshoe Reef, Figure Eight or the Molar. There's decent diving along the chain of islands called 'La Cordillera,' east of Las Cabezas de San

---

ALL THAT GLISTENS IS NOT GOLD

Puerto Rico is blessed with three bioluminescent bays filled with tiny organisms that give off an eerie glow to warn away predators. Bringing tourists through these bays at night is big business, but there's a problem: pollution. Engine oils kill the organisms, and so does bug spray with DEET (see p269).

To avoid damaging these endangered bays, only book tours with operators who use kayaks or electric motors. Golden Heron Kayaks (p156) is on Vieques, which has the best bay of the three.

Yokahú Kayaks (p128) covers the Fajardo bay, which is the second-best option.

Sadly, in La Parguera (p185), home to the third bay, most tour operators use only motorized engines. The bioluminescence has been greatly reduced as a consequence. If you're offered a ride, check that it will be in a boat that's safe for the environment. If not, turn the operator down, and make sure to tell them why you are saying no.

Compact and easily carried, *Snorkeling Guide to Marine Life* by Paul Humann is an excellent guide, which lists all the fish, corals, invertebrates and plants found in less than 15ft of water. Great photographs, too.

Juan (in the Fajardo area), with about 60ft to 70ft visibility. Catch the Drift or the Canyon off Humacao. Spectacular wall dives lie 6 miles out of La Parguera on the south coast. From the Rincón area, consider a trip to the fringe reefs and caves at Isla Desecheo. If you're not limited by money, and true adventure diving is your thing, you must take a multiday diving trip to the virgin reefs 50 miles west of Mayagüez at uninhabited Isla Mona, where visibility can be 150ft. See p213 for information about guided hiking and diving trips to Isla Mona.

Travelers planning a dive expedition should get Lonely Planet's *Diving & Snorkeling Puerto Rico*.

SURFING

Since the 1968 world surfing championships at Rincón, surfers the world over have known that Puerto Rico ranks with a few sites in Mexico (such as Puerto Escondido, Oaxaca) and Costa Rica for some of the biggest and best winter surfing in all of the Americas. Check out the surfers map below for a rundown on the best spots to surf the island.

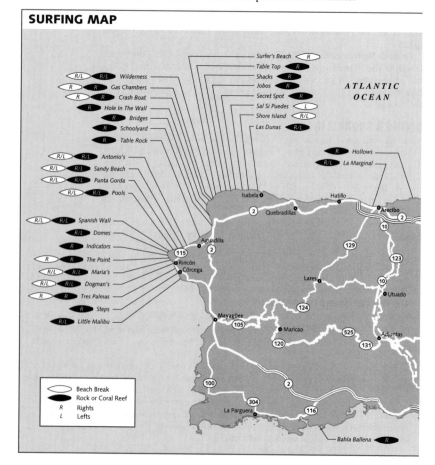

SURFING MAP

If you stay close to San Juan, you will find the *surferos'* scene at the beaches eastward from Isla Verde (p85). But for the big stuff, you need to make a pilgrimage west to Rincón (p202) and Isabela (p219), which host numerous important competitions each year. Stop at the West Coast Surf Shop (p205) for current information on where it's breaking. These breaks are for seasoned surfers only because there are hazards such as submerged rocks, undertows and surf that can often go way over 12ft during the winter months.

Colleen Ryan and Brian Savage's *The Complete Diving Guide: The Caribbean (Volume 2)* has instructions, directions, depths and visibility for just about every dive in the Caribbean.

WINDSURFING

Puerto Rico played host to the Ray Ban Windsurfing World Cup in 1989, and the sport has been booming here ever since. Hotdoggers head for the surfing beaches at Isla Verde or – better yet – the rough northwest coast. Some of the favorite sites here include Playas Crash Boat and Wilderness (p217) in Aguadilla and Playas Shacks and Jobos (p219), near Isabela.

If you are just getting started, try the Laguna Condado in San Juan or Bahía Honda at Culebra, where there are windsurfing schools, constant

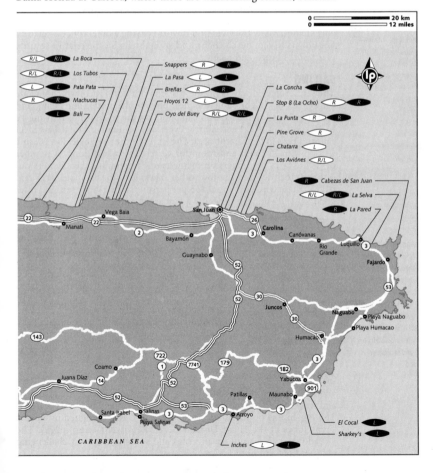

For constantly updated information and insider tips on the best diving spots around Puerto Rico, see www.prdiving.com.

wind and no waves. The protected waters off Wyndham El Conquistador Resort & Golden Door Spa (p129) and the Palmas del Mar Resort (p132) on the east coast are great for novices, as are the bays at La Parguera (p185) and Boquerón (p193). All the shoreside resort hotels have board rentals and instruction.

SWIMMING

With about 750 miles of coastline, Puerto Rico offers travelers a host of swimming beaches. Public beaches, called balnearios, feature lockers, showers and parking at nominal rates, but do not necessarily provide professional lifeguards. These beaches are closed on Monday, Election Day (usually in early November) and Good Friday. Hours are 9am to 5pm in summer, 8am to 5pm in winter. For a complete list, contact the **Departamento de Recreación y Deportes** (Department of Recreation & Sports; ☎ 787-722-5668).

The Puerto Rico Trench that surrounds the north coast is the deepest point in the Atlantic – approximately 27,880ft.

All the balnearios are in lovely settings, but travelers should beware: these beaches can be packed on weekends when island families flee their urban apartments, and some of the beaches draw unsavory crowds. In contrast, some of these beaches look like ghost towns during the week. In general, if a beach and its clientele do not seem safe to you, they probably are not. Many travelers find it worth paying a hotel concessionaire a few dollars to rent beach chairs and an umbrella for the relative security of a resort's beach and facilities.

SAILING

The semiprotected waters off the east end of Puerto Rico, which include the islands of Culebra and Vieques, provide the setting for racing and cruising aboard sailboats. You can count on the trade winds blowing 12 to 25 knots out of the east almost every day. A number of marinas meet sailors' needs in the Fajardo area. The largest is the Puerto del Rey Marina (p127), with 750 slips and room for vessels up to 200ft long. A number of yachts carry passengers on picnic/snorkeling/sailing day charters out of Puerto del Rey and the four other marinas in the area (see p127 and p128). These trips cost about $55 per person for a six-hour sail, and offer good value if you want to enjoy a day of the cruisers' life.

FISHING

Sailors and yacht-lovers shouldn't go anywhere without a copy of *A Cruising Guide to Puerto Rico Including the Spanish Virgin Islands* by Stephen J Pavlidis, which has crucial information for anyone who wants to try and tack between islands.

Puerto Rico hosts many deep-sea fishing tournaments, including the prestigious International Billfishing Tournament in August/September, which is the longest-held billfish tournament in the world. You can fish for tuna all year long. Marlin is a spring/summer fish, sailfish and wahoo run in the fall, and dorado show up in the winter. Charters run from the San Juan Bay Marina; see p89. You can also charter out of docks in Fajardo, Palmas del Mar, La Parguera and Puerto Real.

If you bring your own equipment, you can fish for large-mouth bass, sunfish, catfish and tilapia in the island's freshwater lakes. For more information, contact the Departamento de Recursos Naturales y Ambientales (DRNA; p74).

GOLF

With 10 championship golf courses on the island, Puerto Rico has well and truly earned the reputation of being the 'Scotland of the Caribbean.' The top course on the island is the 18-hole course designed by Robert Trent Jones at the Hyatt Dorado Beach Resort & Casino (p229). The Dorado courses feature ocean vistas and some of the most challenging holes in the Caribbean.

Gary Player designed the 18-hole course at the Palmas del Mar Resort (p132), on the east end of the island, where holes 11 to 15 have been called the 'toughest five successive holes in the Caribbean.' Also on the east end of the island, golfers will find a challenge with the 200ft changes in elevation on the course at the Wyndham El Conquistador Resort & Golden Door Spa (p129) in Fajardo, and two courses by Greg Norman and Tom and George Fazio at the Westin Río Mar Beach Resort & Country Club (p123). The Berwind Country Club course is also in this area (see p123).

If you are on the west coast and craving a game, consider the Club Deportivo de Oeste (p194) at Cabo Rojo, or head north to Aguadilla at Punta Borinquen Golf (p217).

HORSEBACK RIDING

The Palmas del Mar Resort (p132) in Humacao has the island's largest equestrian facility, Rancho Buena Vista, which serves the public with more than 40 horses. Here you will find instruction, trail rides and schooled hunters for jumping. Riders should also check out Tropical Trail Rides (p220) in Isabela and Hacienda Carabaldi (p123) in Mameyes, near Luquillo, at the east end of the island. Horses at these stables will cost you around $30 an hour.

BICYCLING

The high density of automobiles on the island makes bike touring difficult, particularly on the thickly settled north coast of the island. And rugged terrain and frequently slick turf (from tropical showers) on the prime mountain-biking trails of the Central Mountains make freelancing one of these trails risky. Since there is safety in numbers, most travelers do their touring or mountain biking through one of the adventure tour operators.

The best area for cycle touring is along the secondary roads on the southwest coast of the island, through the gently rolling hills of the coastal plain around Guánica, Cabo Rojo and Sabana Grande, the site of the International Cycling Competition each May.

For more information, contact the **Cycling Federation** (☎ 787-721-7185) or bike shops in San Juan such as Condado Bike Rentals (p90), and the **Bike Stop** (☎ 787-782-2282). These shops know the touring and trail-riding scenes out on the island, and they can point you to an expanding network of safe bike routes around San Juan as well.

If you really want to feel comfortable just tooling around on a bike from day to day, head to the less densely populated islands of Vieques or Culebra, where the terrain is gentle, the roads are open and the scenery is rural. You can rent bikes through guesthouses and vendors: see p144 and p156.

If you require lots of information about camping, hiking and generally enjoying the great outdoors in Puerto Rico, check out http://camping.about.com /cs/campgrounds /a/puertorico.htm.

The Islands and the Sea: Five Centuries of Nature Writing from the Caribbean by John A Murray features nature writing from the past 500 years, including original accounts by Columbus.

John Kingsbury's 200 Conspicuous, Unusual, or Economically Important Tropical Plants of the Caribbean is an easy-to-follow guide to shore fauna, with color photographs and short descriptions.

Food & Drink

With the plethora of fast-food restaurants and sudden influx of exotic fusion dishes in restaurants, getting hold of authentic Puerto Rican food – *comida criolla* or *cocina criolla* – can be quite a challenge! Similar in many ways to Central and Latin American cuisine, *comida criolla* features a lot of deep-fried salty snacks, inventive combinations of yucca (a root vegetable similar to a yam and also known as manioc or cassava), plantains (green bananas) and fragrantly spiced rice dishes. For an island, Puerto Rico's surprisingly light on fish dishes, but chicken and beef are present at just about every meal.

STAPLES & SPECIALTIES
Soups & Stews

Soups and stew are staples in *comida criolla*, and in these brews you can taste a fusion of Taíno, European and African recipes and ingredients. Many soups use unique island vegetables to add texture, taste and vitamins. Some of these vegetables, such as yautia (tanier), *batata* (sweet potato), yucca, chayote (squash), *berzas* (collard greens) and *grelos* (turnip greens) might seem odd to North Americans and Europeans. But you'll learn to love these sprouts and tubers when the greens are simmering in a *caldero* (iron/aluminum kettle) with a peculiar mix of criollo spices. *Sancocho* (Caribbean soup) is a blend of many of the vegetables mentioned earlier, along with plantains – peeled and diced – and coarsely chopped tomatoes, green pepper, chili pepper, cilantro leaves, onion and corn kernels. To this mix, the cook adds water, tomato sauce, chopped beef and a few pork ribs for flavoring before cooking it over a low heat.

Perhaps the best-known island concoction to come from a simmering *caldero* is *asopao de pollo*. This is a rich and spicy chicken stew that is fragrant with the ever-present and distinctive seasoning called adobo (garlic, oregano, paprika, peppercorns, salt, olive, lime juice and vinegar crushed into a paste for seasoning meat). Adobo comes from Spain and exists in many Spanish-inspired cuisines, including Filipino, with which it's most often associated.

In addition to adobo, another seasoning that infuses the taste of many criollo dishes is *sofrito*. You can now buy this seasoning on the spice shelves of pueblo supermarkets, but discerning diners say there is nothing like the taste of *sofrito* made from scratch. Certainly the smells that waft from the mix of garlic, onions and pepper browned in olive oil and capped with *achiote* (annato seeds) are enough to make the effort worth it to many cooks.

Meat

Puerto Ricans claim that the modern barbecue descends from the pork roast that the Taínos called *barbicoa*. In this vein, *lechón asado* (roast suckling pig), cooked on a spit over a charcoal fire, is the centerpiece of fiestas and family banquets, particularly at holiday gatherings. Of course, this barbecued pig has been liberally seasoned with adobo, and cooks baste it with *achiote* and the juice from *naranjas* (the island's sour oranges). When cooked to crispness, the meat is served with *ajili-mójili* (a tangy garlic sauce).

For less festive occasions, Puerto Rican dinners will almost always include the staples of *arroz con habichuelas* (rice and beans) and *tostones*,

Puerto Rico: Grand Cuisine of the Caribbean by José Luis Diaz de Villegas is an excellent exploration of the ways in which comida criolla (traditional Puerto Rican cuisine) is infusing and being infused by other culinary cultures. It features many renowned island chefs.

If you've got a hankering to try your hand at aranitas, maduritos or seafood asopao, grab Puerto Rican Cuisine in America: Nuyorican and Bodega Recipes by Oswald Rivera. It's a truly mouthwatering book.

which are fried green plantains, or *panapen* (breadfruit). To these staples, the cook almost always adds a meat dish such as roasted *cabro* (kid goat), *ternera* (veal), *pollo* (chicken) or *carne mechada* (roast beef) – all seasoned with adobo.

Seafood

Surprisingly, Puerto Ricans do not eat a lot of fish. But one of the most popular ways to prepare a variety of fish – from *pulpo* (octopus) to *mero* (sea bass) – is *en escabeche*. This technique yields a fried then chilled seafood pickled in vinegar, oil, peppercorns, salt, onions, bay leaves and lime juice. Fried fish generally comes with a topping of *mojo isleño* (a piquant sauce of vinegar, tomato sauce, olive oil, onions, capers, pimentos, olives, bay leaves and garlic). Land crabs – *jueyes* – have long been a staple of islanders who can simply gather the critters off the beaches. An easy way to enjoy the taste is to eat *empanadillas de jueyes,* in which the succulent crab meat has been picked from the shells, highly seasoned and baked into a wrap made of casabe paste, a flour made from yucca. Of course, grilled or boiled *langosta* (local tropical lobsters without claws) is a pricey delicacy for both islanders and travelers alike. Also try the *ostiones* (miniature oysters) if you like shellfish. Fish lovers should also try a bowl of *sopón de pescado* (fish soup), with its scent of onions and garlic and subtle taste of sherry.

Recipes that come with a sprinkling of history end up tasting twice as sweet. Written by Berta Cabanillas, a professor in Puerto Rico, *Puerto Rican Dishes* explains a lot about the island's culinary history.

Fruits

Puerto Rico grows and exports bananas, papayas, fresh and processed pineapples, as well as a bewildering variety of exotic tropical fruits such as guavas, *tamarindos* (tamarinds), *parchas* (passion fruit) and *guanábanas*

MOFONGO!

No, it's not a curse – it's the unofficial national dish. You'll see it all over the island in a million different guises. Everybody does it differently (unless you are cooking a traditional mofongo, of course), but the core ingredient is always the same: plantains. Some recipes call for pork, some for seafood or chicken, but many recipes, when followed strictly, can be eaten by vegans (no butter or lard allowed – only olive oil). Make sure bacon and/or pork rind aren't included. Here's a recipe to try at home.

Ingredients:

- 3 large green plantains
- 3 cups water mixed with ½ tablespoon salt
- 3 garlic cloves, peeled and chopped
- 3 sweet chili peppers, seeded and minced
- ¼ cup extra virgin olive oil
- salt and pepper to taste
- ¼ cup corn oil

Peel the plantains and cut them into half-inch slices, dropping them into the salted water. Combine the garlic, chili peppers, and olive oil and season with salt and pepper. Heat the corn oil and fry the plantain slices until golden brown. Drain on paper towels. Put a few teaspoons of the garlic/oil mix in a mortar. Add five or six slices of plantain. Mash and press firmly into the mortar. Invert onto a plate. Repeat the process five more times.

(soursops). It's also the third-largest producer of citron – behind Italy and Greece – and you'll see a long swath of fields around Adjuntas dedicated to this fruit.

DRINKS
Nonalcoholic Drinks

Fruit juices, like *guanábana* juice, are locally made and popular with Puerto Ricans (there are carbonated and noncarbonated versions). Other local favorites are carbonated and noncarbonated cans of piña colada (the creamy mix of pineapple juice and coconut cream that can form the basis for a rum drink). *Mavi* is something like root beer, made from the bark of the ironwood tree. As in much of the tropics, beach and street vendors sell chilled green coconuts – *cocos fríos* – to the thirsty.

Coffee, grown in Adjuntas and many of the mountain regions, is a staple at all hours and hardly a meal ends without a cup of steaming java.

Informative and comprehensive, www.wguides.com covers all of Old San Juan, Isla Verde and Condado, but also has reviews and information on Río Piedras, Santurce and lesser-visited parts of the city.

Alcoholic Drinks

Because Puerto Rico is a major producer of alcoholic beverages – and since the government has not levied outlandish taxes on alcohol – Puerto Rico is clearly one of the cheapest places to drink in the Caribbean, and perhaps the world. The importance of rum to Puerto Rico can hardly be exaggerated. Simply put, *ron* (rum) is the national drink. Puerto Rico is the largest producer of rum in the world, and the distilleries bring hundreds of millions of dollars into the island economy. The headquarters for the famous Bacardi Rum Factory is in Cataño (p111), but most locals drink the locally made Don Q, Ronrico, Castillo and Captain Morgan (spiced rum).

There are two island-brewed beers that generally cost no more than $2 in local bars. The India brand has been around for years; Medalla is a popular light pilsner that quite a few islanders drink like water.

CELEBRATIONS

Food is an intrinsic part of Puerto Rican culture, so it's no wonder festivals celebrating regional specialties take place practically year round. The southern region of Salinas, known for seafood, is host to the Salinas Carnival in April. Shrimp lovers should consider visiting the western town of Moca in May for the Festival del Camarón de Río (River Shrimp Festival), where local restaurants and kiosks hold tastings and showcase local recipes. In Lares, located in the mountains, one can sample at least 12 varieties of bananas at the Banana Festival. Those with a sweet tooth should visit the island during the last weekend of August for the Puff Pastry Festival in the western town of Añasco. In October, the northern town of Corozal hosts the National Plantain Festival. The coastal town of Arecibo, where the sardine is considered a delicacy, holds the annual Cetí (a miniature relative of the sardine) Festival. These are just a few of the culinary celebrations that visitors traveling to Puerto Rico might stumble across at any time of year.

Plantains are in such demand they be must imported from the Dominican Republic.

LATIN LIBATIONS

Home-grown rum is the spirit of choice for most cocktails in Puerto Rico (Don Q is the brand favored by locals). Splash in some Coke and you have a Cuba Libre; grenadine and orange juice and it's a Sunrise; coconut and pineapple juice for a Piña Colada. The variations are endless, but the essential ingredient is always *ron*.

WHERE TO EAT & DRINK

There's room for all price ranges in Puerto Rico. Budget-minded diners can easily eat for under $12, while a midrange meal will set you back between $15 and $25. Top end ($30 plus) can go as high as you want it – but you'll get your money's worth.

Usually eaten between about 7am and 9am, typical Puerto Rican breakfasts are light and simple, except on weekends and holidays, when people have more time to cook egg dishes such as *tortilla española* (Spanish omelette) or French toast. You can get American breakfasts at chains like Denny's…and many Puerto Ricans do. More traditional islanders stop at a *repostelría* (bakery) for a long, sweet cup of *café con leche* (a blend of coffee and steamed milk) and a couple of slices of *pan criollo* (a bit like French bread) with butter or *queso de papa* (a mild island cheese). Folks with more of an appetite may get a sandwich. Those with a sweet tooth favor *la mallorca* (a type of sweet pastry that is covered with powdered sugar).

Recipes from La Isla by Robert and Judith Rosado features an extensive listing of recipes, using traditional cooking methods and ingredients (but sometimes with healthier substitutions). Also describes the authentic tools and techniques originally used.

Lunch is available between 11:30am and 2pm. Puerto Ricans usually go cheap on this event, flocking to fast-food outlets for burgers and the like, or gathering around *friquitines* (street vendors) selling a variety of fried finger foods. To a large degree, islanders avoid leisurely luncheon meals in upscale restaurants, and you will find the noon meal the best time of day to sample good Puerto Rican cooking; the restaurants are not crowded and you can often find fixed-price specials for as little as $6.

Dinners, served between about 6pm and 10pm, are more expensive, and a legion of prosperous islanders have developed a tradition of going out to restaurants – especially on Thursday, Friday and Saturday – as a prelude to a long 'night on the town.' Be prepared to wait for a table if you do not call ahead for reservations at popular spots (some of the better restaurants require reservations). The same is true for the big Sunday afternoon *cena* (lunch) at resort destinations near the beach, in the mountains or at a parador. Dinner specials may also be available, but they are usually quite a bit more expensive than virtually the same lunch specials.

Travelers who want to take some of the risk out of sampling island cuisine can take advantage of the Mesones Gastronómicos program, sponsored by the **Puerto Rico Tourism Company** (PRTC; www.gotopuertorico.com). This program has identified a collection of restaurants around the island that feature Puerto Rican cuisine, and has screened those restaurants according to the highest standards of quality. The PRTC publishes a list of these restaurants in its bimonthly magazine, *Qué Pasa*.

At www.meetpuertorico .com you will find lots of reviews of the newest San Juan restaurants by locals, plus a cultural overview of nightlife and entertainment.

Quick Eats

There's hardly a long stretch of highway in mainland Puerto Rico where you won't find street-side shacks (called *friquitines* by most, but also

---

PUERTO RICO'S TOP FIVE

- Tío Danny's (p98) – the best place to unwind in Old San Juan
- El Picoteo (p99, Old San Juan) – can't help responding to the Spanish vibe
- Kiosko La Poceña (p146, Culebra) – homemade food served on a little hill
- Pako's (p172, Ponce) – exquisite food served in front of art from Asia, Africa and Europe
- La Mallorquina (p100, Old San Juan) – savory *asopao* and succulent shrimp every night

buréns in Loíza Aldea) serving up some kind of tasty deep-fried snack. Most of these treats are calorie-laden but delicious; it's rare you'll find anything that hasn't been deep-fried in grease.

Hygiene is pretty much hit or miss. You'll find some vendors who are running a bare-bones operation but are still pretty careful with utensils, grease and refrigeration. Other larger *friquitines* can be much sloppier. Assess things carefully and take time to look around as you approach. If your instincts say no, move on.

If you can't stomach a kiosk, hit any of the numerous fast-food outlets on the island.

VEGETARIANS & VEGANS

The traditional recipes are good in *A Taste of Puerto Rico* by Yvonne Ortiz, but more intriguing are the descriptions of some of the more modern dishes appearing on the island, especially the new emphasis on healthy seafood.

There are a growing number of vegetarian restaurants in Puerto Rico, particularly in Old San Juan and San Juan, but even regular restaurants often carry vegetarian dishes nowadays. It's noted in this book when a restaurant specifically does vegetarian/vegan food, but chefs in many restaurants are very often willing to prepare vegetarian dishes upon request.

Vegans want to be very careful, as butter or meat renderings often find their way into beans and rice, and many other dishes that can be listed as 'vegetarian' by people who don't fully understand that an absence of actual meat doesn't automatically make a meal vegan.

EATING WITH KIDS

Children are welcomed everywhere in Puerto Rico, but it would be a faux pas to bring extremely young children to some of the sleeker restaurants in San Juan. Generally most restaurants are happy to do things like heat up a baby bottle for you, but know that microwaves aren't employed widely outside of San Juan. Baby chairs are often available (especially in fast-food restaurants) and you will see entire families dining out at a wide range of restaurants; you needn't worry that you'll be the only one with kids.

HABITS & CUSTOMS

Yucca turnovers is just one of the old-fashioned recipes found in Carmen Aboy Valldejuli's *Puerto Rican Cookery*, and hardly a page can be turned without finding similar deep-fried starchy dishes.

There are very few tricks to dining out easily in Puerto Rico – you can eat with your left or right hand, hold your utensils American or British style, follow basic table manners and get along fine.

Breakfast and lunch tend to be quick, unless you're having a business meal – they can drag on forever. Dinner in restaurants is always a social and festive affair, so solitary diners will stick out a bit. Lunch is much easier to navigate solo. Smoking and belching are best taken outside, but otherwise there's little you can do that will upset easygoing Puerto Ricans (aside from criticizing their cooking, that is).

If invited to someone's house, bringing a bottle of rum, beer or wine will be well received (more so than flowers). Don't argue when the hosts serve you a gargantuan portion; it's probably more than they would eat in a week, but as their guest, you get special treatment.

EAT YOUR WORDS
Useful Phrases

See the Language chapter (p270) for other useful Spanish words and phrases, and pronunciation guidelines.

Table for ..., please.
  Una mesa para ..., por favor.   *oo·*na *me·*sa *pa·*ra ... por fa·*vor*
Can I see the menu please?
  ¿Puedo ver el menú, por favor?   *pwe·*do ver el me·*noo* por fa·*vor*

How late are you open?
    ¿El restoran está abierto hasta cuándo?   el re·sto·*ran* e·*sta* a·*byer*·to ha·sta *kwan*·do

Is this the smoking section?
    ¿Aquí se puede fumar?   a·*kee* se *pwe*·de foo·*mar*

Is there a table with a view available?
    ¿Hay una mesa con vista?   ai *oo*·na *me*·sa con *vis*·ta

I'm a vegetarian.
    Soy vegetariana/o.   soy veg·khe·ta·*rya*·na/o

What's in this dish?
    ¿Qué ingredientes tiene este plato?   ke een·gre·*dyen*·tes *tye*·ne es·te *pla*·to

What is today's special?
    ¿Cuál es el plato del día?   kwal es el *pla*·to del *dee*·a

I'll try what she/he's having.
    Probaré lo que ella/él está comiendo.   pro·*ba*·ray lo ke e·lya/el es·*ta* ko·*myen*·do

Can I have a (beer) please?
    Una (cerveza), por favor.   *oo*·na (ser·*ve*·sa) por fa·*vor*

Thank you, that was delicious.
    Muchas gracias, estaba buenísimo.   *moo*·chas *gra*·syas es·*ta*·ba bwe·*nee*·see·mo

The check/bill, please.
    La cuenta, por favor.   la *kwen*·ta por fa·*vor*

Food Glossary

Following is a handy list of common Puerto Rican menu items.

aguacate	a·gwa·*ka*·te	avocado
ajo	*a*·kho	garlic
alcapurrias	al·ka·*pu*·ree·as	fish, pork or crab fried in a batter of ground plaintains
amarillos en dulce	a·ma·*ree*·lyos en *dul*·se	ripe plaintains fried in sugar, red wine and cinnamon
almejas frescas	al·*me*·khas *fres*·kas	cherrystone clams
al ajillo	al a·*khee*·lyo	with garlic or cooked in garlic
a la parilla	a la pa·*ree*·lya	grilled
al horno	al *or*·no	oven-baked
asado	a·*sa*·do	roasted and seasoned with sofrito
asopao	a·sa·*pa*·o	an island specialty, a delicious thick stew often with seafood
arroz	a·*roz*	rice
bacalaítos	ba·ka·la·*ee*·tos	fried codfish fritters
bien-me-sabe	byen·me·*sa*·be	a coconut sauce over sponge cake
bistec pizzaola	bi·*stek* pit·za·o·la	breaded beef cutlets
caldo de gallina or *sopa de pollo criollo*	*kal*·do de ga·*lyee*·na *so*·pa de *po*·lyo kree·o·lyo	creole chicken soup

---

DOS & DON'TS

■ Do tip 15% (20% if service was fantastic).

■ Don't insist on paying unless you've specifically invited someone as your guest.

■ Do politely ask if there's a nonsmoking section if someone is indulging next to you.

■ Don't insist on smoking if the restaurant doesn't allow it.

■ Do compliment the food if it's well done, and especially if you're at a private home.

■ Don't use a toothpick at the table, or if you must, shield the action with your hand.

■ Do try to clean your plate. Puerto Ricans hate to waste food.

camarones	ka·ma·*ro*·nes	shrimp
carrucho	ka·*roo*·cho	conch
cebolla	se·*bo*·lya	onion
chicharrones de pollo	chee·cha·*ro*·nes·de *po*·lyo	chicken crisps
chicharrón	chee·cha·*ron*	crisp pork rind
chillo	*chee*·lyo	snapper
chuletas	choo·*le*·tas	pork chops
churrasco	choo·*ra*·sko	charcoal-broiled Argentinean steak
cocina del kiosko	ko·*see*·na del·*kyo*·sko	food-stand offerings
dulce de leche	*dul*·se de *le*·che	candied milk
empanadilla	em·pa·na·*dee*·lya	plantain or yucca dough stuffed with meat or fish and fried
ensalada mixta	en·sa·*la*·da *mik*·sta	mixed salad
ensalada verde	en·sa·*la*·da *vair*·de	green salad
flan	flan	custard
filete a la criolla	fi·*le*·te a la kree·*o*·la	creole steak
filete a la parrilla	fi·*le*·te a la pa·*ree*·lya	broiled steak
frito	*free*·to	fried
guineas al vino	gee·*nay*·as al *vee*·no	guinea hen in wine
guisado	gee·*sa*·do	stewed
habichuelas	ha·bee·*chwe*·las	beans
langosta	lan·*gos*·ta	lobster
lechón asado	le·*chon* a·*sa*·do	roast pig
maní	ma·*nee*	peanuts
mariscos	ma·*ris*·kos	shellfish
medallon de filete	me·da·*lyon* de fi·*le*·te	beef medallions
mero	*me*·ro	seabass
mofongo	mo·*fong*·go	balls of mashed plaintains mixed with pork rind and spices and fried; sometimes stuffed with crab or lobster
parrillada	pa·ree·*lya*·da	spicy grilled steak
natilla	na·*tee*·lya	ice cream
pastelillos de chapin	pa·ste·*lee*·los de cha·*pin*	fried dumplings of trunk fish
pescado	pe·*ska*·do	fish
pionono	pyo·*no*·no	cone of mashed plantains stuffed with seasoned ground meat, deep-fried in batter
piragua	pee·*ra*·gwa	cup of shaved ice covered with a fruity syrup in the tradition of a US snow cone
pulpo	*pul*·po	octopus
sopa	*so*·pa	soup
tembleque	tem·*ble*·ke	pudding made from coconut
tostones	tos·*to*·nes	twice-fried plantains, sometimes coated with honey
vegetales	ve·khe·*ta*·les	vegetables

San Juan

When in Puerto Rico you must accept that all roads lead to San Juan, and not just because it's home to more than one-third of all islanders. This is where the island's heartbeat is – a place of great economic opportunity, beautiful, gleaming casinos and hotels, a university, multiple art galleries, museums and a sophisticated nightlife.

And who would want to overlook San Juan, anyway? It's not just the glamorous high-rise hotels and sleek condos along the beaches of Condado, Isla Verde and Ocean Park that you'd miss, but also the working-class charm of Santurce, the raucous student energy of Río Piedras, and the turbulent pace of downtown Hato Rey.

Then there's the crown jewel, the magnificent walled city that the world has come to know as Old San Juan (Viejo San Juan). This working, breathing community, characterized by cobblestone streets, pastel-colored town houses, Romanesque arches, wrought-iron balconies, intimate courtyards and striking vistas, has the look and feel of a Spanish colonial city. Chock-full of restaurants, clubs, bars, shops and museums, Old San Juan offers the traveler more entertainment per square foot than New York City – at a laid-back, Latin pace.

Beyond the walls of Old San Juan, the modern city demands attention, with flashing neon lights advertising casinos, hotels and fast-food restaurants. But it has its hidden joys, as well; look for them in the neighborhoods where artists paint, and the songs of the next generation of salsa legends fill the streets. Or go for a complete change of pace and follow *sanjuaneros* on their weekend jaunts to nearby Piñones or Loíza Aldea for deep-fried seafood snacks and a taste of bohemian beach life. You can experience many things in San Juan, but boredom isn't one of them.

HIGHLIGHTS

- Get carried away by history while walking the ramparts of **El Morro** (p74)
- Lose yourself in the cobblestone wonder of **Old San Juan's** (p74) colonial streets
- Explore the gastronomic delights of sexy **SoFo** (south end of Calle Fortaleza, p82)
- Admire the incredible artwork on display at Santurce's **Museo de Arte de Puerto Rico** (p84)
- Hit the **beaches** (p88) along Isla Verde and Condado by day and the **discos** (p104) by night

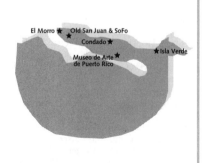

El Morro ★   Old San Juan & SoFo ★
       Condado ★
                    ★ Isla Verde
   Museo de Arte ★
   de Puerto Rico

- POPULATION: 1.6 MILLION
- DRINK: MOJITO

HISTORY

It's hard to believe that San Juan was once a deserted spit of land dominated only by dramatic headlands and strong trade winds, but that was the case when Spaniards first arrived with long-term intentions in the early 1500s. Unable to stave off constant Indian attacks or mosquito-borne malaria in the lower lands, they retreated to the rocky outcrop in 1521 and christened it Puerto Rico ('Rich Port'). (A Spanish cartographer accidentally transposed San Juan Bautista – what Spaniards called the island – with 'Puerto Rico' on some maps a few years later, and the name change permanently stuck.)

The gigantic fortress of El Morro, with its 140ft-high ramparts, quickly rose above the ocean cliffs. The Catholic Church arrived en masse to build a church, a convent and a cathedral. For the next three centuries, San Juan was the primary military and legislative outpost of the Spanish empire in the Caribbean and Central America. But economically it stagnated, unable to prosper from the smuggling that was pervasive elsewhere on the island.

That all changed after the Spanish-American War of 1898. The US annexed the island as a 'territory' and designated San Juan as the primary port. Agricultural goods such as sugar, tobacco and coffee flowed into the city. *Jíbaros* (country people) flocked to the shipping terminals for work and old villages like Río Piedras were swallowed up.

The unchecked growth surge was a nightmare for city planners, who struggled to provide services, roads and housing. By the 1980s, franchises of US fast-food restaurants were everywhere, but there were few places to get a gourmet meal featuring the island's *comida criolla* (traditional Puerto Rican cuisine). Housing developments blighted much of the area; unemployment was rampant, and crime was high. Ironically, Old San Juan was considered the epicenter of all that was wrong with the city. Tourists kept to the overdeveloped beaches of Condado, Isla Verde and Miramar.

In 1992, the world marked the 500-year anniversary of Columbus' 'discovery' of the Americas. That celebration gave city leaders the impetus needed to focus on the historic restoration of Old San Juan. The energy and finesse that characterized that effort waned slightly as the decade ended. Several modern projects – like the Tren Urbano, which is supposed to provide cheaper, quicker transportation to locals – haven't gotten the political push needed to finish them off.

CLIMATE

San Juan is blessed with strong trade winds that keep mosquitoes at bay and somewhat lessen the sun's vigor. In the summer months (June, July, August and September), the city gets increasingly hot and humid, averaging in the high 80s. Rains come from late September through early November. San Juan isn't hit as hard as the El Yunque area to the east, but gets a good amount of overflow. December through May the weather is at its best – highs in the mid-80s, lows in the high 70s (sometimes those trade winds will have you reaching for a sweater at night) with little humidity.

ORIENTATION

Starting at the westernmost tip of the city and working backwards toward the Aeropuerto Internacional de Luis Muñoz Marín (LMM), you've got Old San Juan, the tourist center and most visually appealing part of town. Following the coast, Condado is next, flashy and full of big buildings and hotels along Av Ashford. Miramar and Santurce, to the north and south of Condado, respectively, and set back from the beach, are mostly filled with working-class families. Ocean Park is a private community (with gates) lying along the water between Condado and Isla Verde; its big street is Av McLeary. The final stop in the city is Isla Verde (although, technically speaking, it is in Carolina, a suburb of San Juan). Av Isla Verde is a long stretch of hotels and casinos along a narrow but pretty white beach; the only drawback is the proximity of the airport. Large jets thunder overhead every 20 minutes or so for most of the day.

Hato Rey is the name of the business district of high-rise banks and offices that flanks Av Ponce de León, south of Santurce. Further south, beyond Hato Rey, is Río Piedras, home to the largest campus of the Universidad de Puerto Rico (UPR).

Maps

Travelers will find tourist maps of Old San Juan, Condado and Isla Verde readily available through the tourist information offices run by the Puerto Rico Tourism Company (p74).

If you are driving or want a more complete view of the city, Rand McNally and Metro Data publish fold-out maps of San Juan/Puerto Rico that include a detailed overview of the metro area. These maps are widely available from most bookstores and drugstores in the city's tourist zones for about $5. See p252 for maps covering other island destinations.

Once you have a map, study it with someone who has good local knowledge regarding traffic jams, damaged roads and crime (p74).

INFORMATION
Bookstores
Bell, Book & Candle (Map pp84-5; ☎ 787-728-5000; 102 Av José de Diego, Condado) Pulls in the vacation crowd and offers a wide range of English titles.

Bookshop (Map pp76-7; ☎ 787-724-1815; 201 Cruz near Plaza de Armas, Old San Juan) A great place to familiarize yourself with the latest Puerto Rican authors, in English translation or original Spanish.

Bookworm (Map pp84-5; ☎ 787-722-3344; 1129 Av Ashford) Gay literature in Spanish and English as well as mainstream picks. Very helpful and friendly staff.

Emergency
Beware: you may find that the telephone directory and tourist publications list non-functioning local numbers for emergency services. In *any* kind of emergency, call ☎ 911.

Fire (☎ 787-722-1120, 343-2330)
Hurricane warnings (☎ 787-253-4586)
Isla Verde police (☎ 787-449-9320)
Medical emergencies (☎ 787-754-2550)
Rape crisis hotline (☎ 877-641-2004, 800-981-5721, 787-765-2285)
Río Piedras police (☎ 787-765-6439)
Tourist zone police (☎ 911, 787-726-7020; ☽ 24hr) English spoken.

Internet Access
Crew Station Internet Café (Map pp76-7; ☎ 787-289-0345; La Marina; per 15min $4) Phone cards, fax, web cam, scanner and more available.

Cybernet Café Condado (Map pp84-5; ☎ 787-724-4033; 1128 Av Ashford; per hr $5-6); Isla Verde (Map p86; ☎ 787-791-3138; 5575 Av Isla Verde; per hr $5-6)

Diner's Internet (Map pp76-7; ☎ 787-724-6276; 311 Tetuan, Old San Juan)

Laundry
Rates run about $1.50 to $2 per wash and 50c per 10 minutes to dry.

La Lavandería (Map pp76-7; ☎ 787-717-8585; 201 Sol near Cruz, Old San Juan) The laundromat with the best view in town.

Laundry Condado Cleaners (Map pp84-5; ☎ 787-721-9254; 63 Calle Condado) Promises a fast turnaround, and delivers too.

Medical Services
Ashford Memorial Community Hospital (Map pp84-5; ☎ 787-721-2160; 1451 Av Ashford) This is probably the best-equipped and most convenient hospital for travelers to visit..

Walgreens Old San Juan (Map pp76-7; ☎ 787-722-6690; cnr Cruz & San Francisco); Condado (Map pp84-5; ☎ 787-725-1510; 1130 Av Ashford; ☽ 24hr) US drugstore chains like Walgreens are all over the city.

Money
Banco Popular LMM airport (☎ 787-791-0326; Terminal C); Old San Juan (Map pp76-7; ☎ 787-725-2635; cnr Tetuán & San Justo) Near the cruise ship piers and Paseo de

SAN JUAN

SAN JUAN

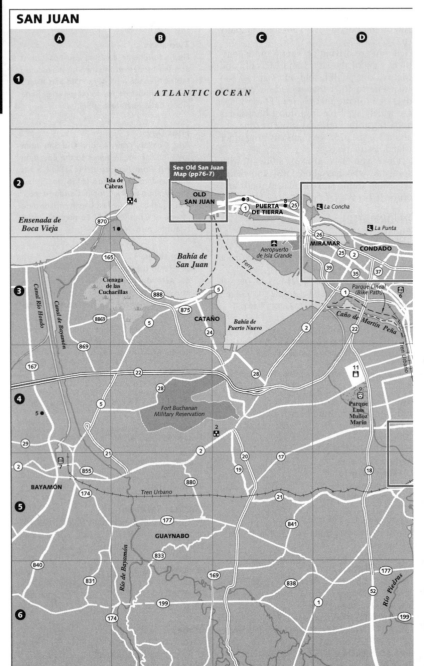

ATLANTIC OCEAN

See Old San Juan
Map (pp76-7)

OLD
SAN JUAN

Isla de
Cabras

☒ 4

● 1

Ensenada de
Boca Vieja

870

165

●3
● 1

PUERTA
DE TIERRA

8
●

25

La Concha

La Punta

MIRAMAR
26

CONDADO
25 2

35 37

39

Parque Lineal
(Bike Path)

6

Bahía de
San Juan

Ferry

Aeropuerto
de Isla Grande

Cienaga
de las
Cucharillas

888

875

CATAÑO

24

Bahía de
Puerto Nuevo

2

1

Caño de Martín Peña

22

Tren Urbano

Canal Río Hondo

Canal de Bayamón

8869

5

869

167

5

5

22

28

28

Fort Buchanan
Military Reservation

2
☒

2

20

19

17

11
☒

9
☒

Parque
Luis
Muñoz
Marín

5 ●

29

21

2

855

174

BAYAMÓN

Tren Urbano

880

21

18

GUAYNABO

177

833

841

840

831

Río de Bayamón

169

838

177

199

1

52

Río Piedras

174

199

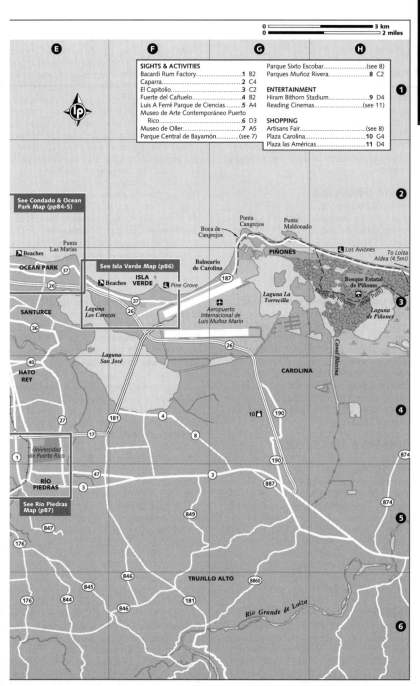

SIGHTS & ACTIVITIES
Bacardi Rum Factory..........................**1** B2
Caparra...**2** C4
El Capitolio.......................................**3** C2
Fuerte del Cañuelo...........................**4** B2
Luis A Ferré Parque de Ciencias.........**5** A4
Museo de Arte Contemporáneo Puerto
  Rico..**6** D3
Museo de Oller.................................**7** A5
Parque Central de Bayamón............(see 7)

Parque Sixto Escobar......................(see 8)
Parques Muñoz Rivera......................**8** C2

ENTERTAINMENT
Hiram Bithorn Stadium......................**9** D4
Reading Cinemas...........................(see 11)

SHOPPING
Artisans Fair..................................(see 8)
Plaza Carolina.................................**10** G4
Plaza las Américas..........................**11** D4

la Princesa; Condado (Map pp84-5; Av Ashford); Isla Verde (Map p86; Av Isla Verde) Charge only 1% commission to cash traveler's checks.

Post

Greater San Juan has about 20 post offices. **Main Post Office** (Map pp72-3; ☎ 787-767-2890; 585 Av Roosevelt, Hato Rey; ☒ 7:30am-4:30pm Mon-Fri, 8:30am-noon Sat) General delivery mail comes here. **Old San Juan Post Office** (Map pp76-7; ☎ 787-723-1281; 153 Fortaleza; ☒ 7:30am-4:30pm Mon-Fri, 8:30am-noon Sat) The one likely to be most convenient for travelers.

Tourist Information

Puerto Rico Tourism Company (PRTC) distributes information in English and Spanish at two venues in San Juan, the LMM airport and La Casita in Old San Juan. At the airport, stop at the information counter between Terminals B and C or visit the PRTC's desk on the lower (arrivals) areas of Terminals B and C.

Departamento de Recursos Naturales y Ambientes (DRNA; Department of Natural Resources; Map pp84-5; ☎ 787-724-8774; www.drna.gobierno.pr in Spanish; Av Muñoz Rivera, Pda 3½, Puerta de Tierra) For information on camping, including reservations and permits, contact this department or visit its office.
Puerto Rico Tourism Company (PRTC; ☎ 800-223-6530, 787-721-2400; www.prtourism.com) LMM airport (☎ 787-791-1014; ☒ 9am-5:30pm); Old San Juan (Map pp76-7; ☎ 787-722-1709; La Casita, Calle Comercio & Plaza de la Darsena near Pier 1)

DANGERS & ANNOYANCES

Under no circumstances should you walk into La Perla (p81), the picturesque yet poverty-stricken enclave outside the north wall of Old San Juan. Avoid the neighboring cemetery at night as well. Some travelers have been mugged during daylight hours along the eastern end of Old San Juan's Calle Norzagaray by drug addicts who hang out in the alleys and park near here. Puerta de Tierra is also a no-no once the sun sets. Avoid Calle Loíza in Santurce and the Plaza del Mercado in Río Piedras at night.

SIGHTS

Most of San Juan's major attractions, including museums and art galleries, are in Old San Juan. There are a few things worth visiting in Condado, Santurce and Río Piedras, but schedule serious time for the old town.

Old San Juan   Map pp76–7

It's possible to devote days, weeks or even months to soaking up the tropical flavor of **Old San Juan** and yielding to the town's mood swings, from pensive mornings to passionate nights. The old town is comprised of lots of crisscrossing cobblestone streets on a hilly incline leading to El Morro, but it's compact: even visitors with severe limits on their time and money can get a feel for this Unesco World Heritage site. Remember to reserve the midday heat for a long lunch in a dark, cool restaurant, a swim or a siesta.

Visitors should note that on weekends Old San Juan is a magnet for Puerto Ricans from all over the island. Also, many cruise ships disgorge their passengers here Saturday through Tuesday. Thursday and Friday tend to be the quietest days, but the town turns wild on those evenings as flocks of night owls descend from all over the city and its suburbs.

COLONIAL FORTS AND BUILDINGS
El Morro

A six-level fort with a gray, castellated lighthouse, **El Morro** (Fuerte San Felipe del Morro; San Felipe Fort; ☎ 787-729-6960; www.nps.gov/saju /morro.html; adult/child/senior $3/1/2; ☒ 9am-5pm, free tours at 10am & 2pm in Spanish, 11am & 3pm in English) juts aggressively over Old San Juan's bold headlands, glowering across the Atlantic at would-be conquerors. The 140ft walls (some up to 15ft thick) date back to 1539, and El Morro is said to be the oldest Spanish fort in the New World. The National Park Service (NPS) maintains this fort and the small military museum on the premises. Displays and videos in Spanish and English document the construction of the fort, which took almost 200 years, as well as El Morro's role in rebuffing the various attacks on the island by the British and the Dutch, and later the US military. It was declared a Unesco World Heritage site in 1983. The lighthouse on the 6th floor is the island's oldest and still in use today.

If you do not join one of the free guided tours, at least try to make the climb up the ramparts to the sentries' walks along the **Sta Barbara Bastion** and **Austria Half-Bastion** for the views of the sea, the bay, Old San Juan, modern San Juan, El Yunque and the island's mountainous spine. On weekends, the fields leading up to the fort are alive with picnickers, lovers and kite flyers. The scene makes an impromptu festival with food vendors' carts on the perimeter. Keep your receipt for free entrance to Fuerte San Cristóbal.

Fuerte San Cristóbal

Just a five-minute walk down Calle Norzagaray, the street veers away from the ocean and the city's wall butts up against **Fuerte San Cristóbal** (San Crisobal Fort; ☎ 787-729-6777; www .nps.gov/saju/sancristobal.html; adult/child/senior $3/1/2; ☻ 9am-5pm Jun-Nov, 9am-6pm Dec-May), which is the old city's other major fortification. In its prime, San Cristóbal covered 27 acres with a maze of six interconnected forts protecting a central core with 150ft walls, moats, booby-trapped bridges and tunnels. The fort was constructed to defend Old San Juan against land attacks from the east via Puerta de Tierra. The imaginative design for Fuerte San Cristóbal came from the famous Irish mercenary Alejandro O'Reilly and his compatriot Thomas O'Daly (hired by Spain); construction began in 1634 and lasted well over a century. As with El Morro, the NPS maintains the fort, which includes a small museum, a store, military archives and a reproduction of a soldier's barracks. Because San Cristóbal attracts far fewer tourists than El Morro, it retains the austere ambience of its working days. Entry is free with admission receipt from El Morro.

La Fortaleza

Recinto Oeste makes a steep climb to the top of the city wall and the guarded iron gates of **La Fortaleza** (The Fortress; ☎ 787-721-7000 ext 2211 or 2358; admission free; ☻ 9am-3:30pm Mon-Fri). Also known as El Palacio de Santa Catalina, this imposing building is the oldest executive mansion in continuous use in the Western Hemisphere, dating from 1533. Once the original fortress for the young colony, La Fortaleza eventually yielded its military pre-eminence to the city's newer and larger forts, and was remodeled and expanded to domicile island governors for more than three centuries. If you are dressed in respectful attire, you can join a guided tour that includes the mansion's Moorish gardens, the dungeon and the chapel. Free guided tours generally run on weekdays except holidays; tours in English leave on the hour, in Spanish on the half hour. Call in advance to make sure the grounds are not closed for a government function.

El Arsenal

On the point of land called La Puntilla is a low, gray fortress with a Romanesque proscenium entrance. This is **El Arsenal** (The Arsenal; ☎ 787-724-1877, 724-5949; admission free; ☻ 8:30am-4pm Mon-Fri), a former Spanish naval station that was the last place to house Spanish military forces after the US victory in the Spanish-American War. Today, the arsenal is home to the fine- and decorative-arts divisions of the Instituto de Cultura Puertorriqueña, and hosts periodic exhibitions in three galleries.

Puerta de San Juan

Spanish ships once anchored in the cove just off these ramparts to unload colonists

---

INSIDER TIPS

Unsuspecting visitors tear into Old San Juan like there's no tomorrow, but the maze of alleys and sights can deplete your energy in no time. Here's how the locals handle things.

■ Avoid rushing. See those picturesque cobblestones on the streets? They're really ankle-twisting traps. Proceed at a leisurely pace, and that goes extra for anyone in high heels.

■ Take the path of least resistance. You want to see El Morro. On the map it looks like a straight climb. It is, if you go that way. But the Spaniards cleverly designed the crisscrossing streets as a ladder. Move horizontally, and each successive block works like a rung. You'll arrive at El Morro much less exhausted and a good deal cooler.

■ *Sol y sombra*. Another trick those wily Spaniards used to beat the heat. Building tall houses on narrow streets means one side is always shaded *(sombra)*. Note that you'll never see a local walking down the sunny *(sol)* side in midafternoon.

■ Wet your whistle. There's a bar on every corner (and several in between) because you need to hydrate often in the tropics. Step inside and set a spell. You'll be in good company.

SAN JUAN

OLD SAN JUAN

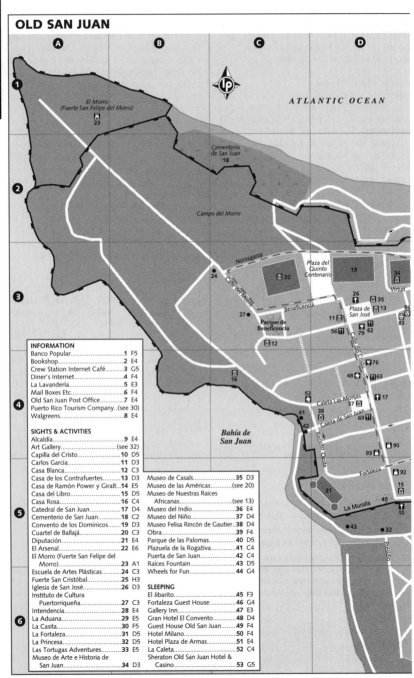

El Morro
(Fuerte San Felipe del Morro)
23

ATLANTIC OCEAN

Cementerio
de San Juan
18

Campo del Morro

Norzagaray

Plaza del
Quinto
Centenario

24

Calle del Morro

20

19

34

Virtud

26

35

Beneficencia

Plaza de
San José

13

86

27

11

79

62

83

Parque de
Beneficencia

56

12

16

Bahía de
San Juan

52

Caleta Las Monjas

48

76

63

17

41

38

37

69

42

Caleta de San Juan

Recinto Oeste

93

90

Fortaleza

31

92

15

La Muralla

40

10

43

32

Presidio

INFORMATION
Banco Popular.............................1 F5
Bookshop....................................2 E4
Crew Station Internet Café.........3 G5
Diner's Internet...........................4 F4
La Lavandería..............................5 E3
Mail Boxes Etc............................6 F4
Old San Juan Post Office............7 E4
Puerto Rico Tourism Company..(see 30)
Walgreens...................................8 E4

SIGHTS & ACTIVITIES
Alcaldía......................................9 E4
Art Gallery.............................(see 32)
Capilla del Cristo.......................10 D5
Carlos Garcia.............................11 D3
Casa Blanca...............................12 C3
Casa de los Contrafuertes.........13 D3
Casa de Ramón Power y Giralt..14 E5
Casa del Libro...........................15 D5
Casa Rosa..................................16 C4
Catedral de San Juan................17 D4
Cementerio de San Juan............18 C2
Convento de los Dominicos.......19 D3
Cuartel de Ballajá......................20 C3
Diputación.................................21 E4
El Arsenal..................................22 E6
El Morro (Fuerte San Felipe del
  Morro).................................23 A1
Escuela de Artes Plásticas.........24 C3
Fuerte San Cristóbal..................25 H3
Iglesia de San José....................26 D3
Instituto de Cultura
  Puertorriqueña......................27 C3
Intendencia................................28 E4
La Aduana.................................29 E5
La Casita....................................30 F5
La Fortaleza...............................31 D5
La Princesa.................................32 D5
Las Tortugas Adventures...........33 E5
Museo de Arte e Historia de
  San Juan...............................34 D3

Museo de Casals.......................35 D3
Museo de las Américas...........(see 20)
Museo de Nuestras Raíces
  Africanas.............................(see 13)
Museo del Indio.......................36 E4
Museo del Niño.........................37 D4
Museo Felisa Rincón de Gautier..38 D4
Obra...39 F4
Parque de las Palomas...............40 D5
Plazuela de la Rogativa..............41 C4
Puerta de San Juan....................42 C4
Raíces Fountain.........................43 D5
Wheels for Fun..........................44 G4

SLEEPING
El Jibarito..................................45 F3
Fortaleza Guest House...............46 G4
Gallery Inn.................................47 E3
Gran Hotel El Convento.............48 D4
Guest House Old San Juan........49 F4
Hotel Milano..............................50 F4
Hotel Plaza de Armas.................51 E4
La Caleta...................................52 C4
Sheraton Old San Juan Hotel &
  Casino..................................53 G5

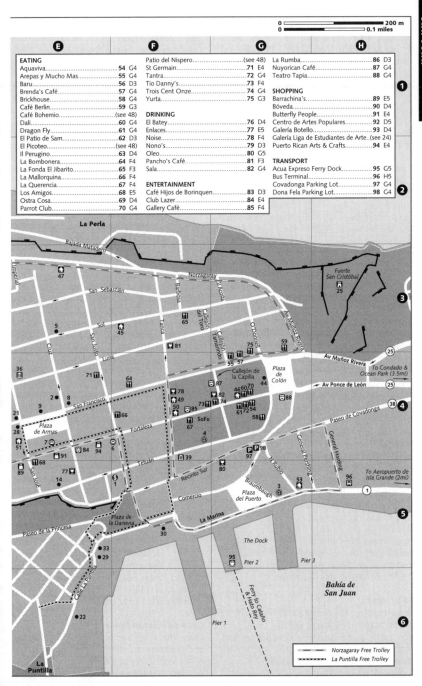

EATING
Aquaviva	**54** G4
Arepas y Mucho Mas	**55** G4
Baru	**56** D3
Brenda's Café	**57** G4
Brickhouse	**58** G4
Café Berlin	**59** G3
Café Bohemio	(see 48)
Dali	**60** G4
Dragon Fly	**61** G4
El Patio de Sam	**62** D3
El Picoteo	(see 48)
Il Perugino	**63** D4
La Bombonera	**64** F4
La Fonda El Jibarito	**65** F3
La Mallorquina	**66** F4
La Querencia	**67** F4
Los Amigos	**68** E5
Ostra Cosa	**69** D4
Parrot Club	**70** G4

Patio del Nispero	(see 48)
St Germain	**71** E4
Tantra	**72** G4
Tio Danny's	**73** F4
Trois Cent Onze	**74** G4
Yurta	**75** G3

DRINKING
El Batey	**76** D4
Enlaces	**77** E5
Noise	**78** F4
Nono's	**79** D3
Oleo	**80** G5
Pancho's Café	**81** F3
Sala	**82** G4

ENTERTAINMENT
Café Hijos de Borinquen	**83** D3
Club Lazer	**84** E4
Gallery Café	**85** F4

La Rumba	**86** D3
Nuyorican Café	**87** G4
Teatro Tapia	**88** G4

SHOPPING
Barrachina's	**89** E5
Bóveda	**90** D4
Butterfly People	**91** E4
Centro de Artes Populares	**92** D5
Galería Botello	**93** D4
Galería Liga de Estudiantes de Arte	(see 24)
Puerto Rican Arts & Crafts	**94** E4

TRANSPORT
Acua Expreso Ferry Dock	**95** G5
Bus Terminal	**96** H5
Covadonga Parking Lot	**97** G4
Dona Fela Parking Lot	**98** G4

Norzagaray Free Trolley

La Puntilla Free Trolley

SAN JUAN

and supplies, all of which entered the city through a tall red portal known as **Puerta de San Juan** (San Juan Gate). This tunnel through the wall dates from the 1630s. It marks the end of the Paseo de la Princesa, and stands as one of three remaining gates into the old city (the others lead into the cemetery and the enclave of La Perla). Once there were a total of five gates, and the massive wooden doors were closed each night to thwart intruders.

La Casita

Looking like a yellow gatehouse, **La Casita** (Little House) greets visitors near the cruise ship docks in 'lower' Old San Juan, in the outskirts of the walled city that rises on the hill to the north. The Department of Agriculture & Commerce built this miniature neoclassical structure with its red-tiled roof in 1937 to serve the needs of the burgeoning port. Today, La Casita is the information center for the PRTC (see p74). Stop here for maps, or check out the weekend craft market. Also look for the food vendors selling icy *piraguas* (delicious snow cones).

Paseo de la Princesa

Stretching to the west of the La Casita is the **Paseo de la Princesa** (Walkway of the Princess), a 19th-century esplanade lined with antique street lamps, shade trees, royal palms, statues, fountains, benches, tables, a food court, fruit vendors' carts and street entertainers on weekends. The paseo is very popular with families from all over the city who come to stroll, listen to street musicians and sample classic island treats such as coconut *tembleque* or *mavi* – a root-beer-like beverage made from the bark of the ironwood tree.

This entire promenade was restored in the 1990s, and its new pink paving stones lead strollers to the brink of the Bahía de San Juan. From here you can catch the cooling breezes off the water, and watch merchant and cruise ships navigating in and out of the busiest harbor in the Caribbean.

La Princesa

Poised against the outside wall of the city is **La Princesa**. Once a harsh jail, the long, gray and white stone structure now houses the main offices of the PRTC (p74) and an **art gallery** (admission free; ◷ 9am-4pm Mon-Fri) with welcome air-conditioning and frequently

changing shows by first-rate island artists. The bronze statue in front depicts San Juan's revered mayor from 1946 to 1968, Doña Felisa Gautier (see opposite).

Casa Rosa

The tropical villa in the foreground of the field leading up to El Morro is the **Casa Rosa** (Pink House). Built as a barracks for the Spanish militia in the early 19th century, this house long served as officers' quarters. The structure has since been restored and now serves as a plush day-care facility for the children of government employees.

Casa Blanca

Beyond the far right corner of the Parque de Beneficencia you'll find the iron gateway leading to the **Casa Blanca** (White House; ☎ 787-724-4102; adult/child $2/1; ◷ 9am-noon & 1-4:30pm Tue-Sun, guided tours Tue-Fri by appointment), the ancestral home for 250 years of the descendants of Puerto Rico's founder, Juan Ponce de León. Laid out before you is a secluded garden with shade trees, a chain of fountains and a courtyard. The restored 'house' – really a compound – in the heart of the garden revives the grandeur attendant on the lives of 17th- and 18th-century Spanish gentry. Ponce de León's son-in-law started construction on this house in 1521; it was intended as a retreat for the colony's founder, but the explorer died in his quest for the fabled Fountain of Youth before he could move in.

Cementerio de San Juan

Sitting just outside the northern fortifications of the old city, the neoclassical chapel in the **cemetery** provides a focal point among the graves of the colony's earliest citizens – as well as that of the famous Puerto Rican freedom fighter Pedro Albizu-Campos. This Harvard-educated chemical engineer, lawyer and politician led the agricultural workers' strikes in 1934 and was at the forefront of the movement for Puerto Rican independence until his arrest and imprisonment in 1936. A number of muggings have occurred here, so beware.

Casa de Ramón Power y Giralt

Once the residence of a political reformer and representative to the Spanish court, this restored 18th-century **house** is now the headquarters for the **Conservation Trust of Puerto Rico**

(☎ 787-722-5834; 155 Tetuán; admission free; ⏰ 9am-5pm Wed-Sun) and a must-see for historic preservation types. The house contains limited exhibits of Taíno artifacts and a small gift shop, and the staff can be helpful in arranging a visit to some of the trust's other island properties, including the Hacienda Buena Vista (p175) near Ponce.

Casa de los Contrafuertes

The **Casa de los Contrafuertes** (House of Buttresses; ☎ 787-724-5949; admission free; ⏰ 9am-4:30pm Wed-Sun), on the Plaza de San José, is considered the oldest colonial residence on the island, dating from the 18th century. The building houses the **Museo de Nuestras Raíces Africanas** (Museum of Our African Roots; admission free; ⏰ 9:30am-5pm Mon-Fri, 10am-5pm Sat). You will find masks, sculptures, musical instruments, documents and prints that highlight Puerto Rico's connections to West Africa. One exhibit recreates living conditions in a slave ship.

MUSEUMS
Instituto de Cultura Puertorriqueña

Once a home for the poor, this buff building with green trim, close to the Intersection with Calle Norzagaray, now houses the executive offices of this **institute** (Institute of Puerto Rican culture; ☎ 787-724-0700; www.icp.go bierno.pr; s/n Paseo Del Morro; admission free; ⏰ 9:30am-5pm Tue-Sun). The agency has been shepherding the flowering of the arts and cultural pride on the island since the 1950s. Its plazas are tranquil.

Cuartel de Ballajá & Museo de las Américas

Built in 1854 as a military barracks, the **cuartel** (off Calle Norazaragay) is a three-story edifice with large gates on two ends, ample balconies, a series of arches and a protected central courtyard that served as a plaza and covers a reservoir. It was the last and largest building constructed by the Spaniards in the New World. Facilities included officer quarters, warehouses, kitchens, dining rooms, prison cells and stables. Now its 2nd floor holds the **Museo de las Américas** (Museum of the Americas; ☎ 787-724-5052; admission free; ⏰ 10am-4pm Mon-Fri, 11am-5pm Sat & Sun, guided tours available weekdays 10:30am, 11:30am, 12:30pm & 2pm) which gives an overview of cultural development in the New World. It features changing exhibitions and Caribbean and European American art, most notably an impressive *santos* collection.

Hours for both the barracks and the museum are the same. The barracks' eastern door opens on to a courtyard that leads to the **Plaza del Quinto Centenario** (Quincentennial Plaza), which was built in 1992 to honor the 500-year anniversary of Christopher Columbus's first voyage to the Americas.

Museo de Arte e Historia de San Juan

Located in a Spanish colonial building at the corner of Calle MacArthur, the **Museo de Arte e Historia** (☎ 787-724-1875; 150 Norzagaray; admission free but donations accepted; ⏰ 9am-4pm Tue-Fri, 10am-4pm Sat & Sun) features galleries with rotating fine-arts exhibits. This is a good place to step into air-conditioned comfort and see a half-hour documentary about the history of San Juan (in Spanish and English).

Museo del Indio

If you are interested in Puerto Rico's indigenous people, but do not have the time to visit the related historic sites out on the island, head uphill on Calle San José, one block from the plaza, to the site of this **museum** (Indian Museum; ☎ 787-724-5477; 119 San José; admission free; ⏰ 9am-4pm Tue-Sat). Also known as Casa de los Dos Zaguanes (House of the Two Foyers), the museum is small but not without merit because of its strong collection of artifacts, including the little stone gods called *cemíes*.

Museo del Niño

The pink and green building that sits on the edge of a small, shady park houses this **museum** (Children's Museum; ☎ 787-722-3791; 150 Calle del Cristo; adult/child $4/3; ⏰ 9:30am-3:30pm Tue-Thu, 10am-5pm Fri, 12:30-5pm Sat & Sun). Kids love these hands-on exhibits! A particular favorite is the short-wave radio display that lets them talk with children in other countries, the miniature town touting the benefits of recycling and a tour through the human heart.

Museo Felisa Rincón de Gautier

This **museum** (☎ 787-723-1897; 51 Caleta de San Juan; admission free; ⏰ 9am-4pm Mon-Fri) is an attractive neoclassical town house that was once the long-time home of San Juan's beloved mayor. Doña Felisa presided over the growth of her city with personal style and political acumen for more than 20 years during the Operation Bootstrap days of the 1940s, '50s and '60s. This historic home is a monument to the life of an accomplished public servant.

Casa del Libro

Tucked away on a very pretty street is the **Casa del Libro** (House of Books; ☎ 787-723-0354; 255 Calle del Cristo; admission free; ☽ 11am-4:30pm Tue-Sat, closed holidays), yet another of the old city's tiny museums. This restored 18th-century town house contains more than 5000 manuscripts and texts that date back 2000 years. The collection includes one of the most respected assemblages of *incunabula* (texts produced prior to 1501) in the Americas, including documents signed by Ferdinand and Isabela.

Escuela de Artes Plásticas

The monumental gray-and-white building with a red-roofed rotunda across from El Morro is actually the **Escuela de Artes Plásticas** (Academy of Fine Arts; s/n Calle Nozagaray). Built as an insane asylum during the 19th century, this grand building looks more like a seat of government with its symmetrical wings, columns, Romanesque arches, porticos, courtyards and fountains. Today it is the source of more than a few jokes by contemporary art students about the mad dreams that continue to take shape within its walls. See for yourself when student shows go on display at the end of each academic term, or take a look at the sculpture court on the right-hand side of the building, where students can be seen chipping new images from granite. The courtyard on the left-hand side has a kiosk.

Museo de Casals

On Plaza de San José is the **Museo de Casals** (Casals Museum; ☎ 787-723-9185; adult/child $1/50c; ☽ 9:30am-5:30pm Tue-Sat). A native of Spain's proud but repressed province of Catalonia, world-famous cellist Pablo Casals moved to his mother's homeland of Puerto Rico in 1956 to protest the dictatorial regime of Francisco Franco in Spain. He quickly established the respected Festival Casals for classical music, which became a principal force in the subsequent flowering of the arts on the island (p44). If you loved the man, you'll love the museum.

CHURCHES
Catedral de San Juan

Every Spanish colonial city must have its cathedral, and the **Catedral de San Juan** (☎ 787-722-0861; 153 Calle del Cristo; admission free; ☽ 8am-4pm) fills the local need a block west of the Museo del Indio, where Calle Luna meets the little plaza and the Gran Hotel El Convento. The building dates back to 1521 and includes pieces of the original Gothic ceiling and staircase constructed in 1529. The current whitewashed structure is largely a 19th-century neoclassical affair, and has been lovingly restored in recent years. Most people visit to see the marble tomb of Ponce de León and the body of religious martyr St Pio displayed under glass. You can get quite a show here on Saturday afternoons when the limos roll up with bridal parties putting on the Ritz. The main entrance to the cathedral faces Calle del Cristo, a shady street of posh boutiques, trendy bars and restaurants that capture the fancy of both tourists and islanders alike.

Capilla del Cristo

Over the centuries, tens of thousands of penitents have come to pray for miracles at the **Capilla del Cristo** (Christ's Chapel; ☽ 10am-4pm Tue), the tiny outdoor sanctuary adjacent to Parque de las Palomas (Dove Park). One legend claims that the chapel was built to prevent people from falling over the city wall and into the sea. Another claims that citizens constructed the chapel to commemorate a miracle. As the story goes, a rider participating in a race during the city's San Juan Bautista festivities miraculously survived after his galloping horse carried him down Calle del Cristo, off the top of the wall and into the sea. Some historians claim the rider actually died (no mention of the horse's fate). Nevertheless, over the years, believers have left hundreds of little silver ornaments representing parts of the body – called *milagros* (miracles) – on the altar before the statues of the saints as tokens of thanks for being cured of some infirmity. You can see the chapel any time, but the iron fence across the front is only open during the listed hours.

Iglesia de San José

Facing the Plaza de San José is the **Iglesia de San José** (☎ 787-725-7501; admission free; ☽ 8:30am-4pm Mon-Sat, mass noon Sun), the second-oldest church in the Americas. Established in 1523 by Dominicans, this church with its vaulted Gothic ceilings still bears the coat of arms of Juan Ponce de León, whose family worshipped here, a striking carving of the Crucifixion and ornate processional floats. For 350 years, the remains of Ponce de León rested in a crypt here before being moved to the city's cathedral, down the hill. Another relic missing from the chapel is a Flemish carving of the Virgin of Bethlehem, which came to the island during the first few years of the colony and disappeared in the early 1970s. It's also the final resting place of José Campeche (p42), one of Puerto Rico's most revered artists.

Convento de los Dominicos

Next to the Iglesia de San José is the **Convento de los Dominicos** (☎ 787-721-6866; ⏰ 9am-noon & 1-4:30pm Wed-Sun), a Dominican convent which dates from the 16th century. After centuries of use as a convent, the building became a barracks for Spanish troops and was later used as a headquarters for US occupational forces after the Spanish-American War of 1898. It has been restored to its colonial grandeur and houses the arts/crafts/music/book store of the Instituto de Cultura Puertorriqueña, as well as a small chapel museum. Cultural events are sometimes held in the patio, and art exhibitions in the galleries.

PARKS & PLAZAS
Plaza de Armas

Follow Calle San Francisco into the heart of the old city and it opens on to the **Plaza de Armas** (Army Plaza). Here you see the city's central square, which was laid out in the 16th century with the classic look of plazas from Madrid to Mexico's Mérida and San Miguel de Allende. In its time, the plaza has served as a military parade ground (hence its name), a vegetable market and a social center. Shade trees, banks of seats, open-air cafés and musical entertainment once made the plaza the destination of choice for couples making their evening stroll. Despite the addition of chain stores, it still retains a lot of its colonial image.

One of the highlights of the plaza is the **Alcaldía** (City Hall; ☎ 787-724-7171; ⏰ 9am-5pm Mon-Fri), which dates from 1789 and has twin turrets resembling those of its counterpart in Madrid. This building houses the office of the mayor of San Juan and is also the site of periodic exhibitions. The Alcaldía is closed on holidays.

At the western end of the plaza, the **Intendencia** (Administration Building) and the **Diputación** (Provincial Delegation Building) are two other functioning government buildings adding to the charms of the plaza. Both represent 19th-century neoclassical architecture, and come complete with cloisters.

La Perla

Walking along Calle Norzagaray as it runs parallel to the northern wall of the city presents truly striking vistas of the Atlantic. In the foreground, accessed by a steep road and steps leading down the outside of the wall to the beach, is a warren of terraced, whitewashed and pastel homes known as **La Perla** (The Pearl). Often called the most picturesque slum in the world, La Perla has been home to centuries of dispossessed, desperate people who have survived by their wits, creating their own microculture based on street crimes. The district gained international infamy when Oscar Lewis wrote his novel *La Vida* (1966), which detailed the tragic cycle of poverty and prostitution lived out by people growing up in La Perla.

For anyone who has seen the *favelas* of Rio, the *ranchos* of Caracas or the *barrios* of Mexico City, La Perla might look innocuous by comparison. But it remains the prized turf of lawless people who will be only too happy to rough you up and rob you if given the opportunity. Despite the sometimes incredible beauty of the colors of the houses along this area – turbulent blues, glinting greens and foamy browns that seem pulled right from the ocean – this is not a place to wander into.

Plazuela de la Rogativa

This tiny gem of a park, the **Plazuela de la Rogativa** (Small Plaza of the Religious Procession), has lovely vistas overlooking the bay and is home to a whimsical bronze sculpture of the bishop of San Juan and three women bearing torches. According to legend, the candles held by the women who walked through this plaza one night in 1797 tricked British lieutenant Abercromby – who was getting ready to lay siege to San Juan with his 8000 troops and flotilla of more than 50 vessels – into believing that reinforcements were flooding the city from out on the island. Fearful of being outnumbered, Abercromby and his fleet withdrew.

Plaza de Colón

Tracing its roots back more than a century to the 400-year anniversary of the first Columbus expedition, the **Plaza de Colón** (Columbus Plaza) lies across the street from the lower part of Fuerte San Cristóbal. The city wall on this end of Old San Juan has been torn down, and the plaza, with its statue of the 'Discoverer' atop a pillar, stands on the site of one of the city's original gated entries, Puerta Santiago. Today, the plaza acts as a gateway to much of the traffic entering the city from Av Muñoz Rivera. Bus stops are along the plaza's south side.

Parque de las Palomas

Parque de las Palomas (Pigeon Park), on the lower end of Calle Cristo, is a cobblestone courtyard shaded with trees at the top of the city wall. People come here for the view it affords of Bahía de San Juan and to feed the pigeons that live in the park. (You can buy birdseed from a vendor by the gate.) Devout Christians have long believed that if you feed the birds and one 'anoints' you with its pearly droppings, you have been blessed by God.

Plaza de San José

Adjacent to the uppermost terrace of the Plaza del Quinto Centenario, where it meets Calle San Sebastián, is the **Plaza de San José**. This relatively small cobblestone plaza is dominated by a statue of Juan Ponce de León, cast from an English cannon captured in the raid of 1797. The plaza is probably the highest point in this city and serves as a threshold to four cultural sites on its perimeter. The neighborhood around the plaza, on San Sebastián and the intersecting Calle del Cristo, is the original home of the restaurant, bar and café scene that began in Old San Juan more than a decade ago. There are still plenty of places to grab a bite to eat in a shady building or outside in the plaza. See p98 for a description of your options…or just follow your nose. The smells of *sofrito* (an island seasoning), grilled chicken, garlic, fresh dorado and lime permeate the air.

Puerta de Tierra

Less than 2 miles in length and only one-quarter of a mile broad, this district oc-

cupies the lowland, filling the rest of the area that was colonial San Juan. **Puerta de Tierra** (Map pp72–3) takes its name from its position as the 'gateway of land' leading up to the walls of Old San Juan, which was the favored route of land attack by waves of English and Dutch invaders. For centuries, Puerta de Tierra was a slum much like La Perla, although far less picturesque. It was a place where free blacks and biracial people lived, excluded from the protection of the walled city where the Spaniards and *criollos* (islanders of European decent) postured like European gentry and maneuvered for political favor.

Today, the district is a hodgepodge of commonwealth government buildings, Navy and Coast Guard facilities, shipping docks, modest residences and sleazy bars… along with a park, a fort and a dramatic coastline at the eastern end of the island. It is a desolate area at night, and you will see desperate characters lurking in the shadows here by day. Beware.

FUERTE SAN GERÓNIMO

Completed in 1788 and meant to guard the entrance to the Condado Lagoon, this small **fort** (see Map pp84–5) barely had a chance to get up and running before the British ripped through during their 1797 invasion. Entered via the walkway (not always open)

SOFO CULINARY WEEK

The foodie cognoscenti know that 'SoFo' is the nickname given to south Fortaleza (what appears on the maps as the eastern end of Calle Fortaleza), an area packed with bars and restaurants (see p97). Some are upscale and trendy, others bohemian and earthy, and the foods range from Caribbean to Asian to whatever works for the chef in between. Twice a year – the week before Christmas Day and the weekend of Father's Day in June – SoFo and Recinto Sur are closed to traffic, and cute tables with sunshades sprout up on the cobblestones as chefs display all their culinary skill to an appreciative public. The week-long experiment in al fresco dining (with a touch of hedonistic block party thrown in) has been so successful the government is considering permanently closing SoFo to traffic.

behind the Caribe Hilton, the property is controlled by the Instituto de Cultura, which currently does not open the interior of the fort to visitors, though the exterior walls and ramparts are sometimes accessible. The chief reason to visit the site is to climb to the top of the ramparts, where you can catch a sea breeze and enjoy the vistas of Condado across the inlet.

EL CAPITOLIO

El Capitolio (The Capitol; Map pp72–3; ☎ 787-721-6040; admission free; ⏱ 9am-4pm Mon-Fri, tours by appointment only) of the commonwealth lies between Avs Muñoz Rivera and Ponce de León, just east of Fuerte San Cristóbal. The building looks a little like the US Capitol (albeit a bit more Romanesque): monumental and out of place crushed between two highways. The much-revered constitution of the commonwealth, which moved the island a step closer to its citizens' dreams of freedom from colonialism in 1951, is on display inside the 80ft rotunda. Regular sessions of the legislature meet inside, while rallies for and against statehood occur outside every time the government calls for an islandwide plebiscite on the issue.

PARQUES MUÑOZ RIVERA & SIXTO ESCOBAR

Spanning half the width of Puerta de Tierra, at the east end between the Atlantic and Av Ponce de León, this green space, known as **Parque Muñoz Rivera** (Map pp72–3), dates back over 50 years. It has shade trees, trails, recreation areas for children, and the Peace Pavilion, which sometimes hosts community events. An artisans' fair is held here and at the adjacent **Parque Sixto Escobar** (Map pp72–3; ☎ 787-277-9200) on most weekends.

Parque Sixto Escobar was the site of the eighth Pan American Games, held in 1979, and is now home to an Olympic athletics track, an historic powder magazine with a small museum, and the Balneario Escambrón. It also hosts the annual Heineken Jazz Festival, which never fails to bring jazz luminaries from all around the island and the Caribbean for a fabulous event.

Condado & Ocean Park   Map pp84–5

These areas have little to offer but the beaches – at least, in terms of sights and attractions. It's hard to believe that ritzy **Condado** (the name derives from the royal title for 'count' in Spain) was once a den of inequity, but 'tis true. In the 1950s the region was grossly overdeveloped and promoted as the 'next Miami Beach.' But as decades passed and destinations went in and out of fashion for the jet set, this strip of international-style high-rise resort hotels, casinos and apartment buildings drew an unsavory crowd of prostitutes, pimps, drug dealers and high rollers.

As mainstream tourism declined, the long-standing laissez-faire ambience of Condado attracted both island-born and traveling gays. Today, hotels and guest houses hum, and the nightlife howls with mixed throngs of gays and straights, islanders and travelers.

At the east end of Condado, past the San Juan Marriott, is a mile of broad beach called **Ocean Park**, with its associated neighborhood of **Punta Las Marías**, a largely residential collection of private homes and beach retreats that include a number of seaside guest houses.

Miramar & Santurce   Map pp72–3

Tucked behind Condado is the upscale neighborhood of **Miramar**, distinguished by the yachts berthed at the Club Náutico, near the Laguna del Condado bridge, the Aeropuerto de Isla Grande jutting out into the bay to the west, and a mix of fancy homes and condominium towers. Alas, there is no beach. Miramar is the place to live if you work in the commercial heart of San Juan (and earn a princely salary) because you can avoid rush-hour commutes from the suburbs by taking public transportation or even walking to work.

Bordering Condado to the south is **Santurce**, a thriving business and residential area during the Operation Bootstrap days of the 1950s. But, for the last 20 years, the area has been in decline. Businesses are moving to the nearby money pit of shiny, new Hato Rey, while longtime Santurce residents flee to the suburbs south of the city.

The Museo de Arte de Puerto Rico represents positive changes, however, and an influx of artists has given a bohemian softness to an otherwise gritty neighborhood. There's plenty of nightlife here (see Habana Club, p104 and Stargate, p104), and while it's not wise to wander around in the darkness like a lost tourist, getting a taxi to drop you off and pick you up is safe enough.

SAN JUAN

MUSEO DE ARTE DE PUERTO RICO

One of the biggest and newest art museums in the Caribbean, the **Museo de Arte de Puerto Rico** (MAPR; Map pp72-3; ☎ 787-977-6277, for tours ext 2230 or 2261; www.mapr.org; 299 Av José de Diego, Santurce; adult/child/senior $6/3/3; ☉ 10am-5pm Tue-Sat, to 8pm Wed, 11am-6pm Sun) opened in 2000. Located just south of the Condado tourist district, the MAPR consists of 130,000 sq ft of facilities. The west wing is a neoclassical structure, built in the 1920s as part of the Municipal Hospital of San Juan. The historical building is the main entrance to the museum and houses the permanent collection in 18 exhibition halls.

The east wing of the museum is a modern five-story structure. The facility boasts a five-

acre sculpture garden, a three-story atrium, a conservation laboratory and a computer-learning center (ActivArte). As well, there are studios and workshops, a 400-seat theater, a museum shop and the very highly regarded **Pikayo** (☎ 787-721-6194) restaurant.

The collection traces the island's contributions in the visual arts from Campeche in the 18th century to contemporary masters. You can park in a four-story underground parking lot.

Do not miss the opportunity to take a walk through the gardens, where winding paths invite visitors to stroll past 14 sculptures commissioned from Puerto Rican artists, and more than 100,000 plants make a peaceful green oasis.

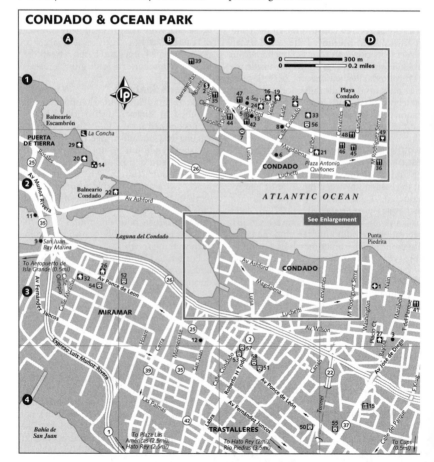

MUSEO DE ART CONTEMPORÁNEO DE PUERTO RICO

It's hard for the small **Museo de Arte Contemporáneo de Puerto Rico** (Map pp72-3; ☎ 787-727-5249; www.museocontemporaneopr.org; Universidad del Sagrada Corazon, Edificio Barat; admission free; ⏰ 8am-noon & 1-5pm Mon-Fri, 9am-noon, 1-5pm Sat) to compete with the massive MAPR down the street, but it has a thought-provoking exhibit of contemporary art – much of it with a political edge. Follow Av Ponce de León north to Calle Rosale and enter the campus. Look for a large blue building; the museum is on the 2nd floor.

Isla Verde   Map p86

Technically speaking this newly developed stretch of beach is in Carolina, a busy sub-urb of San Juan. But **Isla Verde**, replete with glamorous boutique hotels and dimly lit casinos, has absolutely nothing in common with that working-class neighborhood. Aside from the occasional rumble of a jet passing overhead (the international airport is just around the corner), Isla Verde is very insulated from the outside world.

The hotels tend to be the all-inclusive type – you can spend days just wandering from bed to beach to casino and bar. Some islanders criticize this area as being too devoid of Puerto Rican culture, but there's no doubt that for those travelers who want to de-stress with sun, sand and surf (which means not having to venture into Puerto

0 _____ 500 m
0 _____ 0.3 miles

INFORMATION
Ashford Memorial Community
  Hospital...1 D3
Banco Popular.................................2 B1
Bell, Book & Candle.......................3 D3
Bookworm..4 C1
Cybernet Café.................................5 C1
Departamento de Recursos Naturales y
  Ambientales...........................(see 11)
Laundry Condado Cleaners..........6 C2
Main Post Office.............................7 C2
Walgreens..8 C1

SIGHTS & ACTIVITIES
Anticipation Harbor Cruises.........(see 9)
Captain Mike Benitez.....................9 A3
Captain Mike's Sport Fishing Center..(see 9)
Caribbean School of Aquatics......10 E3
Caribe Aquatic Adventures.......(see 29)
Club Náutico...................................11 A2
Compania de Baile de Rumba de
  Fuego...12 B3
Condado Bike Rentals...................13 C1
Fuerte San Gerónimo....................14 A2
Museo de Arte de Puerto Rico...15 D4
Wave Rider...................................(see 20)

SLEEPING
Alelí by the Sea............................16 C1
Arcade Inn....................................17 E3
At the Wind Chimes Inn..............18 E3
Atlantic Beach Hotel....................19 C1
Caribe Hilton.................................20 A2
Casa del Caribe.............................21 C2
Condado Plaza Hotel & Casino...22 A2
El Canario by the Sea...................23 C1
Embassy Guest House...................24 C1
Hostería del Mar..........................25 F3
Hotel Excelsior..............................26 A3
Iberia Hotel...................................27 D3
L'Habitation Beach.......................28 F3
Normandie Hotel..........................29 A2
Numero Uno..................................30 F3
Ocean Park Beach Inn..................31 F3
Olimpo Court Hotel......................32 A3
San Juan Marriott Resort & Casino...33 C1
Tu Casa Boutique Hotel...............34 F3

EATING
Ajili-Mójili....................................35 B1
Antonio's.......................................36 D2
Augusto's....................................(see 32)
Chayote.......................................(see 26)
Che's..37 H3
Dunbar's Pub................................38 F3

Hacienda Don José.......................39 B1
Kasalta's...40 F3
La Patisserie...................................41 D3
Migas...42 C1
Pepin's...43 H4
Ramiro's..44 C1
Salud..45 D2
Via Appia.......................................46 D2
Yerba Buena..................................47 C1
Zabo's..48 D2

DRINKING
Kali's..49 D2
La Fiesta Lounge........................(see 22)

ENTERTAINMENT
Asylum...50 C4
Eros..51 C4
Fine Arts Cinema...........................52 B3
Habana Club..................................53 C4
Kouros..54 A3
Luis A Ferré Center for the Performing Arts
  (Bellas Artes)............................55 D4
Pleasure.....................................(see 57)
Rio Bar & Club...............................56 C1
Stargate...57 C4
Stellaris Casino...........................(see 33)
Teatro Metro.................................58 C4

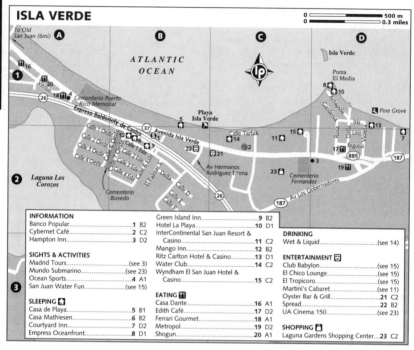

ISLA VERDE

INFORMATION	
Banco Popular..............................**1** B2	
Cybernet Café...............................**2** C2	
Hampton Inn.................................**3** D2	

SIGHTS & ACTIVITIES	
Madrid Tours..............................(see 3)	
Mundo Submarino.....................(see 23)	
Ocean Sports...............................**4** A1	
San Juan Water Fun...................(see 15)	

SLEEPING ☐	
Casa de Playa................................**5** B1	
Casa Mathiesen..............................**6** B2	
Courtyard Inn................................**7** D2	
Empress Oceanfront......................**8** D1	

Green Island Inn.............................**9** B2	
Hotel La Playa...............................**10** D1	
InterContinental San Juan Resort &	
Casino...**11** C2	
Mango Inn.....................................**12** B2	
Ritz Carlton Hotel & Casino........**13** D1	
Water Club....................................**14** C2	
Wyndham El San Juan Hotel &	
Casino...**15** C2	

EATING 🍴	
Casa Dante....................................**16** A1	
Edith Café......................................**17** D2	
Ferrari Gourmet.............................**18** A1	
Metropol.......................................**19** D2	
Shogun..**20** A1	

DRINKING	
Wet & Liquid.............................(see 14)	

ENTERTAINMENT 🎭	
Club Babylon.............................(see 15)	
El Chico Lounge.........................(see 15)	
El Tropicoro...............................(see 15)	
Martini's Cabaret.......................(see 11)	
Oyster Bar & Grill.........................**21** C2	
Spread..**22** B2	
UA Cinema 150...........................(see 23)	

SHOPPING ☐	
Laguna Gardens Shopping Center...**23** C2	

Rican traffic every time you want a meal), Isla Verde is the perfect location.

Hato Rey
Map pp72–3

Av Ponce de León skirts the southern edge of Santurce and veers south to the 'Miracle Mile' business district of **Hato Rey**. High-rise office buildings dominate the scene here, displaying the names of both local and offshore banks like Chase Manhattan and Spain's ubiquitous Banco Santander. There are plenty of business restaurants in the area, a few business-oriented hotels and a plethora of shopping opportunities. But Hato Rey doesn't have much you haven't seen in two dozen other cities, and this district becomes a desolate place after dark.

Río Piedras
Map p87

As you head south of Hato Rey, on Av Ponce de León, the landscape begins to rise above the marsh and landfill of Hato Rey. Here you enter the academic enclave of **Río Piedras**. Not only is this the site of the vast Universidad de Puerto Rico campus, but it is a busy indoor/outdoor discount-shopping zone reminiscent of the markets and bazaars of Asia. One of the major attractions here is walking around the campus and mingling with the students, who support the restaurants and bars that fan out along the streets from the intersection of Avs Ponce de León and José Gandara.

MERCADO DE RÍO PIEDRAS

If you like the smell of fish and oranges, the bustle of people, and trading jests in Spanish as you bargain for a bunch of bananas, this **market** (Paseo de Diego; ☉ 9am-6pm) is for you. As much a scene as a place to shop, the market continues the colonial tradition of an indoor market that spills into the streets.

The four long blocks of shops and inexpensive restaurants lining Paseo de Diego, and facing the market, have been closed to auto traffic, turning the whole area into an outdoor mall. Here you can shop or just watch as the local citizens negotiate for everything from *chuletas* (pork chops) and *camisas* (shirts) to cassettes featuring Puerto Rican pop-music wonders like Menudo. *Sanjuaneros* know that the market probably

RÍO PIEDRAS

0		500 m
0		0.3 miles

Aventuras.................................1 A1
Biblioteca Lazaro.....................2 C1
Centro de Públicos del Oeste.....3 D2
Centro Públicos del Este...........4 D2
Estación Experimental Agrícola
de Puerto Rico.....................5 B3
Los Mexicanos..........................6 C2
Mercado de Río Piedras (Plaza
del Mercado)........................7 C2
Museo de Antropología, Historia
y Arte.................................8 C1

has the largest and freshest selection of exotic fruits in the city at the best prices. Shoppers will find the market and stores along Paseo de Diego open from early morning to late evening, Monday to Saturday.

JARDÍN BOTÁNICO

This 75-acre tract of greenery is the site of the **Estación Experimental Agrícola de Puerto Rico** (Experimental Agricultural Station of Puerto Rico; ☎ 787-763-4408, 787-767-1710; admission free; ☺ 10am-6pm, closed holidays, tours available), but open to the public. Hiking trails lead to a lotus lagoon, an orchid garden with more than 30,000 flowers, and a plantation of more than 120 species of palm. The air smells of heliconia blossoms, as well as of nutmeg and cinnamon trees.

One of the reasons the garden is so serene is that it's difficult to find. The entrance is nearly hidden on the south side of the intersection of Hwy 1 and Hwy 847, a walk of about a mile from the center of the UPR campus. Call ahead to book a tour, although it can be difficult to get the phone answered.

MUSEO DE ANTROPOLOGÍA, HISTORIA Y ARTE

This small but quite engaging **museum** (☎ 787-764-0000 ext 2452; admission free; ☺ 9am-4:30pm Mon-Sat) of anthropology, history and art is worth a stop to see examples of the trove of Indian artifacts unearthed by university scholars in recent digs. In addition, this museum features revolving art shows and offers scholarly perspectives on island history. Finally, visiting the museum gives travelers a legitimate reason to be snooping around the university campus and opens opportunities for connecting with the students and faculty. The opening hours vary, so call ahead. It lies just inside the entrance to the UPR campus, next to the **Biblioteca Lazaro**.

CASA-FINCA DE DON LUIS MUÑOZ MARÍN

This house and farm was once home to the godfather of the Partido Popular Democrático (PPD) and the man who shepherded Puerto Rico into commonwealth status – as well as a 20th-century industrialized market economy in the 1950s and '60s. Today, it is a **museum** (☎ 787-755-7979; Hwy 181 Km 1.3; admission $3; ☺ 10am-2pm Wed-Sun) honoring the memory of this legendary Puerto Rican figure, and it also serves as a venue for concerts and experimental theater. Call for events, and visit if you are interested in learning more about the legend behind Luis Muñoz Marín and his astounding political career. Also take a minute to check out the great vegetation and expansive grounds. Look for the house on the east side of Río Piedras.

BEACHES

Go east, beach lover! As a general rule of thumb, beaches improve as you head in that direction. Don't swim near or around Old San Juan – the water is badly polluted.

Puerta de Tierra

The closest safe beach to Old San Juan is **Balneario Escambrón** (Map pp84–5), at the eastern end of Puerta de Tierra on Av Muñoz Rivera, inside Parque del Tercer Milenio, which encompasses Parque Sixto Escobar. There are lifeguards, restrooms, snack bars and a large parking lot. You can even get in some decent snorkeling in the early morning. Stay away at night – when the sun goes down, some dirty deals start to take place.

Condado

The official public beach for Condado is **Balneario Condado** (Map pp84–5), which has calm waters on the shore of the inlet (packed with local teens on weekends). It's actually quite close to Puerta de Tierra. A line of rocks breaks the water, so kids feel safe. Lifeguards are here on weekdays and snack bars are open daily, but bathrooms are few and far between. You can rent beach chairs.

You can just walk a little further east and join the fray on the rest of Condado's beaches – they are very popular, especially among gay men, who seem to like the stretch of sand in front of Calle Condado. Although you have to pick your way through condo developments to get to these beaches, they are open to the public.

Ocean Park

Far less famous than neighboring Condado, these beaches (Map pp84–5) are nonetheless quite lovely. Just pick a road and follow it toward the water and you'll eventually find an access point.

Playa Isla Verde

This is the best beach (Map p86) in San Juan, although it often has light seaweed. The broad beach stretches for well over a mile in front of the condo towers and chic hotels like the Water Club and Wyndham El San Juan. This is the Copacabana of Puerto Rico, alive with tourists, local beach bunnies, *playeros* (beach hippies) and water sports/umbrella/beach-chair vendors. All of the hotels sport beach-front pubs and restaurants.

Balneario de Carolina

An incredible strip of white sand and gorgeous blue waters, this is San Juan's best public beach. **Balneario de Carolina** (Map pp72–3; Rte 187; parking $3; ☺ 8am-6pm) actually lies about 1 mile east of Isla Verde in the suburb of Carolina, but it's easily found. The same road also takes you to Piñones. On weekdays (except holidays), this beach is practically empty. There's ample parking, lifeguards, bathrooms, showers, barbecue pits, food vendors and a playground.

ACTIVITIES
Hiking

A favorite store for climbers and hikers in Puerto Rico, **Aventuras** (Map p87; ☎ 787-766-0470; www.aventuraspr.com; 268-A Av Jesús T Pinero, Río Piedras; day trip $150; ☺ store 10am-6pm Tue-Sat, tours available upon demand) is also a tour group specializing in rock climbing and rappelling trips to the Río Camuy caves (p224). Guides also take people on trips through Río Tanama and Angeles Cave, and there's a very good trip for children to Yuyu cave in the karst region. Novices welcome – all expeditions begin with a short lesson.

Diving & Snorkeling

While Puerto Rico is well known for its first-class diving, San Juan is not the best place for it. Strong winds often churn up the water. Condado has an easy dive that takes you through a pass between the inner and outer reefs into coral caverns, overhangs, grottoes and tunnels.

Eco-Action Tours (☎ 787-791-7509; ecoactiontours@ yahoo.com; tours $40-130) can do just about any tour imaginable, but for far less than you'll pay if you book the same trip through your hotel; they operate out of a van and come to you. Snorkeling, diving and kayaking trips are available.

Karen Vega operates **Caribe Aquatic Adventures** (Map pp84-5; ☎ 787-281-8858; www.diveguide .com/p2046.htm; tours $65-135) from inside the Normandie Hotel, but you needn't be a guest to use her services. This outfit does dives near San Juan, but also further afield: the islands off the coast of Fajardo (Icacos for snorkeling· and Palomino and Palominito for diving). Lunch and transportation from San Juan are included in trips to Fajardo. Snorkeling and diving equipment rental is available, and fishing trips, catamaran picnics, windsurfing, kayaking and jet-skiing excursions can be arranged. It is very kid-friendly, too.

Captain Luis Torres of **Mundo Submarino** (Map p86; ☎ 787-791-5764; www.mundosubmarino.net; Laguna Gardens Shopping Center, 10 Av Laguna, Isla Verde; 2-tank dives $75) knows all the very best places to dive around San Juan and can recommend other dive spots and captains around the island. Rental equipment is available, too.

At **Ocean Sports** (Map p86; ☎ 787-268-2329; www .osdivers.com; 77 Av Isla Verde; dives $50-90), Carlos Felix will organize shore dives, deep dives, night dives, wall dives and cavern dives. He's also got a full service facility that provides Nitrox, Trimix and rebreathers.

Kayaking

At **Las Tortugas Adventures** (Map pp76-7; ☎ 787-725-5169; www.kayak-pr.com; 4 La Puntilla), with the owner Gary as your leader, you can get a good workout and some thrills as you circle the island that is home to Old San Juan and Puerta de Tierra. He also has two- and four-hour tours of the Laguna Piñones, as well as trips off the south coast and the east coast.

Copladet Nature & Adventure Tours (☎ 787-765-8595; www.copladet.com in Spanish; 528 Calle Soller) also offer lots of good tours, including kayaking on the Laguna de Piñones (p109).

Sailing & Fishing

Captain José Castillo of **Castillo Tours & Watersports** (☎ 787-791-6195; www.castillotours.com; 2413 Laurel, Río Piedras; trips $45-450) puts together catamaran sailing trips and snorkeling excursions that include equipment, instruction, lunch and transportation. Deep-sea fishing for blue marlin, wahoo, tuna and mahimahi also available.

If you want one of the most experienced charter captains in the Caribbean, call **Captain Mike Benitez** (Map pp84-5; ☎ 787-723-2292; San Juan Bay Marina, Miramar), who has carried the likes of former US President Jimmy Carter. Another Mike runs **Captain Mike's Sport Fishing Center** (Map pp84-5; ☎ 787-721-7335; San Juan Bay Marina, Miramar), which also has a reputation for bringing home the trophies. Prices for both range from $400 to $800 and higher.

Call **Makaira Hunter** (☎ 787-397-7028) for deep-sea fishing aboard a 20-passenger vessel.

At **San Juan Water Fun** (Map p86; ☎ 787-643-4510; www.waterfun-pr.com; Wyndham El San Juan Hotel & Casino, Isla Verde Beach; rental $50-125) Kenneth Pastor can provide you with anything that floats: banana boats, wave runners, Hobie Cats, jet skis, kayaks, water skis and knee boards. Or get airborne with some parasailing.

To rent a small sailboat or powerboat, contact the **Caribbean School of Aquatics** (Map pp84-5; ☎ 787-728-6606; 1 Calle Taft, suite 10F, Condado).

For a cruise around Bahía de San Juan, call **Anticipation Harbor Cruises** (Map pp84-5; ☎ 787-725-3500; San Juan Bay Marina; party cruise adult/ child $12/6). Its evening, one-hour party cruise with free munchies, open wine and soda bar, live music and dancing is good value.

Surfing

You will find the best waves and biggest *surferos* scene east of Isla Verde, when the morning and evening breezes glass off a 4ft swell. Popular breaks include Pine Grove, Los Aviónes and La Concha (in Bosque Estatal de Piñones) along Hwy 187.

Respected island surf daddy Stephen Rivera at **Wave Rider** (Map pp84-5; ☎ 787-722-7103; 51 Av Muñoz Rivera; short boards/long boards per day $25/30), in Puerta de Tierra next to the Caribe Hilton, has all the local knowledge and gear you're looking for.

Velauno (☎ 787-728-8716; www.velauno.com; 2430 Loíza, Isla Verde; long boards/windsurfers per day $35/75) is a great place to start learning how to surf, windsurf or kitesurf. On weekends they rent equipment right from the beach, and there is a discount for rentals longer than a day. Classes in all three disciplines offered.

Learn how to maneuver a catamaran, or rent a surfboard, Hobie Cat, sunfish, windsurfer or kayak at **Beach Cats** (☎ 787-727-0883; 2434 Loíza, Isla Verde). Surfboard repair also done.

Bicycling

Rent a bike from **Wheels for Fun** (Map pp76-7; ☎ 787-725-2783; 204 O'Donnell; per day $20), across from the Plaza de Colón, and head for the hills around El Morro. On just about any given evening you'll find other bikers there getting in a work out. You can also rent scooters here for $40 an hour.

You can rent new trail bikes at **Condado Bike Rentals** (Map pp84-5; ☎ 787-722-6288; 1106 Av Ashford; 1/3 days $20/50). The shop has trail maps for the city and sponsors mountain-biking tours.

In 2000 the government opened the Paseo de Pin bike trail, which runs from the east end of Isla Verde along the shores of Playa Pin, and into the Bosque Estatal de Piñones, where you can rent bikes (p109).

WALKING TOUR

Starting at **La Casita** (**1**; **p78**), check out the docking cruise ships and busy activity at Pier 1, the most-trafficked port in the Caribbean.

Head west along the Paseo de la Princesa (p78), a 19th-century esplanade leading strollers to the brink of the Bahía de San Juan. From here you can catch the cooling breezes off the water and take a peek at **La Aduana** (**2**; Customs House), the big pink building on your left.

Follow Calle La Puntilla south a short distance to **El Arsenal** (**3**; p75), a former Spanish naval station that was the last place to house Spanish military forces after the US victory in the Spanish-American War. Further along the paseo, poised against the outside wall of the city, is **La Princesa** (**4**; p78), formerly a jail. As the promenade reaches the edge of the Bahía de San Juan, you will see an imposing bronze sculpture

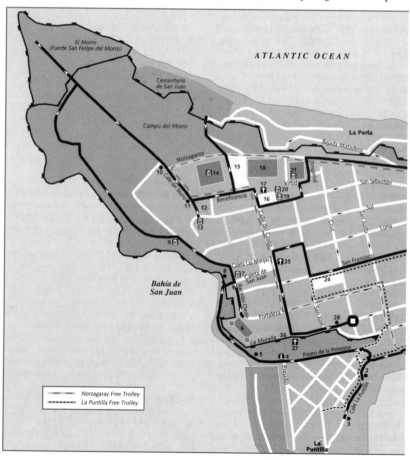

and fountain called **Raíces (5)**. The sculpture's figures depict the Taíno, European and African ancestors of modern Puerto Ricans.

From the fountain, follow the Paseo de la Princesa to the north along the perimeter of La Muralla (City Wall) as it squeezes along the very edge of the bay. Here you can see an excellent example of the kind of walls – with turreted guard towers called *garitas* – the Spaniards built to fortify their colonial cities. Completed in the late 1700s,

Distance: 2.5 miles
Duration: Three to four hours

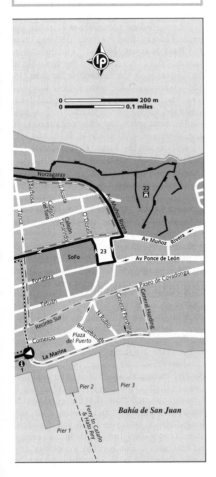

the wall's 20ft-thick sandstone construction shows one reason why British and Dutch assaults on the city failed over the centuries. Spanish ships once anchored in the cove just off these ramparts to unload colonists and supplies, all of which entered the city through a tall red portal known as Puerta de San Juan (p75). This tunnel through the wall dates from the 1630s.

As soon as you pass through the gate, turn right on Recinto Oeste. Follow the steep cobblestone street to the guarded iron gates of **La Fortaleza (6**; p75) and step inside for a guided tour. Then retrace your steps down the hill to Recinto Oeste until you reach the corner of Caleta San Juan and the **Museo Felisa Rincón de Gautier (7**; p79), a museum dedicated to San Juan's first female mayor. Continue uphill on Recinto Oeste to a side street called Caleta Las Monjas. Take a moment to gaze out over the water from the **Plazuela de la Rogativa (8**; p81) and enjoy the sculpted art work on the ramparts. Resuming your walk northwest along the rim of the fortified wall overlooking the entrance to the Bahía de San Juan, you pass through a gate ushering you onto the Campo del Morro, a vast field leading up to the imposing Fuerte San Felipe del Morro fortress, colloquially known as El Morro. As you pass through the gate, the tropical villa to your left in the foreground is the **Casa Rosa (9**; p78). Take some time to really enjoy this place – even if guns and war don't stir your blood, the fresh breezes and panoramic views will keep you occupied for a while.

Leaving El Morro by Calle del Morro, the main road, visitors will see the **Escuela de Artes Plásticas (10**; p80) on the left and a courtyard with snack kiosks. Just beyond the facade of the arts academy lies the **Instituto de Cultura Puertorriqueña (11**; p79), a building well worth entering. It has fine exhibits, but also several tranquil gardens that give respite from the heat. Continuing back down towards the heart of Old San Juan, beyond the far right corner of the **Parque de Beneficencia (12)**, you'll find the iron gateway leading to the **Casa Blanca (13**; p78), the ancestral home for 250 years of the descendants of Juan Ponce de León.

Behind the Parque de Beneficencia is the Cuartel de Ballajá and **Museo de las Américas (14**; p79). Note the **Plaza de Quinto Centenario (15)** alongside the *cuartel*; it was built in 1992

GETTING STRANGE IN SAN JUAN

How do you feel about walking backwards into the ocean in the middle of the night? Good, because that's a major feature of the Fiesta de San Juan Bautista (opposite). It brings good luck, apparently. You could also have a candlelit dinner for two served right on the beach (vegetarian options available). Go to Numero Uno's (p96) and start wiggling your toes. The Gallery Inn (p95) is nothing if not quirky, and if you like knickknacks decorated with butterflies, you'll love Butterfly People (p106). If you harbor a 'Dirty Dancing' fantasy, hit El Chico Lounge (p104) for some real bump-n-grind. (FYI – the professional dancers at the big hotels generally gather on weekend nights after their shifts end, around 3am, and head somewhere to *really, really* let loose. If you want to see some mind-blowing Latin dancing, ask the pro at your hotel what's on for the 'after' party.)

to commemorate Christopher Columbus' 'discovery' of the New World. Adjacent to the uppermost terrace of the Plaza del Quinto Centenario, where it meets Calle San Sebastián, is the **Plaza de San José** (16; p82), with its statue of Juan Ponce de León, cast from an English cannon captured in the raid of 1797.

Facing the plaza is the **Iglesia de San José** (17; p80), the second-oldest church in the Americas. Next to the Iglesia de San José is the **Convento de los Dominicos** (18; p81), a Dominican convent restored to its colonial grandeur. It houses the arts/crafts/music/book store of the Instituto de Cultura.

Also on the plaza is the **Casa de los Contrafuertes** (19; p79). The final sight on the plaza is **Museo de Casals** (20; p80), dedicated to Pablo Casals, whose mother was Puerto Rican. The final historical attraction on the Plaza de San José is the Casa de los Contrafuertes. The building houses the Museo de Nuestra Raices Africanas. You will find masks, sculptures, musical instruments, documents and prints that highlight Puerto Rico's connections to West Africa. One exhibit recreates conditions in a slave ship.

After a break in the area around Plaza San José, make your way east along Calle San Sebastián (away from El Morro and all of

the sites described earlier) and take your first left on Calle Virtud. This street opens onto a market square, and the former market building in front of you now houses the **Museo de Arte e Historia de San Juan** (21; p79). Following Norzagaray will bring you alongside La Perla (p81), Puerto Rico's most picturesque slum. As you continue east along Norzagaray, you come to **Fuerte San Cristóbal** (22; p75), the old city's other major fortification. Across the street from the lower part of Fuerte San Cristóbal is the **Plaza de Colón** (23; p82). From the northwest corner of Plaza de Colón, follow Calle San Francisco back into the heart of the old city. This is one of the busiest commercial streets in Old San Juan, and a good place to shop with the islanders in the boutiques, bookstores and markets.

After strolling the narrow sidewalk for several blocks, find the street opening on to the **Plaza de Armas** (24; p81). On the corner where Calle Luna runs into the Gran Hotel El Convento is the **Catedral de San Juan** (25; p80), where noted Puerto Ricans worship. The main entrance to the cathedral faces Calle del Cristo. Head south on that, past all the boutiques and chic restaurants, to the lower end of that street. Here you will be able to see the **Parque de las Palomas** (26; p82) and maybe get a 'blessing.'

Capilla del Cristo (27; p80), is an outdoor sanctuary adjacent to the park and has some lovely works by José Campeche. The final leg of this walk takes you along Calle Tetuán, a block-and-a-half east to the **Casa de Ramón Power y Giralt** (28; p78). From this stop you are just a few blocks up the hill and to the west from your starting point on the Paseo de la Princesa.

SAN JUAN FOR CHILDREN

Puerto Ricans love children – it doesn't matter who they belong to. And they love family. So traveling with youngsters is rarely a hassle, because the Puerto Ricans are doing it too. There are some hotels that won't take children under a certain age, but they are few. Several museums and hotels offer children rates or discounts – don't be afraid to ask. If renting a car, make sure that the rental agency has a car seat for you, and if taking a taxi any long distance, bring one with you. Children should carry some form of ID in case there's an emergency. You'll rarely encounter any icy or disdainful looks when dining out with

---

MUST-SEE GALLERIES FOR GALLERY NIGHT

On the first Tuesday of every month from February to May and September to December galleries stay open late for Noches de Galerías.

Obra (Map pp76-7; 301 Tetuan) Look for pieces by Augusto Marin, Myrna Báez and Rafael Tufino, as well as world-famous glass artist Chihuly.

Carlos Garcia (Map pp76-7; 55 Calle del Cristo) Puerto Rican, Latin American and African art from renowned painters and sculptors.

Galería Botello (p106) Dedicated to the work of the late artist Angel Botello, as well as up-and-comers from around the Caribbean.

---

your child, but some of the trendier places in Old San Juan, Condado and Isla Verde would be the exception to that rule.

In and around San Juan there are several attractions that children really enjoy. The Museo del Niño (p79) is always a big hit, as is the Casa de Ramón Power y Giralt (p78). The Río Camuy caves and Arecibo observatory (both p223), just a short drive away, are just right for kids, and the Luis A Ferré Parque de Ciencias (p112) is a favorite. Habana Club (p104) has an alcohol-free salsa night once a month for youngsters.

Baby-sitters are not easily found in San Juan, or elsewhere in Puerto Rico. There are no organizations that offer this service, but all the larger hotels have vetted baby-sitters on speed dial – usually staff who are happy to make some extra money on the side.

TOURS

Legends of Puerto Rico (☎ 787-605-9060; www
.legendsofpr.com) Debbie Molina-Ramos is a well-respected guide whose wildly popular 'Night Tales in Old San Juan' tour books up pretty fast. She also does 'Legends of San Juan' and many others, including a coffee plantation tour, an eating and drinking tour, and tours to El Yunque. Bus trips are available, as are special discounts for families with children (and child-friendly tours, too), as well as wheelchair-accessible tours (advance booking required). Debbie's also working on developing tours with a sign language interpreter, and one for the visually impaired.

Madrid Tours (Map p86; ☎ 787-791-8777, ext 1023; Hampton Inn, 6530 Av Isla Verde) Trips to Old San Juan and the Bacardi Rum Factory, as well as El Yunque and Playa Luquillo. Pick up from hotel included, but tours only leave when enough people have signed up. Reservations required.

FESTIVALS & EVENTS

Unless otherwise noted, information on the following events can be obtained by contacting the PRTC (p74).

Festival Casals (www.festcasalspr.gobierno.pr) Renowned soloists and orchestras come here from all over the world to join the Puerto Rican Symphony Orchestra in giving night after night of virtuoso concerts, primarily at the Luis A Ferré Center for the Performing Arts. Tickets run around $40, but there are deep discounts for students, children and seniors. Dates vary.

Noches de Galerías (Gallery Nights; first Tuesday of every month February to May and September to December) Galleries stay open late to showcase special exhibitions and present up-and-coming talent. Enthusiastic art lovers have also turned this into something of a pub crawl (see the boxed text, below), especially along Calle San Sebastián, Plaza de Armas, Calle del Cristo and Plaza San Sebastián. Look for nearby museums like El Arsenal and Museo de las Américas to hold special exhibits for this event.

Festival La Casita (Saturdays year-round, starting 6pm) La Casita, adjacent to Pier 1 in Old San Juan, forms the backdrop for free performances of traditional music and dance, craft exhibitions, puppet theater and sunset trio concerts.

Festival San Sebastián (Mid-January) Held in the old city's famous party street, Calle San Sabastián. For a full week in mid-January it hums with semi-religious processions, music, food stalls and larger-than-ever crowds. During the day, it's folk art and crafts, at night drunken revelry.

Jazz Festival (Late May to early June) Puerto Rico's largest jazz fest, courtesy of Heineken, attracts the best Latin jazz artists from all over the Caribbean. The late, great Tito Puente sometimes played here, and Eddie Palmieri still does.

Fiesta de San Juan Bautista (June 24) Celebration of the patron saint of San Juan and a summer solstice party, Latin style. Staged during the week preceding June 24,

---

MUST-VISIT BARS FOR GALLERY NIGHT

When the galleries are open late on the first Tuesday of every month, from February to May and September to December, you might like to visit one of these bars.

Nono's (Map pp76-7; 107 San Sebastián) This place is famous for potent cocktails and a friendly crowd.

El Batey (p102) It looks like a dive, but many say this is the best bar in Puerto Rico. Shoot pool, chat people up and enjoy the casual vibe.

Café Hijos de Borinquen (p104) Grab a partner and hit the floor – it will never get any less crowded, so you might as well wade in.

GAY & LESBIAN SAN JUAN

There's really no such thing as 'gay' San Juan. Much like Miami Beach, gay and lesbian professionals have made their mark in the tourism world and created a remarkably tolerant and open
culture. Of course, San Juan still has touches of the stereotypical 'macho' attitude, but more
often than not, crowds in many local clubs and restaurants are visibly and openly mixed. And
'gay night' at a club doesn't mean that straight people aren't welcome – in fact, quite the opposite is true. In any case, so many businesses in San Juan are gay owned or operated that the
finer points of one's sexual preference are pretty much irrelevant anyway. You'll find the highest
concentration of gay activity – mostly for men – along the Condado beach area. Lesbians have
fewer options set aside just for them, but are a large part of the general 'scene.' You can start
to get the lay of the land by stopping on a weekend night at the terrace bar in the Atlantic
Beach Hotel (opposite). Weekday nights draws a steady crowd as well. Sunday is gay night at
the popular club Asylum (p104). There's also Eros (p104), Kouros (p104) and Cups (p104).

the heart of the action – including religious processions,
wandering minstrels, fireworks, food stalls, drunken sailors
and beauty queens (straight and otherwise) – is in Old
San Juan, but the rest of the city gets into the act as well
and parties down on the last day of the fiesta at Playa
Isla Verde.

Fiesta de Película (October) Screens about 100 new films
during the one week, all of which relate to the Caribbean in
some way. Given the number of Puerto Ricans/Nuyoricans
making good on the big screen – J Lo, Benicio del Toro,
Jimmy Smits (and Raul Julia, who was given a state funeral
when he died of cancer in 1994) – this event has been
pulling in bigger luminaries each year.

Fiesta Artisanos de Bacardi (Bacardi Artisans Fair; first
two Sundays of December) It has the feel of a big county
fair back in the USA (complete with carnival rides); the
fiesta also brings together the largest collection of artisans
on the island. As many as 125 crafters show up to compete,
display and sell their wares. This is a good place to see an
array of folk art, including *santos*, and shop for bargains.
The *bomba y plena* singers add a touch of tradition to the
whole affair.

SLEEPING

You'll find ample accommodations in San
Juan for every price range except one –
budget traveling. Outside of a few affordable guest houses, it's slim pickings for those
watching their money. On the up side, rates
for places to stay in San Juan vary significantly (sometimes more than 30%) from
season to season. In general, rates are highest from December 15 to June 1, and lowest
from September 1 to December 14, so good
deals can be found.

Aside from that, San Juan is wide open.
Upscale, midscale, boutique or B&B: there's
something for everyone. Condado and
Ocean Park have the highest concentra-

tion of guest houses and big resort hotels.
Isla Verde's got a few ritzy boutique options flanked by mega-resorts, and Old San
Juan's got a little bit of everything (except
a beach, of course).

Old San Juan   Map pp76–7
BUDGET

La Caleta (☎ 787-725-5347; www.thecaleta.com; 11
Caleta Las Monjas; apt per week from $350) Situated
on a quiet street, this three-story apartment
building has some balconies that catch the
trade winds, and overlook La Fortaleza
and the Plazuela de la Rogativa at the entrance to Bahía de San Juan. Some rooms
are plainer than others; the best deal is the
bright and sunny penthouse apartment.
All rooms have kitchenettes. The owner,
Michael Giessler, also has 35 rooms to rent
around the island.

Guest House Old San Juan (☎ 787-722-5436; 205
Tanca; r with fan/air-con $40/55; 🔀) The cheapest
rooms are minuscule and a bit dingy – the
shared bathrooms slightly unappealing.
Larger rooms are somewhat more attractive.
But then again, it's probably the most affordable place in Old San Juan and it's on a
beautiful street with lots of great attractions
just steps away.

El Jibarito (☎ 787-725-8375; 280 Sol; r $60) You
won't go hungry because this small guest
house is right over a restaurant of the same
name. Basically you are renting a room in
the owner's house, and if you are comfortable with that, then this is a good, clean,
affordable option.

Fortaleza Guest House (☎ 787-721-7112; 361
Fortaleza; r without bathroom per week from $65) Only
Spanish at this guest house! Tiny rooms in

homey settings are quite a bargain at weekly prices. There's not much privacy and you'll see a few multi-legged creatures skittering by (ants, not roaches), but overall it's a safe and fun place to stay.

MIDRANGE

Gran Hotel El Convento (☎ 787-723-9020; www.el convento.com; 100 Calle del Cristo; r $165-400; 🐕 🏊 P) The front door says it all – solid wood, built in the 1600s, and still guarding the entrance to El Convento, which literally was a convent once for wealthy women from Spain widowed in the New World. El Convento sits in a beautiful section of the old town and is worth a visit whether you stay overnight or not. Anyone is welcome to check out the restful atrium inside and drink or eat at any of the upbeat bars or restaurants (p99). To go upstairs, just call on the white courtesy phone in the lobby or ask at the front desk. The super-friendly staff will let nonguests take a supervised peek at the upper floors, but most rooms are off limits in the interest of guest privacy. The Mother Superior suite is utterly fascinating – not so much opulent as it is elegant, and steeped in a very unique kind of Old World charm. No matter what room you stay in, however, a night at El Convento is a very special experience.

Gallery Inn (☎ 787-722-1808; www.thegalleryinn .com; 204-206 Norzagaray; r with breakfast $145-350; P 🐕) This is a series of connecting town houses overlooking the ocean from a perch near the city's northern wall. Jan D'Sopo and her husband, Manuco Gandía, have decorated this 18th-century compound with a vast collection of their own art. Overall, the inn is eclectic and whimsical, the rooms quite beautiful and the patio view to die for.

Hotel Milano (☎ 787-729-9050; www.hotelmilanopr .com; 307 Fortaleza; r with continental breakfast $95-155; 🐕) A renovated 19th-century building on one of the busiest streets in the heart of Old San Juan, the Milano's right on Fortaleza, just steps from the hottest restaurants in Old San Juan. Rooms are bland but clean and comfortable, rather like a chain hotel but with slightly more personality. If you're looking for a midrange hotel with nice amenities in the hippest section of town, the Milano is for you.

Hotel Plaza de Armas (☎ 787-722-9191; www.ihp hoteles.com; 202 Calle San Jose; r $90-175; 🐕) In the heart of Old San Juan, this modern and new

hotel offers little to attract the eye inside but does offer every possible convenience in terms of location. Rooms are a bit stuffy and not particularly charming, but the bathrooms are in order.

TOP END

Sheraton Old San Juan Hotel & Casino (☎ 787-721-5100; 101 La Marina; r $225-575; P 🐕 🏊) Facing the cruise ship docks, this nine-story, convention-style hotel, which used to be a Wyndham, offers 240 rooms with all the amenities for the luxury-minded, including a major casino. While comfortable, it is a chain hotel. Bland decor and atmosphere come with the territory.

Condado & Ocean Park   Map pp84–5
BUDGET

Embassy Guest House (☎ 800-468-0615; 1126 Sea View; r $65-90; P 🐕 🏊) A favorite budget spot among gay travelers – although others like it too – the Embassy encourages guests to have fun in its Jacuzzi with bar. The rooms show their age a bit, but since the oceanfront location is sublime, it's hardly worth fussing about.

Arcade Inn (☎ 787-728-0668; 8 Taft; r $75-80; 🐕) Families like the beach-cottage vibe of this almost-but-not-quite waterfront B&B. The rooms are bright and inviting, and there's plenty of shared space for wee ones to run about. Kitchen available.

Aleli by the Sea (☎ 787-725-7313; 1125 Sea View; r $65-110; P 🐕) In the heart of Condado this inn has nine units with private bathrooms, as well as shared living room, kitchen and seaside sundeck. If you can pony up for the higher-priced rooms the stay will be much more enjoyable – the less expensive ones are a bit depressing and sterile.

Casa del Caribe (☎ 787-722-7139; 57 Caribe; r $75-165; 🐕) A bit run-down and shabby in places, this B&B isn't a bad option if you just want to sit on the beach and relax, returning to your room just to catch some zzzzs. In the off-season, when the prices are sure to be low, this is an even better deal. Dogs welcomed.

MIDRANGE

Atlantic Beach Hotel (☎ 787-721-6900; www.atlantic beachhotel.net; 1 Vendig; r $105-155) The Atlantic Beach has been the soul of San Juan's gay community for decades. This place has a knowledgeable and funny staff, and 37 spacious plain rooms right on the broadest part of Condado beach. The Atlantic Beach is also home to an on-site restaurant and a popular terrace bar.

At Wind Chimes Inn (☎ 800-946-3244; www.at windchimesinn.com; 53 Taft; r $85-115; P ⊠ 🖥 🛋) At Wind Chimes is modeled along the lines of a Spanish villa and feels quite homey, with passably pretty rooms and a nice pool with Jacuzzi. Prices will fall in off-season, making this even more of a bargain.

Hostería del Mar (☎ 787-727-3302; hostelria@ caribe.net; 1 Tapia; r $70-145; ⊠) This medium-size guest house (17 units) is on the beach in Ocean Park. There is no pool here, but there's a great vegetarian restaurant (p100) in an enclosed gazebo overlooking the beach.

Iberia Hotel (☎ 787-723-0200; 1464 Av Wilson; r $95-115) Another gay-friendly option, this Spanish-looking small hotel with 30 units is in an exclusive residential neighborhood of Condado. You get all the amenities plus a terrace, solarium and restaurant. This place offers a lot of style and attention to detail for the price.

Numero Uno (☎ 787-726-5010; 1 Santa Ana; r $115-215; P ⊠ 🛋) Just east of Condado beach in Ocean Park, there is a lot of charm in this distinctive whitewashed beach house surrounded by coconut palms. Owned by a former New Yorker who's spruced everything up nicely, Numero Uno lives up to its name.

Ocean Park Beach Inn (☎ 787-728-7418; 3 Elena; r $90-165) Catering to gay men and women, the inn features 10 rooms with private entrances, fridges, baths and ocean/garden views just one block from the beach.

L'Habitation Beach (☎ 787-727-2499; www.habit ationbeach.com; 1957 Italia; r $90-120) A very popular guest house often frequented by gay couples, L'Habitation welcomes everybody with equal enthusiasm. Rooms are big, clean and decorated in a very homespun style. The private beach is quite nice, and there's an on-site bar.

El Canario by the Sea (☎ 787-533-2649; www .canariohotels.com; 4 Calle Condado; r $100-115; ⊠) There are actually three different Canario inns around Condado – agents here at the 'By the Sea' can assist you in reserving at any one of the properties. Each of the small hotels has 25 to 40 units with cable TV,

phone and continental breakfast. You get a quiet, clean, well-lit place.

Tu Casa Boutique Hotel (☎ 787-727-5100; 2071 Cacique; r $99-200; P ⊠ 🛋) A very pretty boutique hotel just two blocks from the beach, Tu Casa also rents bicycles to zip around on. Rooms are beautifully coordinated, and the romantic suite is a real knockout.

TOP END

Condado Plaza Hotel & Casino (☎ 727-721-1000; 999 Av Ashford; r $300-1350; 🛋) The hotel steals the show with a fitness center, spa, bi-level suites, seven restaurants, live entertainment and great salsa. The hotel even has its own private beach facing Fuerte San Gerónimo across the inlet.

Caribe Hilton (☎ 787-721-0303; www.hiltoncaribbean .com/sanjuan; Rosales; r $260-450) Situated on Calle Rosales off Av Muñoz Rivera in Puerta de Tierra, this is a good bet if you want luxury near Old San Juan, as well as access to a beach and tennis courts. With 672 newly renovated rooms and nine restaurants, this place is really an all-inclusive resort.

Normandie Hotel (☎ 787-729-2929; www.norman diepr.com; Av Muñoz Rivera; r $200-325) Next door to the Caribe Hilton, more affordable and smaller with 189 units, this hotel is an art-deco masterpiece. It echoes with the ghosts of the jet set who used to scandalize the island 50 years ago by cavorting nude in the pool. For a large hotel, this place has soul.

San Juan Marriott Resort & Casino (☎ 787-722 7000; www.marriotthotels.com; 1309 Av Ashford; r $265-525; 🛋) After rising from the ashes of the burned-out Dupont Plaza in 1995, this Marriot has turned into a pretty beachfront property, with two pools and 525 units.

Isla Verde   Map p86

BUDGET

Mango Inn (☎ 787-726-4230; www.themangoinn .com; Calle 1 Este; $70-105; P ⊠) It's all good but the location – it just happens to be on the wrong side of the highway. If you don't mind a hop over to the beach, then the Mango is perfect for a budget traveler. The pool is small but cute, and fresh flowers adorn the rooms.

Casa Mathiesen (☎ 787-726-8662; 14 Calle 1 Este; r $70-89; P 🛋) A pedestrian bridge over the expressway connects you to the beach and restaurant. Rooms come with kitchenette, but are tiny. Those are the only drawbacks,

THE AUTHOR'S CHOICE

Water Club (Map p86; ☎ 787-728-3666; www
.waterclub.com; 2 Calle Tartak; r $289-995; ☒
☐ ☎ P) This is such a refreshing change
from the blandness of chain hotels that
overwhelm parts of San Juan. It is light,
both in ambience and decor, and the staff
is truly attentive. And unlike many other
'boutique' hotels, the Water Club manages
to be daring in a welcoming way. The tink-
ling waterfall, glass doors from Venice and
brilliant lighting make you feel as if you're
staying inside a sunlit atrium instead of
four walls.

And how can you not like a hotel that
has custom-designed beds positioned to
face the ocean? Not to mention an open-
air 11th-floor bar (with a rooftop fireplace
to ward off any chills) and a swimming pool
so close to the sky you could use the clouds
to towel yourself off. It's trendy all right, but
also something special.

This is one of the island's best deals. Right
on the beach (sunshades, chairs and towels available) with two beautiful pools, an
open-air bar and more formal restaurant
inside, it's also got a casino that's small but
fun – a good choice for beginners, since
croupiers don't mind explaining the rules.

TOP END

Ritz Carlton Hotel & Casino (☎ 800-241-3333; www
.ritzcarlton.com; 6961 Av of the Governors; r $325-2500;
P ☒ ☐ ☎) A huge, square monolith with
festive lights strung all year round, the Ritz
keeps a tight grip on its front door – nonguests aren't exactly welcomed (that's why
it's the favorite celebrity hangout). Rooms
are, as you would expect, swanky, swell and
sumptuous. The beds are bigger than most
hotel rooms.

Wyndham El San Juan Hotel & Casino (☎ 800-
468-2818; www.wyndham.com; 6063 Av Isla Verde; r $395-
450; P ☒ ☐ ☎) El San Juan still has it, even
after 40 years. You can get lost just walking up
to the front door, the finely tended grounds
are so lush. Rooms are absolutely huge
and decked out with fine brocade spreads
and plush rugs. If you want to turn back
the clock about 50 years, this is the place –
the hotel's advertising claims nightlife here is
reminiscent of 1950s Havana, and this is no
lie. Bring your tux and platinum card.

InterContinental San Juan Resort & Casino
(☎ 800-443-2009; www.intercontinental.com; 187 Av
Isla Verde; r $399-539) Recently refurbished to
bring it up to the standard of the neighboring Wyndham, the InterContinental is once
again an opulent star on the beach. Rooms
are moderately sized, but most have terraces
and are immaculately tricked out. The staff is
very attentive. With five on-site restaurants
(including a good sushi bar) and the popular
Martini's Cabaret (p103), this place is a state-
of-the-art adult playground.

Miramar, Río Piedras

While these areas have none of the seaside
attractions of Old San Juan, Condado/Ocean
Park or Isla Verde, the commercial heart of
the city does offer a number of accommodations options.

Olimpio Court Hotel (Map pp84-5; ☎ 787-724-
0600; 603 Calle Miramar; r $60-135) It's not an elegant
choice by any means, but aside from some
drab decorations and a bit of wear and tear,
there's nothing wrong with the Olimpio.

however, and if you can live with that, this
is a good deal.

Green Island Inn (☎ 800-677-8860; 36 Calle 1 Este;
r $58-78; ☎) The owners also run Casa Math-
iesen, down the street. It's within a mile of
the airport. There's a restaurant and pool
on site.

Casa de Playa (☎ 800-916-2272; 86 Av Isla Verde;
r $75-140; ☒) This is a former private beach
villa set amid an explosion of palms. There
are now 20 units here with all the mod cons.
The beach bar has a loyal following.

MIDRANGE

Hotel La Playa (☎ 787-791-1115; www.hotellaplaya
.com; 6 Amapola; r $95-135) Amid the schlock high-
way art, fast-food joints, car-rental agencies
and condo towers of Isla Verde, this place is
an oasis on the beach. You get a room with
all the comforts in a beachfront property.
There is also a popular, moderately priced
restaurant-bar on the premises.

Empress Oceanfront (☎ 800-678-0757; 2 Amapola;
r $140-200; ☎) For a dramatic location, this
hotel can't be beaten. It commands a small
peninsula at the water's edge. The pool and
restaurant are part of a deck that stands on
pilings over the ocean.

Courtyard Inn (☎ 787-791-0404; www.marriott
.com; 7012 Boca de Cangrejos; r $150-300; P ☒ ☐ ☎)

SAN JUAN

Hotel Excelsior (Map pp84-5; ☎ 787-721-7400; 801 Av Ponce de León; r $130-165; ☒) Geared for business travelers, the Excelsior has an award-winning on-site restaurant as well as a day spa, fitness center and beauty salon. Considering that it's tricked out with many of the same amenities as the five-star hotels along the beach, it's a pretty good deal. The drawback, naturally, is its location.

EATING

Some really top-notch eateries have opened up in San Juan recently. The latest craze is fusion cuisine – expect to see all sorts of creative combinations. When in doubt, head to Calle Fortaleza in Old San Juan. Most restaurants have vegetarian-friendly dishes, although they may not be billed as 'vegetarian.' Vegans may have a more difficult time as butter and meat renderings are common ingredients. In vegie dishes always check that your rice and beans, for example, haven't been seasoned with a bit of meat grease. When a restaurant specifically mentions vegetarian options it's noted below, but don't assume you can't find good vegie dishes at any of these places.

Budget-minded diners can easily eat for under $12, while a midrange meal will set you back between $15 and $25. Top end ($30 plus) can go as high as you want it – but you'll get your money's worth.

All of these places are gay-friendly. In fact, many of them are owned by gay couples.

Old San Juan   Map pp76–7
BUDGET

St Germain (☎ 787-721-7194; http://stgermaincafe .com; 150 San Justo; dishes $1-10; ☺ breakfast & lunch) Perfect for a light breakfast or lunch, this European-style café (cash only) has juices, hot chocolate, espresso, café au lait and all sorts of baked goods – croissants, tarts, baguettes – and for lunch crunchy salads with goat cheese, hummus or chicken breast toppings. Paninis and sandwiches are also served. Vegetarian-friendly.

Yurta (☎ 787-977-0286; 359 San Francisco; dishes $5-12; ☺ lunch & dinner) This small diner has a counter to eat at and also doubles as a tiny market (good source of vegetarian staples). Have a smoothie and swivel on your stool while the friendly staff dish you up some penne with shrimp in white sauce, tortillas filled with cheese and beans and/or chicken

or shrimp. There are also daily specials, grilled sandwiches and at least one vegetarian option on the menu.

Brenda's Café (☎ 787-725-0027; 353 San Francisco; dishes $7-18; ☺ lunch & dinner) One of Old San Juan's more interesting options, Brenda's Café is a vegetarian restaurant that attracts an eclectic, artistic, New Age crowd.

Arepas y Mucho Mas (☎ 787-724-7776; 351 San Francisco; dishes $3-10; ☺ lunch & dinner) A bit blighted by the bright neon sign outside, Arepas is nonetheless a good choice if you want a light lunch or just need a quick bite to tide you over. Delicious *arepas* (baked cornmeal cakes) come filled with meat, cheese and vegies. One is a mouthful, two a filling snack.

Los Amigos (253 San José; sandwiches $2-4; ☺ 8am-5pm) Don't let the completely unprepossessing exterior fool you – this is the best place around for a traditional, inexpensive Puerto Rican breakfast or lunch.

La Bombonera (☎ 787-722-0658; 259 San Francisco; mains $5-10; ☺ 8am-4pm) *Sanjuaneros* claim the baked goods here cannot be matched, and they relish the endless free refills of *café con leche* (coffee with milk).

Brickhouse (☎ 787-559-5022; 359 Tetuan; dishes $8-22; ☺ lunch & dinner) A very American-style restaurant, the Brickhouse serves hefty burgers, fries and bar food. It attracts a young crowd and is a pleasant place to unwind with a beer.

MIDRANGE
Tio Danny's (☎ 787-723-0322; 313 Fortaleza; dishes $8-22; ☺ lunch & dinner) On a hot afternoon in Old San Juan, you can't do any better than this. It's great for a drink or for food. Lots of space, an ample rosewood bar to lean on (the plaques are the names of famous residents or dedicated customers) and a truly convivial atmosphere. Big, steaming plates of *arroz con pollo* (rice and chicken), *lechon asado* (roast suckling pig) and *pez espada* (grilled swordfish) come out of the kitchen with reassuring regularity, and there are plans to serve Mexican food in the al fresco area out back. When you want to get a sense of 'Old San Juan,' far from the madding crowds and steeped in turn-of-the-century courtliness, this is the place to visit.

Tantra (☎ 787-977-8141; 356 Fortaleza; dishes $13-27; ☺ lunch & dinner) A glossy eatery that serves 'Indo-Latin fusion' cuisine, Tantra's got a sexy, slinky vibe. The bar prides itself on innovative drinks (try the Black Martini) and the kitchen prides itself on innovative dishes (sesame crusted sushi tuna with a coco-ginger peanut sauce, chicken and shrimp congee, pan roti with palak paneer and grilled *churrasco*, charcoal-broiled Argentian steak). Everything is served appetizer size so you can pick an array from the menu.

Baru (☎ 787-977-7107; 150 San Sebastián; dishes $13-30; dinner) Very popular with food-lovers and martini drinkers, Baru doubles as a nightspot as well as trendy restaurant. Dishes include 'yuccafongo' (yucca made like a mofongo) with shrimp, beef carpaccio with basil essence or the mahimahi topped with crispy onions.

La Fonda El Jibarito (☎ 787-725-8375; 280 Sol; dishes $8-22; 11am-11pm) Local writers and artists, hip expats and young travelers flock to this place. Largely open to the quiet narrow street, the restaurant's low-lit bistro design actually re-creates the colonial facades of Old San Juan on the interior. Salad, sweet plantains and grilled shrimp will run you $13.

Café Berlin (☎ 787-722-5205; 407 San Francisco; dishes $10-25; lunch & dinner) Outdoor seating, leafy green salads and sinfully sweet desserts. What's not to love? Café Berlin is a favorite hangout for *sanjuaneros*.

El Patio de Sam (☎ 787-723-1149; 102 San Sebastián; dishes $16-28; 11:30am-midnight) Among the restaurant-bars at the crest of the hill on this street, this one stands out for the gauzy light of its hidden interior patio, as well as for its exceptional collection of *comida criolla*, authentic Puerto Rican food.

TOP END

Parrot Club (☎ 787-725-7370; 363 Fortaleza; dishes $18-32; lunch & dinner) Along with a vibrating orange, blue and yellow decor, the Parrot Club features live jazz and the tastes of 'nuevo Latino' cuisine. The fact that the menu is written in 'Spanglish' hints at the fusion cookery that goes into recipes like crabcakes *caribeños* and vegetarian 'tortes.' Some call this the best place in Old San Juan; others say the bloom is already off the rose. For late-night dining it still seems to be the favorite pick of *sanjuaneros* – try a Sunday brunch or dinner if you want to check it out under less chaotic conditions.

Dragon Fly (☎ 787-977-3886; 364 Fortaleza; dishes $10-25; dinner) This is hip eatery number two on Fortaleza, and it's right across the street from the Parrot Club (same owner, too). Word on the street is Dragon Fly is even better: that depends on what you like, but it's definitely different from its older sister. Dragon Fly looks like an intimate Penang bordello with its flaming red walls and fabrics, and it draws a sexy-looking crowd to the bar. Try the 'Dragon Punch' cocktail, but leave room for dinner. The flavor combinations are generally great – shrimp nachos, seviche topped with yucca, grilled snapper with pumpkin and the odd cassoulet to round things out.

Aquaviva (☎ 787-722-0665; 364 Fortaleza; dishes $30-40; dinner) And this makes hip eatery number three. Aquaviva is the most recent addition to the Dragon Fly/Parrot Club family. An 'aquaviva' is a jellyfish, and the glowing white decor inside is offset by blue lamps shaped like that aquatic creature. Very fitting in a place that offers a fresh seafood bar nightly – it's almost impossible to resist. Other menu items include calamari

THE AUTHOR'S CHOICE

It's a trifecta! All three of these favorite places are in Gran Hotel El Convento (p95).

Patio del Nispero (dishes $8-15; breakfast & lunch) Tender flaky croissants in the morning and juicy steak, shrimp and chicken dishes for lunch, El Patio offers the most tranquil al fresco dining found anywhere else.

El Picoteo (dishes $6-20; lunch & dinner) With warm, reddish walls and the Gypsy Kings in the background, this airy spot is reminiscent of a tapas bar in southern Spain. *Sanjuaneros* love to play dominoes and sip sangria while nibbling on classics like *tortilla española* (potato omelette), *gambas al ajillo* (shrimp with garlic) and *albondigas* (meatballs) done Andalusia-style. Also a frequent stop on the bar-hopping route.

Café Bohemio (dishes $12-24 lunch & dinner) Quiet at lunch, restful in the afternoon, Bohemio is unrecognizable at night, especially Tuesday, Thursday, Friday and Saturday. Live music and hip-swaying crowds transform this café into a sizzling dance party with spicy food and frosty drinks.

filled with shredded, seasoned beef, and dorado with lightly grilled green and red bell peppers, seasoned with garlic and served with plantains. The specialty drink is the beach cooler – light, citrusy and deceptively potent.

La Querencia (☎ 787-723-0357; 320 Fortaleza; dishes $16-26; ☽ dinner) A beautifully restored old town house that's full of color – try drinks in the red bar up front and dinner in the warm, candle-lit green room in back. Children who like interesting food do well here; the menu rotates but chef Ana likes to focus on *comida criolla* with an haute cuisine edge – filet mignon with a red wine and mushroom mofongo, garlic and thyme chicken with mashed cassava and caramelized onions, sautéed shrimp with roasted pineapple and coconut-spiced rum vinaigrette. The genial hosts invented a cocktail called the 'Why Not?' and it's the perfect antidote for a long day.

Trois Cent Onze (☎ 787-725-7959; 311 Fortaleza; dishes $12-30; ☽ dinner) Owner Christophe Gourdain came to Calle Fortaleza from his native France via New York, where he met and married his Puerto Rican wife. Trois Cent Onze has billowing white curtains, a zinc bar, flickering candles and tantalizing arches over delightful Moorish-Andalusian tiles. This is the premier French restaurant on the island and it serves succulently creative dishes like sautéed sea scallops with almond-flavored butter, mango and crabmeat salad, and magret of duckling roasted with honey.

La Mallorquina (☎ 787-722-3261; 207 San Justo; dishes $16-35; ☽ lunch & dinner) The grande-dame of Old San Juan eateries, La Mallorquina's been around for 150 years. If nothing else, have a drink at the immense slab of mahogany that is the bar; it's beautiful. The food's delectable, as well. The specialty of the house is *asopao*, a rice broth stewed with all type of herbs, seafood or meat. From the main menu, the shrimp dishes are particularly good.

Ostra Cosa (☎ 787-722-2672; 154 Calle del Cristo; dishes $15-30; ☽ noon-11pm) Touting itself as an 'aphrodisiac restaurant' with eclectic menu offerings like royal smashed potato with octopus, Ostra Cosa's lush garden does make you feel like you've stepped into a secret earthy paradise. Perfect for couples, of course.

Dali (☎ 787-721-0787; 317 Fortaleza; dishes $10-28; ☽ dinner) As you would expect, things are quite a bit surreal in this restaurant (especially the glasses used to serve drinks). But it's refreshingly different and captivating. The cocktails are really great, the food is light and inventive (carpaccio of salmon marinated in citrus, for example), and the late-night atmosphere? Pretty off the wall (see p103).

Il Perugino (☎ 787-722-5481; 105 Calle del Cristo; dishes $22-40; ☽ noon-midnight) Said to be the best Italian in town, Il Perugino serves Umbrian and Tuscan delicacies like veal piccata and carpaccio in a restored town house. With a bottle of wine, a meal for two can easily surpass $100.

Condado & Ocean Park   Map pp84–5

Don't let the prevalence of second-rate hotel restaurants, tourist traps and fast-food chains deter you – there's good eating to be found along this stretch of beach.

BUDGET

Hostería del Mar (☎ 787-727-3302; hostelria@caribe.net; 1 Tapia; dishes around $12; ☽ 11am-10pm) One of the island's great secrets: an intimate vegetarian restaurant right on the beach. The menu changes frequently, but tofu, brown rice and onion dishes with a side salad are staples. See also Sleeping (p96).

Salud (☎ 787-722-0911; 1350 Av Ashford; dishes $5-15; ☽ breakfast & lunch) Vegie eaters will find a pleasant surprise here. Both a health food store and café, this narrow little place serves up a spicy stew of roots and vegetables for $5, and you can stock up on vegie protein if you are heading out of town.

Via Appia (☎ 787-725-8711; Av Ashford; pizzas $7-14; ☽ lunch & dinner) Right next door to Salud, you'll find the Condado area's favorite pizza restaurant, complete with its shady streetside tables.

Kasalta's (☎ 787-727-7340; 1966 McLeary; dishes $4-10; ☽ 6am-10pm) This is a Cuban bakery on Ocean Park's main drag that opens early for those who have watched the sun rise through the open doorway of a bar or club. Inside this old-style cafeteria with display cases filled with treats, you can order up a *cubano* (a delicious pickled and grilled Cuban pork and ham sandwich), omelette or one of a dozen sweet confections to eat with your steaming mug of *café con leche*.

MIDRANGE

Yerba Buena (☎ 787-721-5907; 1350 Av Ashford; dishes $13-30; ☾ dinner) The *ropa vieja* (shredded beef) melts in your mouth, and the accompanying pile of sweet plantains are the perfect side dish. Shrimp are doused in coconut-mango sauce or brandy with mango – your choice. Order a mojito, reputed to the best on the island.

Hacienda Don José (☎ 787-722-5880; 1025 Av Ashford; dishes $5-12; ☾ breakfast, lunch & dinner) A bit touristy, yes, but also right on the beach and serving plentiful dishes at comparatively low prices. Breakfast will set you back less than $5. Drinks are also very affordable, and you can take your meal on the beachfront patio. Not bad.

Dunbar's Pub (☎ 787-728-2920; 1954 McLeary; dishes $7-22; ☾ lunch & dinner) You can follow the party crowd from Kasalta's (next door) to this place. Dunbar's serves up burgers, wings and other American pub favorites; potato skins here go for $6. Sunday brunch with live Brazilian jazz is a great first stop before heading to the beach nearby.

Pepin's (☎ 787-728-6280; 2479 Av Isla Verde; dishes $11-22; ☾ lunch & dinner) In the Punta Las Marías neighborhood, this café and tapas bar gets raves from both locals and expats in the area. Tapas start at $4. Dress up: shorts are a no-no.

TOP END

Ajili-Mójili (☎ 787-725-9195; 1052 Av Ashford; dishes $14-23; ☾ lunch & dinner) The menu is high-end *comida criolla* – such as island-style pork loin with mofongo (mashed plantains) – and the atmosphere is heady and romantic. Candles, sweeping views, lots of attention from the staff – come prepared to be pampered, and dress up rather than down.

Zabo's (☎ 787-725-9494; 14 Candida; dishes $12-30; ☾ lunch & dinner) Very creative dishes like mango and curry rice, and rosemary pork chops with garlic merlot sauce make Zabo's a hit with the foodie crowd in town. The breezy colonial-style building makes you feel like you've stepped miles away from the crowded city street.

Ramiro's (☎ 787-721-9049; 1106 Magdalena; dishes $25-37; ☾ lunch & dinner) Reservations are always a good idea for Ramiro's, which some would say has replaced Ajili-Mójili as the city's 'best' restaurant. Dishes like lamb with spiced root vegetables and guava sauce, and crabmeat

and avocado salad certainly make a good argument on behalf of Ramiro's.

Migas (☎ 787-721-5991; 1400 Magdalena; dishes $15-35; ☾ lunch & dinner) The latest trendy boutique restaurant to open up on Magdalena, Migas is high on the list of bar-hopping *sanjuaneros*. Some come for drinks and others for the food – miso-glazed salmon, classic French steak frites, spicy duck with orange glaze – and others hang out just to enjoy the sleek elegance and fashionable buzz.

Antonio's (☎ 787-723-7567; 1406 Magdalena; dishes $18-30; ☾ dinner) Gourmands will love the duck breast with mango sauce and other foodie-friendly options. Reservations are highly recommended because this is a very popular place. Break out the nice threads, too.

Isla Verde

Ferrari Gourmet (Map p86; ☎ 787-982-3115; 51 Av Isla Verde; dishes $6-14; ☾ lunch & dinner) Try to picture an elegant pizza joint and you'll get a feeling for Ferrari Gourmet – simple pizzas and snacks, but oh so tastefully done. Wine by the glass, too.

Che's (Map pp84-5; ☎ 787-726-7202; 35 Caoba; dishes $12-24; ☾ lunch & dinner) Almost all of the *sanjuaneros* and expats say Che's has the very best Argentinean food around; once you taste the *churrasco* or *parrillada* (grilled, marinated steak), or even the veal chops, you won't disagree.

Casa Dante (Map p86; ☎ 787-726-7310; 39 Av Isla Verde; dishes $14-22; ☺ lunch & dinner) Casa Dante is a family-run restaurant that serves more variations of mofongo than one would think humanly feasible. All are delicious, and you can stick to fajitas or enchiladas or a basic steak, if that's what you prefer.

Edith Café (Map p86; ☎ 787-253-1281; Av Isla Verde, Km 6.3; dishes $6-15; ☺ 24hr) No frills, but good food. Try one of the daily specials or sample the tasty, deep-fried seafood snacks. It's located next to the Hampton Inn.

Shogun (Map p86; ☎ 787-268-4622; 35 Av Isla Verde; dishes $5-14; ☺ lunch & dinner) Lots of Japanese restaurants line the Isla Verde strip. This is one of the most popular, serving standard fare like tuna, maki and California rolls, or specialty rolls that you can put together yourself or choose from the à la carte menu.

Metropol (Map p86; ☎ 787-791-5585; Av Isla Verde; dishes $12-26; ☺ dinner) You can't miss this place – it's right next to the cockfighting arena. It's a neighborhood favorite for the plentiful portions and simple (but not plain) Spanish fare.

Miramar & Río Piedras

Chayote (Map pp84-5; ☎ 787-722-9385; 603 Av Miramar; dishes $22-30; ☺ lunch & dinner) Named for a flavorful island vegetable, Chayote is in the Olimpio Court Hotel (p97). It combines *criollo* cooking with French, Hindu, African, Spanish and Central American cuisines. Like the cooking, the dining room is a golden fusion of traditional wicker and contemporary art and sculpture. Casual but elegant.

Augusto's (Map pp84-5; ☎ 787-725-7700; 801 Av Ponce de León; dishes $22-35; ☺ lunch & dinner) The Austrian-born Augusto Schreiner was executive chef at the Caribe Hilton for six years before opening this highly touted restaurant. Formal and expensive, Augusto's has been designated the best restaurant in San Juan six times. The menu has strong roots in all the major European cuisines and is constantly evolving.

ENTERTAINMENT

If you're looking for bars and restaurants, Old San Juan has the hippest and hottest options. Calle San Sebastián is always busy,

but Calle Fortaleza is also a rising star. Weekend nights see casual crowds enjoying live jazz along Paseo de la Princesa and in the gardens nearby. On busy weekend nights, companies will send out cruises from Plaza de la Darsena that turn into bustling dance parties.

It's a late nightlife in San Juan. Things don't start picking up until about 11pm, and don't really take off until much later. Lines can start forming as early as 9pm at some places on weekends and holidays. Dress sharp and your chances of getting waved inside increase greatly.

One curious thing: happy hour in a lot of tourist bars in Old San Juan follows the American standard of late afternoon half-price drinks until about 7pm. But in many places – especially along Condado and Isla Verde, where the young crowd tends to work in hotels – happy hour will run from 10pm to midnight or midnight to 2am.

Admission prices, when there are any, usually run from $5 to $15, and if you suspect sometimes you're being charged the 'tourist price,' you're absolutely right.

Drinking
OLD SAN JUAN   Map pp76–7

El Batey (101 Calle del Cristo; ☺ 3pm-late) It's not at all good looking – in fact the words 'hole-in-the-wall' come to mind. But it just has a certain something that keeps everybody coming back. Call it character – not always a commodity easily found in tourist-heavy parts of San Juan.

Sala (☎ 787-724-4797; 317 Fortaleza; ☺ 10pm-1am Tue-Thu, 6pm-3am Fri & Sat) If the main entrance is closed, go through the door in Callejón de la Capilla. Sometimes Sala is more of a laid-back bar scene than disco, other times everybody's grooving to live music. In either case, dress carefully.

Pancho's Café (☎ 787-977-3412; 253 Tanca; ☺ 7pm-4am) For younger crowds, this is the latest in a series of cool clubs that have been appearing in Old San Juan. Pancho's does live music, but also features rap, hip-hop and house, courtesy of some of the island's best DJs.

Noise (☎ 787-724-3426; 203 Tanca; ☺ 10pm-late) Ladies get in free on Friday nights, but a $5 to $15 cover generally applies to everyone on other nights. Hip-hop only at this packed club.

Oleo (☎ 787-977-1083; 305 Recinto Sur; 6pm-2am) Loud house music in an art-filled space that's been lovingly decked out in vibrant, flashy colors.

Enlaces (☎ 787-977-0754; 255 Cruz) In Old San Juan, this hip-hop lounge plays some heavy beats and attracts a late-teen, early-twenty-something crowd. There are no set opening hours, and it lasts until 3am or 4am.

CONDADO & ISLA VERDE

Kali's (Map pp84–5; ☎ 787-721-5104; 1407 Av Ashford; 6pm-late Tue-Sat) Sophisticated *sanjuaneros* love this moody, Asian-themed restaurant and bar. Sheer curtains flutter against dark maroon walls while trendy patrons sip cocktails and order Indian-influenced appetizers at a big bar adorned with candles.

Wet & Liquid (Map p86; ☎ 787-728-3666; Water Club, 2 Calle Tartak) Inside the Water Club (p97), this bar is where well-heeled guests mingle with well-heeled drinkers on the make. Fashionable and full of fashionistas, this place is where you are mostly likely to bump into a model (male or female).

La Fiesta Lounge (Map pp84–5; ☎ 727-721-1000; Condado Plaza Hotel & Casino, 999 Av Ashford) This club in the Condado Plaza Hotel & Casino gets very Latin and brassy. Call for the latest program and expect to find yourself with an over-40 crowd of tourists and islanders. You can hear some great salsa here from small combos. Cover charge varies.

Live Music

OLD SAN JUAN   Map pp76–7

Nuyorican Café (☎ 787-977-1276; 312 San Francisco; 7pm-late) Arriving on the scene in 2001, the Nuyorican quickly became the hottest live jazz venue (nightly) in the city. Although the street address is Calle San Francisco, the actual entrance is on the alley, Callejón de la Capilla, between Calle San Francisco and Calle Fortaleza. Some nights also include poetry reading. Also step into the little bar in the alley for a beer; lots of locals and pleasant conversation.

Gallery Café (☎ 787-725-8676; 305 Fortaleza; 7pm-1am) This café in the old city features jazz on Wednesday night, and funk, hip-hop, Latin jazz and techno Thursday to Saturday. Happy hour specials run till 9pm on Friday. You get a well-dressed local yuppie gang here.

CONDADO & ISLA VERDE

Rio Bar & Club (Map pp84–5; ☎ 787-723-8680; 1309 Av Ashford; 5pm-5am) Live salsa and merengue on the beach – that's what keeps this place busy. Young professionals love to unwind here after a hard day at the office with a drink in hand and their feet in sand.

El Tropicoro (Map p86; Wyndham El San Juan Hotel & Casino, 6063 Av Isla Verde; admission around $23) The club is one of the many nighttime attractions at this hotel. There are usually 9pm and 11pm shows nightly during the winter season. You won't get the big names that attract the crowds to Las Vegas shows, and the crowd here is mostly affluent tourists over 50. The shows feature a lot of dancers in tight or scant clothing working their mojo to tropical themes. Picture Havana, Cuba, in the 1950s. Cover includes two drinks.

Martini's Cabaret (Map p86; InterContinental San Juan Resort & Casino, 187 Av Isla Verde; admission around $30) This place has booked headliners such as Whitney Houston and Jay Leno; performances are held on Wednesday, as well as Friday to Sunday. The cover charge includes two drinks. Bringing in a mix of islanders and tourists, the scene is pure Las Vegas.

Dance Clubs

OLD SAN JUAN   Map pp76–7

La Rumba (☎ 787-725-4407; 152 San Sebastián; 11pm-late) This is what you came to Puerto Rico for – a club so packed with people of all races and ages that it matters not if you are an expert twirler or a rank neophyte who can't even spell syncopation. It won't get busy until after 11pm, when the live bands start warming up, but soon enough the trickle of people through the door will turn into a torrent and you'll be caught up in a warm tropical crush of movement. Expect *bomba, plena,* salsa, samba and, of course, rumba music.

Dali (☎ 787-721-0787; 317 Viejo San Juan; 11pm-late) On weekend nights and select weekdays, the room in the back of this restaurant (see p100) is turned into a funky club with either live music or a super-skilled DJ who gets your heart pumping before you even hit the dance floor. It's a scene and a half, with loads of beautiful people flouncing around, but more than a few down-to-earth local types keeping things real in the corners. The fun starts late – after midnight. Drop in during quiet afternoon hours for an advance music schedule from the engaging maitre d': Thursday night often features local musicians specializing in electronica and salsa.

Club Lazer (☎ 787-721-4479; 251 Cruz; ✆ 11pm-late) It's been around for a while, but it's still a big draw. Cruise-ship escapees, employees on a night off, young, old, gay and straight pack into Club Lazer for a wild night of fun. Probably the most 'alternative' of all San Juan discos. The music ranges from house, electronica, reggaeton (sometimes) to rap and hip-hop.

Café Hijos de Borinquen (☎ 787-723-8126; 51 San José; ✆ 8pm-late) Gotta wedge your way in on weekend nights. Come for the 10am happy hour and blaring salsa from the jukebox. It's actually fun to dance to.

CONDADO & ISLA VERDE

Club Babylon (Map p86; ☎ 787-791-2781; Wyndham El San Juan Hotel & Casino, 6063 Av Isla Verde; admission $15; ✆ 6pm-2am) A celebrity hangout, this two-story play palace has a VIP lounge on Saturday nights and hordes of young hipsters hoping to get in. Friday nights are big for the dance music; Saturday it's salsa, house and whatever strikes the DJ's fancy.

El Chico Lounge (Map p86; ☎ 787-791-1000; Wyndham El San Juan Hotel & Casino, 6063 Av Isla Verde; ✆ 10pm-2am) If you want to dance but discos aren't your style, then try El Chico. Professional dancers move among the crowd getting everyone in motion. Live music adds to the fun. Dressy attire required.

Spread (Map p86; ☎ 787-727-3422; 5940 Av Isla Verde; ✆ 11pm-late) On Friday nights, this popular martini bar becomes a club, with a DJ spinning lots of trance and house music while harried staff move through the crowds serving complimentary sushi and other yummy snacks. Saturday night this is the best 'after' party place; expect the crowd to arrive around 3am. Martinis of all flavors and combinations are the house specialty, but regular mixed drinks, wine and beer are also served.

Oyster Bar & Grill (Map p86; ☎ 787-726-2161; Condominio La Posada, Av Isla Verde; ✆ lunch & dinner) Maybe it's the Cajun spices in the crawfish served at dinner, but it seems people can't sit still in the Oyster Bar! It's a dance-happy and salsa-loving crowd which doesn't finish until 1:30am weeknights, and 4am weekends and holidays.

SANTURCE

Stargate (Map p84-5; ☎ 787-725-4664; 1 Roberto H Todd; ✆ 9pm-4am) Calle Roberto H Todd is a major thoroughfare linking the districts of Miramar and Condado east of Laguna del Condado, and here at No 1 you'll find perhaps the most popular disco among *sanjuaneros*. The cavernous interior plays reggaeton while the stylish crowd twists to the beat. The next room is a semi-separate club known as Pleasure, frequented by a college-age crowd that likes R&B and hip-hop.

Asylum (Map pp84-5; ☎ 787-723-3416; 1420 Av Ponce de León; ✆ 9pm-4am) A lot of night owls, of both straight and gay varieties, end their Sunday morning dance-a-thons at Asylum. The crowd is mostly 18 to 23, except on gay nights when it's older.

Habana Club (Map pp84-5; ☎ 787-722-1919; 303 Calle Condado; ✆ 10pm-6am) Weekend nights you can barely breathe for the crowds – Habana Club claims to be the 'home of salsa', and apparently quite a few *sanjuaneros* believe that's true. Don't wait until too late to come or you might not get in.

Gay & Lesbian Venues

Eros (Map pp84-5; ☎ 787-722-1131; 1257 Av Ponce de León; ✆ 10pm-late) If you want a place with a Latin feel, where the disc jockey mixes some of the heavier New York house sounds with a Latin rock and salsa, try here. Eros is next to the Teatro Metro in the Santurce/Miramar district. While basically a gay venue, this hot dance scene on Saturday nights draws free spirits from all quarters of the gay, lesbian, bi and straight world.

Kouros (Map pp84-5; ☎ 787-977-0771; 1515 Av Ponce de León; ✆ 10pm-late Sat & Sun) Open only on the weekends, Kouros is probably the most glamorous disco in town, and it caters to a well-heeled gay male and female crowd (although certainly anyone is welcome). If you want to put on something slinky and get hot and sweaty under a strobe light, check out Kouros.

Cups (☎ 787-268-3570; 1708 San Mateo; ✆ 10pm-late) Bars catering exclusively to women are hard to come by in San Juan, but this one in Santurce is a laid-back women's scene popular with couples and cruisers.

Classical Music, Opera & Ballet

Luis A Ferré Center for the Performing Arts (Bellas Artes; Map pp84-5; ☎ 787-724-4747; 22 Av Ponce de León;

tickets $15-45) Built in 1981 in Santurce, this center has more than 1800 seats in the festival hall, about 700 in the drama hall and 200 in the experimental theater. The three concert halls fill when the Puerto Rican Symphony Orchestra holds one of its weekly winter performances. International stars also peform here, and it stages productions by the Ópera de Puerto Rico and Ballet de San Juan.

Theater

Teatro Tapia (Map pp76-7; ☎ 787-722-0407; Plaza de Colón; tickets $15-30) On the south side of the plaza in Old San Juan, this is an intimate structure in typical Spanish colonial interpretation of the neoclassical style. It dates from 1832, and has been the beneficiary of two recent restorations.

Named for the famous 19th-century Puerto Rican playwright Alejandro Tapia y Rivera, this elegant theater hosts cultural productions of all types. The performances are usually in Spanish and frequently feature new works from Spain or Latin America. The acting is professional and performances attract Puerto Rico's literati and social elite. Opening night is a fashion show of who's who in San Juan.

Cinemas

Movie theaters can be found in most of San Juan's major shopping centers. You can also look in the yellow pages of the phone directory under *Teatros y Cines* (Theaters & Cinemas) for the one nearest you; be sure to ask someone you trust whether the movie house is in a safe area before you go wandering around its locale after dark.

Reading Cinemas (Map pp72-3; ☎ 787-767-1363, 767-3505; Plaza Las Américas) In the Hato Rey district, this is the city's largest multiplex.

Teatro Metro (Map pp84-5; ☎ 787-722-0465; Parada 18, 1313 Av Ponce de León) This classic, restored cinema is in Santurce, edging towards Miramar.

UA Cinema 150 (Map p86; ☎ 787-791-0707; Laguna Gardens Shopping Center, 10 Av Laguna, Isla Verde) This awaits viewers in Isla Verde.

Fine Arts Cinema (Map pp84-5; ☎ 787-721-4288; 654 Av Ponce de León) In Miramar, it has a good selection of independent films from around the world.

Movie buffs should refer to p93 for information on the city's up-and-coming annual cinema festival.

Casinos

San Juan may not be Las Vegas, but a lot of travelers and islanders come for the action. All of San Juan's casinos are associated with resort hotels, and the gaming houses have now expanded to offer Caribbean Stud Poker, Let It Ride, Pai Gow Poker and the Big Six Wheel, as well as the standard blackjack, roulette, craps, baccarat and minibaccarat. Most of the city's casinos are open between noon and 4pm, and 8pm and 4am.

InterContinental San Juan Resort & Casino (Map p86; ☎ 787-791-6100; 187 Av Isla Verde) The massive gaming facilities at this casino in this resort (p97) are reminiscent of those at the casino's Vegas namesake.

Stellaris Casino (Map pp84-5; ☎ 787-722-7000, ext 6759; San Juan Marriott Resort & Casino, 1309 Av Ashford) The tables are new at this casino in the San Juan Marriott Resort.

Wyndham El San Juan Hotel & Casino (Map p86; ☎ 787-791-1000; 6063 Av Isla Verde) Living up to its reputation as the most exclusive hotel (p97) on the island, this is a top-drawer operation where the crowd usually dresses up to play.

Courtyard Inn (Map p86; ☎ 787-791-0404; 7012 Boca de Cangrejos) This small casino doesn't have any of the panache of the larger hotels, but it certainly has its own mojo going on. The croupiers and card dealers are extra patient and explain rules to befuddled novices (sometimes they even offer advice). It's a laid-back place where gamblers tease each other in Spanish and English across the tables, and even egg each other on. See also Sleeping (p97).

Sports

Estadio Sixto Escobar (p83) is a popular place for track and field competitions.

Hiram Bithorn Stadium (Map pp72-3; ☎ 787-725-2110; Plaza Las Americas, Av Roosevelt) Home of the Montreal Expos (at least in the winter), this is a small ball park built on Astroturf. It's named after the first Puerto Rican to play in the majors.

SHOPPING
Arts & Crafts

The best arts and crafts shopping is in Old San Juan, and all the following can be found on the Old San Juan map (Map pp76–7). Calles San Francisco and Fortaleza are the two main arteries in and out of the old city, and both are packed cheek by jowl with shops. Running perpendicular at the west end of the town, Calle del Cristo is home to many of the old city's most chic establishments. Visitors should note that many of the craft vendors in the old city are actually selling imports from South America, so do not proceed with the illusion that you are buying the produce of Puerto Rican artisans. As well, around Plaza de Armas you'll find Marshalls, a Polo/Ralph Lauren Factory Outlet Store, a Coach and many more recognizable names.

Puerto Rican Arts & Crafts (☎ 787-725-5596; 204 Fortaleza; 🕙 9am-6pm Mon-Fri, noon-5pm Sat) For the real thing, check the selection at this place.

Centro de Artes Populares (253 Calle del Cristo; 🕙 9:30am-4:30pm Tue-Sat) This shop is another good source for santos, *mundillo* lace and Carnaval masks (see p40 for detailed descriptions of these popular art forms).

Butterfly People (☎ 787-723-2432; 257 Cruz; 🕙 10am-6pm Mon-Sat) A gallery, antique shop and small restaurant mixed together under walls that are covered with flurries of the little critters. (You can buy the arrangements.)

Galería Botello (☎ 787-723-2879; 208 Calle del Cristo; 🕙 10am-6pm Mon-Sat) This is one of the oldest, most established and avant-garde galleries in town. Don't miss Angel Botello's own work, including his boilerlike sculpture of *The Three Sisters*.

Bóveda (☎ 787-725-0263; 200 Calle del Cristo; 🕙 10am-8pm Mon-Sat) Directly across the street from Botello's gallery, Linda Williams runs one of the street's most imaginative arts, decoration, jewelry and clothing boutiques.

Galería Liga de Estudiantes de Arte (Gallery of Art Students' League; Escuela de Artes Plásticas, Calle del Morro) If you want to see some of the freshest expressions of island artists at affordable prices, head to this place. Opening hours vary.

Barrachina's (☎ 787-725-7912; 104 Fortaleza; 🕙 9am-6pm Mon-Sat) You can sample exotic rums for free (or buy a bottle) when you shop for jewelry and fragrances here. The restaurant portion of this operation claims to have invented the piña colada.

Markets

Artisans Fair (Map pp72-3; Parques Muñoz Rivera & Sixto Escobar, Puerta de Tierra) For more traditional shopping, head here. The market is generally open on weekends, but call the PRTC (p74) ahead of time to inquire about changing hours of operation.

Mercado de Río Piedras (Map p87; Paseo de Diego) Of course, there's also the market for produce, meats and bargain clothing (p86).

Shopping Malls

Plaza Las Américas (Map pp72-3; 🕙 9am-9pm Mon-Sat, 11am-5pm Sun) If the sun or heat get to you, you can always have a thoroughly American experience in air-conditioned comfort visiting the 200 stores. It is just off Hwy 18 (Expreso Las Américas) in Hato Rey.

Plaza Carolina (Map pp72-3; 🕙 9am-9pm Mon-Sat, 11am-5pm Sun) This is a similar operation, which lies to the east of the city, offering US standards such as JC Penney and Sears among its collection of 150 shops. It is off Hwy 26 (Expreso Baldorioty de Castro) in Carolina.

GETTING THERE & AWAY
Air

International flights arrive at and depart from LMM airport about 8 miles east of the old city center. See p257 for information on airport services and for a list of international carriers that fly to San Juan.

Several airlines provide services between San Juan and the other parts of the commonwealth, though Puerto Rico's domestic air network is limited. Private aircraft, charter services and the bulk of the commuter flights serving the islands of Culebra and Vieques arrive at and depart from San Juan's original Aeropuerto de Isla Grande, on the Bahía de San Juan in the city's Miramar district. See p261 for details.

Cruise Ship

More than a dozen cruise lines include San Juan on their Caribbean itineraries, and as the second-largest port for cruise ships in the Western Hemisphere, the city is visited by more than a million cruise-ship passengers a year. All ships dock at the piers along Calle La Marina near the Customs House, just a short walk from the cobblestone streets of Old San Juan. See p260 for details.

Público

There is no islandwide bus system. Públicos form the backbone of public transportation in Puerto Rico and can provide an inexpensive link between San Juan and other points on the island, including Ponce and Mayagüez. Públicos are generally shared taxis in the form of minivans that pick up passengers along predetermined routes.

In San Juan the major público centers include the LMM airport, two large público stations in Río Piedras (Centro de Publicos Oeste and Centro de Publicos Este) and – to a lesser extent – the Plaza de Colón in Old San Juan. See p262 for detailed information.

GETTING AROUND
To/From the Airport

The bus is the cheapest option. Look for the 'Parada' sign outside the arrivals concourse at LMM airport. The B40 bus will get you from the airport to Isla Verde or Río Piedras. From there you can take other buses to Old San Juan or Condado.

There are also airport shuttle vans or limousine kiosks on the arrivals concourse. Chances are you can join some other travelers headed your way. Once the van fills, you'll pay around $7 to Isla Verde, $9 to Condado and $12 to Old San Juan.

Getting to LMM airport from hotels in the San Juan area is easy. Staff at virtually all of the midrange and top-end hotels will arrange for a taxi or airport shuttle van to pick you up in front of your lodging at your request. Depending on how many people share the cost of the ride, you can expect to pay between $4 and $20. If you go it alone, there are fixed prices to/from the airport and the following destinations: Isla Verde ($8), Condado ($12) and Puerta de Tierra/ Old San Juan ($16).

Bus

The **Autoridad Metropolitana de Autobuses** (AMA; Metropolitan Bus Authority & Metrobus; ☎ 787-767-7979) has a main bus terminal in Old San Juan near the cruise ship piers. These are the routes taken most often by travelers (bus numbers are followed by associated route descriptions):

B40 LMM Airport, Isla Verde, Piñones and Río Piedras.
M1 & M9 Old San Juan, Río Piedras via various routes.
B21 Old San Juan, Condado, Stop 18 (Santurce), Plaza Las Américas.
A5 Old San Juan, Stop 18, Isla Verde.
C10 Hato Rey, Stop 18, Condado, Isla Grande.

Beware! The A5 bus from Isla Verde to Old San Juan runs through the dangerous housing project of Loíza. In fact, if you want to go to Condado from Isla Verde, you must

get off near here at Stop 18 in Santurce; the surrounding area is rife with violent crime.

Car

If you can avoid driving in the city, by all means, do so. Traffic, parking, the maze of thoroughfares and the danger of being carjacked make having and using a rental car in the city a challenge. Old San Juan has the city's two safest and most accessible parking facilities: Covadonga parking lot on Recinto Sur just as you enter town, and Dona Fela, next door, which is slightly cheaper. For access to El Morro or the nightlife of Calle San Sabastián, check out the underground lot (beneath Parque Beneficencia off Calle Norzagaray) at the upper end of town. Parking costs $2.50 for the first hour, and 75c for additional hours.

Ferry

A commuter ferry service called the **Acua Expreso** (☎ 787-788-1155; every 30min 6am-9pm, per trip $1) connects the east and west sides of Bahía de San Juan, Old San Juan and Cataño. In Old San Juan, the ferry dock is at Pier 2, near the Sheraton Old San Juan Hotel & Casino.

Taxi

Cab drivers are supposed to turn on the meter for trips around town, but that rarely happens. Insist on it, or establish a price from the start. Meters – when or if they do go on – charge $2 initially and $1.50 per mile or part thereof. You'll also pay $1 per piece of luggage. There's a $5 reservation charge; add a $1 surcharge after 10pm.

Taxis line up at the south end of Calle Fortaleza in Old San Juan; in other places they can be scarce. Don't make yourself a mugging target by standing on a deserted street waiting for one to pass by – call from the nearest hotel. Try **Metro Taxi Cabs** (☎ 787-725-2870) or **Rochdale Radio Taxi** (☎ 787-721-1900); they usually come when you call.

Train

The Tren Urbano, which will connect Bayamón with most of downtown San Juan, started limited test service in December 2004, but nobody knows for sure when service will begin in earnest. The train is already two years behind schedule and about two billion dollars over budget, so it remains to be seen if future plans to run a

Tren Urbano to the airport will be implemented. Fares were supposed to be about $1.50, but that price was set in 2003, before delays ballooned the budget. To learn of the Tren Urbano's current status, check with the PRTC (p74).

AROUND SAN JUAN

PIÑONES

Not fifteen minutes from the hustle and bustle of LMM airport sits a stretch of wildly untamed coastline disturbed only by the occasional incongruous airplane flying high overhead. Of the many arresting cultural contrasts visible in Puerto Rico, none is as striking as the abrupt transition from modern San Juan to pleasantly ramshackle Piñones, gateway to the east coast. The two worlds are linked by Punta Cangrejos, a small bridge on Rte 187 that spans Boca de Cangrejos (Crabmouth Point); once you cross it, you must be prepared to embrace beach town ways.

Do as the visiting *sanjuaneros* do on weekends and saunter along the sandy curves that are backed by spiky pine groves, nosh on seafood snacks and *coco frío* (ice-cold coconut milk) sold at roadside stands, and soak up the strong Afro-Caribbean culture that permeates Loíza Aldea and Carolina, two neighboring towns that maintain strong indigenous identities in the face of urbanization.

The first sign that you are approaching Piñones (if you take Rte 187 east) will be the Balneario de Carolina, a sparkling and well-tended public beach fronted by ample parking and bright red sculptures. You'll have arrived when a smattering of battered shacks rises up on the road in front of you and the smell of freshly cooked seafood wafts through the air. The wild and primitive scenery is almost shocking at first, but it only takes a minute for the beauty of the tall pines, growing right up to the water's edge, and surrounding mangrove forests to sink in.

Both a state forest – Bosque Estatal de Piñones – and a neighborhood of its parent municipality, Loíza Aldea, further to the east, Piñones presents an alternative to the high-rise condos and casino hotels of Isla Verde to the west, and the massive pharmaceutical plants of Carolina to the south. During vacations and on weekends, this entire stretch is filled with *sanjuaneros* and locals enjoying lots of African-influenced music, food and drinks.

Friquitines, also known as *buréns* in Piñones, are food kiosks of all shapes and sizes (and states of hygiene) that line the coastal road. Proprietors roast plantains, whole fish, codfish fritters and skewered pieces of seasoned pork over wood fires (it's a good idea to avoid oysters, seviche and other raw or lightly cooked dishes). Reefs just offshore create good surfing conditions and protect bathers from the full force of ocean swells, and on the days the ocean's just too rough, there's the recently completed Paseo de Piñones, a first-rate nature trail and bike path along the beach and through the forest reserve (opposite).

History

In the 16th century most of this fertile low-lying coastal region was farmed and inhabited by local people. Once the Spanish arrived and took over in 1719, huge tracts of land were turned into massive sugarcane plantations and captured natives were forced to provide the necessary labor, although they resisted mightily. Unable to keep many of their farmhands from melting into the nearby mountains, plantation owners began shipping in African workers, and sometimes stole them from other Caribbean islands. Most of the 30,000 residents living in the municipality today are freed descendants of these Yoruba slaves. The region is justifiably proud of its Afro-Caribbean heritage: Loíza Aldea is named after Luisa, a powerful Taíno *cacique* (chief) who ruled the area before the Spanish conquest.

Orientation

Whatever is happening in laid-back and rural Piñones is happening on Rte 187, which parallels the ocean. Entering from the west side, coming from San Juan, there's a little bridge to cross and then immediately a sign on the left saying '*Bienvenidos a Boca de Cangrejos*' (Welcome to Crabmouth Point). The sign leads up a small incline and onto a cliff overlooking the water. Several popular *friquitines* and restaurants are located there; it's a popular drinking place and offers fabulous views, especially at sunset. The road circles and brings you back down onto Rte 187. Parking is available on the cliff top. About a mile down the road is another concentration of popular beach shacks, set again just a little off the road overlooking the ocean. There are few accommodations and no real sense of the town beyond what is immediately visible along Rte 187; eventually 187 hits Rte 951, which returns to Hwy 3.

Dangers & Annoyances

Avoid walking along deserted strips of beach after nightfall, and be aware that some drug activity takes place on the beaches toward the west side of town. Don't venture onto the beach in that area at night. Do watch your speed while driving; transit cops love to patrol scenic Rte 187.

Beaches

The main attractions of Piñones are the wild (but sometimes trash-laden) **beaches**. To find a pretty beach for a picnic, you can't go wrong at almost any place where Rte 187 parallels the coast. The most picturesque and deserted beaches start around 9km. For swimming, avoid the corals at the western end of the strand of beaches. Unfortunately, this is where most of the food stands are, and it's where the bus from San Juan ends its route. Head about a mile to the east.

Activities

To see a patch of the rarely viewed coastal wilderness, you can join up with a **kayak** flotilla on a three-hour guided ecotour of the Laguna de Piñones and Laguna la Torrecilla. The lagoon features fish, birds and the occasional manatee. Copladet Nature & Adventure Tours (p89) in San Juan can hook you up for $80. So can Gary Horn of Las Tortugas Adventures (p89).

If the **surfing** is good at Piñones, you will see rows of cars with board racks parked by a good break. Or you can check ahead with one of the San Juan surf shops before you go (p89).

For **bicycling**, head across to the 5-mile-long Paseo de Piñones bike trail, running from the east end of Isla Verde along the shores of Playa Piñones and into the Bosque Estatal de Piñones. You can rent bikes from Domiro Sousa Brugal at El Pulpo Loco (p110), a beachfront restaurant on the bike trail, for $10/20 per hour/day. **Piñones Ecotours** (☎ 787-253-0005; tours $10-40) offers bike

---

> **MORNING DIP**
>
> Get wet early and you'll catch the best waves. Always check on area reefs and riptides with local surf shops, and keep an eye out for sharp-toothed denizens of the deep, although no problem with sharks has ever been reported in this area. November through March is the best surfing season on this corner of the island. Beaches favored by the locals include **Aviones, Chatarra, Tacones** and **Vacía Talega** (famous for strange rock formations) in Piñones, **La Pared** and **Costa Azul** in Luquillo, **El Convento, El Faro** and **Racetrack** in Fajardo, and **El Cocal** and **Sharkey's** in Yabucoa.

---

and kayak tours and rentals. Ring them and they will come to you.

Eating & Drinking

Although the ocean vistas, open-air seating and shade from the tall pine trees make the food kiosks a terrific place to kick back with a cold soft drink or beer, hygiene is not always a top concern for vendors in Piñones. If your tummy hasn't acclimatized yet, hit one of the more established restaurants listed below.

Piñones has a well-established nightlife, especially on weekends. There's no specific gay and/or lesbian bar in town, but gay couples won't attract any unwelcome attention at local spots.

Reef Bar & Grill (☎ 787-791-1374; mains $15-20, beers $3; ⏲ noon-10pm Wed-Thu, noon-2am Fri-Sun) This open-air bar and restaurant, on a bluff at the first left after the bridge entering town, wins the best-view competition hands down. And the food's pretty good too – hefty steak and seafood dishes, accompanied by fritters, plantains and a few African-flavored sides. Good for nightlife on weekends, and playing pool in the afternoon. Check out the massive mangrove tree clinging to the veranda, half tipping over the edge, roots exposed. It's lovely to sit and hear the waves slam the rocks right at your feet.

La Terraza (mains $15; ⏲ lunch & dinner) This is another fun place on the same bluff owned by Dominicans and serving *mangú* (their version of mofongo), codfish, seasoned pork and vegetable dishes. There is live music on Saturday night.

Puerta del Mar (mains $13-18; ☯ lunch & dinner) Also fun and on the same bluff, this place serves classic mofongo, fritters, deep-fried fish and burgers. Keep in mind that food choices at these places may be limited during the slow season, and hours may be curtailed.

El Pulpo Loco (☎ 787-791-8382; Rte 187 Km 4.5; mains $6-18; ☯ lunch & dinner) This is further down the road, and the mainstay of this brightly painted restaurant with shaded deck and sea view at the west end of the beach is very filling *criollo* cooking with an African flair. Plain mofongo runs $6. Local land crab with rice is $13.

Soleil Beach Club (☎ 787-253-1033; www.soleil beachclub.com; Rte 187 Km 4.6; mains $8-24; ☯ 7pm-1am Wed-Fri, 10pm-1am Sat, 2-5pm Sun) Just in front of El Pulpo Loco is the town's hottest night spot. While it tends to be a bit slow early in the week and during the rainy season, no place gets more packed during Christmas, spring breaks and on weekends. It's partially the great seafood dishes – shrimp, calamari, conch and crab are the staples – but also the fabulous music, sometimes live and sometimes featuring a DJ lured from San Juan for the weekend. Wednesday to Friday features jazz, '70s and '80s music and salsa, Saturday features blues, and Sunday features *bomba y plena*.

Tropical Fruit Shack (Rte 187 Km 4; breakfast $3) looks a bit dwarfed next to the two-storey Soleil, but the Tropical Fruit Shack offers wholesome *batidos* (shakes) made with local fruit and healthy breakfasts, something hard to come by in Piñones, which has a decided affinity for fried foods.

Getting There & Away

The B40 bus picks passengers up near the Cockfight Arena on Isla Verde and runs all the way to the settlement at the west end of the beach at Piñones. This is not a good place to end up, however, because you have to walk at least a mile further east before you really get to some decent swimming beaches. Your best bet is to rent a car and drive, or a bike and make use of the bike path, open 6am to 6pm.

LOÍZA ALDEA

Take Hwy 187 east from San Juan to catch some fresh air and rural scenery (and escape the commerce and traffic jams on Hwy 3).

The road eventually breaks out of the Piñones forest. When you cross a bridge spanning the island's largest river, the Río Grande de Loíza, the road brings you to the center of Loíza Aldea, commonly called 'Loíza.' This town is a largely rural municipality in the coastal lowlands east of LMM airport, and it includes Piñones as well as three other districts.

Loíza dates from 1719 and has a rich Taíno heritage. Sadly, there's little infrastructure to support tourism, and none of the settlements here are scenic. Most of the 30,000 residents are poor. There are only two reasons for a traveler to visit – a church and a fiesta. You will find some kiosks set up along the roads in Loíza that sell the usual snacks, but there's nowhere to sleep at night. Stay in nearby Piñones, San Juan or at any number of places around Luquillo, El Yunque or Fajardo.

Information

The center of the town is called the Plaza de Recreo, known as La Plaza, and is just east of the bridge over the Río Grande de Loíza. Here you will find the **Loíza Tourism Office** (☎ 787-886-6071; ☯ 8am-noon & 1-4pm Mon-Fri).

Sights

At the northern end of the plaza, **La Iglesia del Espíritu Santo y San Patricio** (Church of the Holy Ghost and St Patrick) appears every bit as proud and colonial as the cathedral in Old San Juan, and stands out from the humble collection of surrounding modern buildings. The church dates from 1646 and took its name from the patron saint of Ireland to honor Puerto Rico's famous Irish mercenaries, who designed many of the fortifications of Old San Juan.

Shopping

Handmade *vejigante* masks carved by local artisans are available in many places in Loíza (and are generally higher quality for less money than what you'll find in San Juan). The most famous shop is town is **Estudio de Arte Samuel Lind** (☯ 10am-6pm). The studio, which is open to visitors when someone is at home, is 3km south of town on Rte 187. Items cost between $15 and $350. To drive there, head toward Río Grande until you see a sign for the studio. Turn left and stop at the third house on the left. Públicos from San Juan to Rio Grande will stop at the studio on request. About 20 other mask makers work in the area. The tourist office will supply details.

Getting There & Away

You can catch a público to Loíza's plaza from Río Piedras in San Juan for about $2, which is not a bad way to go during the Fiesta de Santiago, when traffic into Loíza on Hwy 187 and Hwy 188 can be more frightening than a *vejigante* mask. Públicos return to Río Piedras from a terminal in Loíza (three blocks away from the plaza), but usually only during daylight hours.

CATAÑO & BAYAMÓN

Together, Bayamón and Cataño have a denser concentration of strip malls than any other area in Puerto Rico, which may be one reason why tourists don't seem to be flocking across the bay. Other reasons could be the heavy industrialization, traffic that could make you pull your hair out, and air that's often fouled with noxious chemicals. Nonetheless, there are a few things worth seeing in Bayamón and Cataño, although nothing warrants staying overnight.

To get here, you can take the Acua Expreso ferry from Old San Juan and enjoy a quick harbor tour along the way (p107).

The new Tren Urbano, that began test runs late in 2004, is supposed to link Hato Rey to Bayamón; but then it was supposed to be functional in 2003, so it may be a while longer before that's up and running.

If you head about a mile north of town to where Hwy 165 meets Hwy 870, you can follow the latter to a secluded picnic site amid the dramatic setting of Isla de Cabras.

Bacardi Rum Factory

Called the 'Cathedral of Rum' because of its six-story pink distillation tower, the **Bacardi Rum Factory** (☎ 787-788-8400; Hwy 888 Km 2.6; admission free; ☼ 8:30am-4:30pm Mon-Sat) covers 127 acres and stands out like a petroleum refinery across from Old San Juan, near the entrance to the bay. The world's largest and most famous rum-producing family started their business in Cuba more than a century ago, but they began moving their operation to this site in 1936. Today the distiller produces some 100,000 gallons of rum per day and ships 21 million cases per year worldwide.

In exchange for some freebies you'll be escorted on a tram tour that lasts about 30 minutes. To get to the Bacardi factory, take a público (about $3 per person) from the ferry terminal in Cataño along the waterfront on Calle Palo Seco (Hwy 888). At Km

---

ST JAMES THE MOOR SLAYER

The big event in Loíza Aldea is the **Fiesta de Santiago**. This is the town's *fiesta patronal* (patron saint's festival) and lasts nine days, from the final week of July to early August. With its tradition of colorful costumes, devilish *vejigante* masks and superb *bomba y plena* drummers and singers, Loíza's *fiesta patronal* is probably the best-attended fiesta on the island.

St James (Santiago) became the patron saint of the Yoruba slaves in Loíza as a consequence of the religious syncretism that has come to be called Santería or *espiritismo* on the island. When the Spaniards and the Catholic church denied the African slaves the right to worship their Yoruba *orishas* (gods) and forced them to convert to Christianity, the Africans took consolation in finding that the story of some saints reminded them of legends associated with their *orishas*. In the case of the slaves in Loíza, the story of how Christ's follower St James descended from heaven as a vengeful warrior to help the Spaniards drive the Moorish rulers from Iberia reminded them of their proud god of thunder and lightning, Changó.

So, under the guise of worshipping St James, the Africans worshipped Changó – and dreamed of liberation from their oppressors – drawing on their Yoruba customs of masking, ritualized drumming, entranced dancers and costumed clowns. The tradition continues to this day, focusing on parades celebrating three different effigies of St James.

Those sporting *vejigante* masks during the festival are supposed to represent the bad guys (the Spanish Moors that St James was railing against), but the handsome coconut husk and gourd masks the participants wear, painted with bright colors and vivid decoration, always seem to win them popular support. This festival draws huge crowds (and nightmare traffic), but is definitely worth making an effort to see.

2.6 north of town, look for the Cathedral of Rum and other Bacardi factory buildings to your left, rising above the landscape. Free tours of the plant leave every 30 minutes on the half-hour.

Isla de Cabras & Fuerte del Cañuelo

Located at the end of Hwy 870, north of the Bacardi Rum Factory and the settlement of Palo Seco, **Isla de Cabras** (Goat Island; admission $2) is perhaps the greatest seaside refuge in metro San Juan for travelers craving privacy and nature. There isn't much here except some shade trees, park benches, rocky seashore, waves and litter. You can fish, but the offshore currents are too dangerous for swimming. The ruins at the north end of the island mark a late-19th-century leper colony.

On the island's south end stand the remains of **Fuerte del Cañuelo** (Cañuelo Fort). The fort, which is nothing but ruins today, dates from 1610 and once shared the responsibility of protecting Bahía de San Juan with El Morro, which is across the channel marking the entrance to the bay.

Luis A Ferré Parque de Ciencias

This 42-acre **science park** (☎ 787-740-6868; Hwy 167; adult/child/senior $5/3/3; parking $1; ☯ 9am-4pm Wed-Fri, 10am-6pm Sat & Sun) is located in Bayamón on Hwy 167, south of the exit from the Hwy 22 toll road. Children seem to get a kick out of this science museum, despite the fact that the focal point of the park is education. It features pavilions that include a new planetarium, electrical energy museum, physics museum, rocket plaza, aerospace museum, transportation museum and zoo. There's also an artificial lake that kids can paddle-boat through just for the thrill of it – no educational lesson attached.

PARQUE CENTRAL DE BAYAMÓN

In the old tradition of urban oases like New York's Central Park, this pristine park stands across from the new city hall (the industrial-looking bridgelike structure spanning Hwy 2) in the center of Bayamón. It is remarkable for its landscaping and the preserved country house located on the grounds. The train running around the park's perimeter is one of the last vestiges of the days when sugarcane railways laced the northern lowlands of the island.

MUSEO DE OLLER

Located in the former city hall on the plaza of Bayamón's historic district, this art and history **museum** (☎ 787-785-6010; admission free; ☯ 8:30am-4pm Mon-Fri) pays tribute to native son Francisco Oller (1833–1917), considered the first Latin American impressionist. Most of Oller's great works are displayed elsewhere, but the restored neoclassical museum building is worth a peek if you are in the area. The collection includes some Oller portraits, Taíno artifacts, and sculptures.

CAPARRA

This is the site of Juan Ponce de León's first settlement on the island, established in 1508. The site was rediscovered in 1936, and only the foundations of a few buildings remain. There is a small **museum** (☎ 787-781-4795; Hwy 2 Km 6.6; admission free; ☯ 8:30am-4:15pm Tue-Sat) featuring Taíno artifacts that is open irregularly. Located on a highly commercial section of Hwy 2 east of Bayamón in Guaynabo, the site is only worth a visit to ponder why the great conquistador ever imagined this spot on the fringe of a mammoth swamp could possibly be suitable as a location for a colony. On the other hand, this is the same guy who got himself killed in search of the fabled Fountain of Youth.

East Coast

Shimmering clouds of a purplish hue seem to hang perpetually over the interior of this region, dumping considerable amounts of moisture onto the splendid mountains of the Sierra de Luquillo, a range that's dominated by the anvil-shaped peak of El Yunque, amid the only tropical rainforest in the US National Forest System. More than a million people visit each year, making this the most popular natural attraction on the island. Hikers, bird-watchers, campers and botanists come from around the world to revel in the deep greens and dark corners of this mysterious inland wilderness.

But if it's sunshine you're looking for, the east coast has plenty of that, too. The entire coastline is full of renowned beaches and spots for surfing, snorkeling and diving – all within easy reach of one another.

Most of the beach action kicks off at Playa Luquillo, just a short drive down to sea level from the heights of El Yunque. The crescent-moon shape of this balneario is backed by plenty of picnic tables, bathrooms, showers and the ubiquitous *friquitines* (food stalls) that offer salty seafood snacks and creative takes on *comida criolla* (traditional Puerto Rican cuisine). Dining among the rickety (but colorful) *friquitines* may not be for everyone, but many Puerto Ricans consider it an essential part of island life.

Surfers and solitude-seekers enjoy the less-trammeled beaches of Playa Azul and La Pared; divers marvel at the chaotic aquatic life of coral reefs near a string of archipelago islands near Fajardo, a bustling seaport. Near the sleepy little villages of Humacao, Naguabo and Yabucoa, the central mountain range tumbles down into the sea. Punta Santiago, an attractive sweep of beach that juts out into the bright, blue Caribbean, is as laid-back and undeveloped as Luquillo used to be 20 years ago.

HIGHLIGHTS

- Marveling at the tremendous aquatic life around the coral reefs of **La Cordillera** (p128)
- Gliding through **Laguna Grande** (p127), Fajardo's bioluminescent bay
- Slipping and sliding across 27 miles of rainforest trails in **El Yunque** (p115)
- Trading glances (from a safe distance) with the wild monkeys on **Cayo Santiago** (p131)
- Enjoying seaside snacks while watching the surf crash against **Punta Santiago** (p132)

- POPULATION: 450,000
- DRINK: EL COQUITO

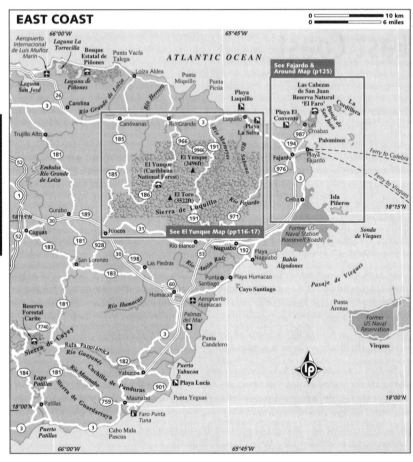

EAST COAST

History

Much of this region was once covered with lighter variations of the dense foliage now found only in El Yunque, but native Taínos did manage to successfully farm the fertile land around the low-lying coasts. All that changed when the Spanish arrived en masse around 1700. The tremendous wealth of natural resources in El Yunque – lots of fresh water and timber, for example – attracted settlers, and existing farmlands were quickly turned into massive sugar plantations by colonizers. A small gold rush added to the need for a strong labor force, and after most of the indigenous population was either wiped out by disease or forced deep into the mountains, the Spanish brought in African slaves

in considerable numbers. Descendants of those Yoruba people make up the bulk of the 30,000 residents who live in the municipalities around El Yunque today. The next wave of colonization came when the US took control of the island in 1898, eventually setting up the commonwealth status that continues to this day. Most of the highways and existing infrastructure on this part of the island were built by the US military, which maintained a base near Fajardo until 2003.

Climate

The east coast tends to follow the same weather patterns as San Juan. The exception to that rule is El Yunque, with weather catering to the unique needs of its ecosystem. Sudden surges of light rain can occur anytime during the year in this dense rainforest, but that goes with the territory – throw on some protective gear and get on with your day. During the island's hurricane season – late June through mid-November – El Yunque gets very wet indeed. Some trails might be closed down due to mudslides, and streams swell enormously. It's a good idea to check in at the visitors center for the latest weather update before heading out for a trek. Winter nights in the Luquillo Sierra can be damp and a little chilly.

Getting There & Around

Most of the east coast is traversable via Hwy 3, which – while far from pretty – gets the job done with relative efficiency. Once you leave San Juan, be it on Rte 187 (which dips into Piñones and behind Loíza Aldea for about 10 scenic miles before rejoining the major road) or on the main drag of Hwy 3, be prepared for bursts of concentrated development (fast-food restaurants, several strip malls and the occasional pharmaceutical plant) followed by surprisingly rural stretches. Plan your accommodations at least one day ahead whenever possible; although distances between towns are never large, not every town in this region is big enough to have a hotel or resort. Also, towns themselves can be very spread out; depending on where you stay, you might have to drive 10 minutes to get to the nearest restaurant. A rental car is definitely the easiest option if you're planning a long trip.

There is little to no public transportation in this region, but El Yunque is easily accessed by car. There are public vans running between Fajardo and San Juan, but to traverse that stretch quickly it's best to drive or arrange for a pickup from a tour operator (see p93). To see the many sights that are set back from the main highway or to leisurely explore the coastline, drive yourself. The trip from San Juan to Fajardo takes about two hours (without traffic); note that on weekends and late afternoons it can be quite snarled on Hwy 3. From San Juan to Yabucoa it's about three hours (again, without traffic).

EL YUNQUE

Covering some 28,000 acres of land in the Luquillo mountains, this verdant tropical rainforest, officially known as the Caribbean National Forest, is but a shadow of what it was before wood-hungry Spanish conquerors arrived on the scene. Nonetheless, what remains of the island's dense and fecund foliage is impressively healthy and bountiful, and some of the oldest trees remain (1000 years and growing!). The views of the valleys, Atlantic, Caribbean and eastern islands are inspiring; the temperatures are cool; the hiking is heart-pounding; and the streams and waterfalls are rejuvenating. Some people claim you can hear the voices of the ancient Taínos in the songs of the wind, the birds and the beloved coquí. The name of nearby Luquillo comes from Yukiyú, the spirit of happiness and well-being that Taínos believed resided in these mountains; and *yuque*, the Taíno word for white sand, was transformed by the Spanish into El Yunque, which in Castilian means 'the anvil' – a fair description of the peak when viewed from the north.

More than 240 species of tree and 1000 species of plant thrive in this forest, including 50 kinds of orchid, as the area receives up to 200in of rain per year. Six major rivers trace their sources here. Most of the remaining population of the highly endangered Puerto Rican parrot *(el higuaca)* and more than 60 other species of bird live in El Yunque. The forest is also home to nine species of rare freshwater shrimp, the coquí frog, anole tree lizards, the 7ft-long Puerto Rican boa and a substantial collection of common rats.

Four forest zones define El Yunque. The tabonuco forest grows below 2000ft and receives less than 100in of rain. This area is characterized by tall, straight trees such as the tabonuco and ausubo, and palms, epiphytes (including many orchids), flowers and aromatic shrubs of many kinds.

The palo colorado forest grows above 2000ft in the valleys and on gentle slopes. Here annual rainfall averages as much as 180in. This area is lush with ancient colorado trees (some more than 1000 years old). Vines and epiphytes hang from the trees.

Above 2500ft, look for sierra palms along the streams and on the steep valley slopes. The so-called mountain palm tree dominates here in the third zone, the Palma Sierra Forest, with mostly ferns and mosses growing beneath.

The highest forest zone, the so-called 'cloud forest,' grows above the Palma Sierra Forest and sees up to 200in of rain per year.

EL YUNQUE

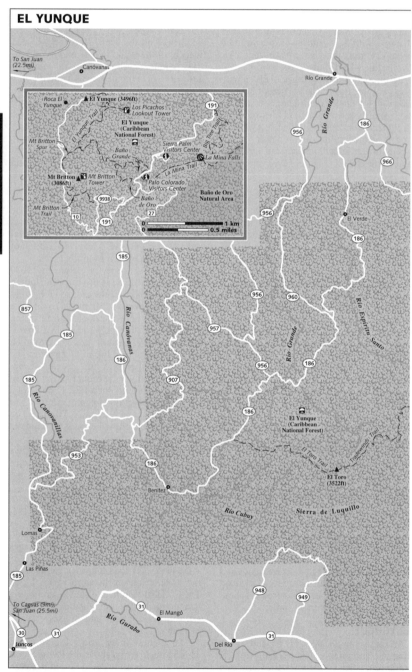

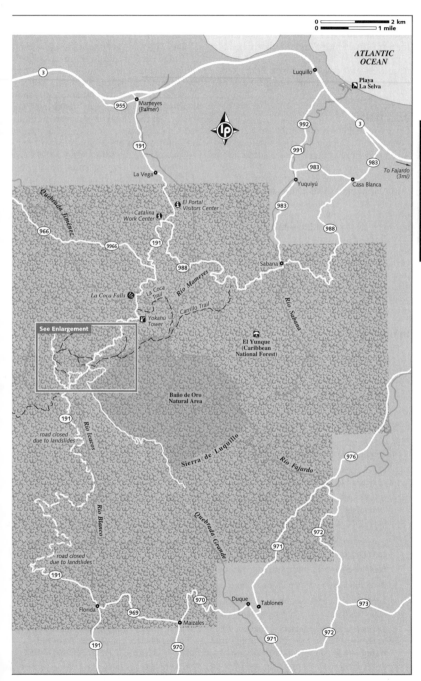

Trees here are generally twisted from strong trade winds and are less than 12ft tall (hence the term 'dwarf forest' commonly applied to this ecosystem). Mosses and lichens hang from trees and cover the forest floor. Red-flowering bromeliads stand out like beacons in the fog.

Orientation

Once you've entered the Caribbean National Forest (see p121 for directions), all of the forest's visitors centers, major attractions and trailheads appear as Hwy 191 twists, turns and climbs steeply on its way south toward the summit. Although maps can make it seem like Hwy 191 descends through the forest to the south side, note that the road has been closed for quite some time due to landslides. Mountain-bike enthusiasts get their workout on this closed road, which is the *only route* open to bikers within the forest. It's also possible to follow Hwy 186 along the west side of El Yunque, but if you want to experience the forest's heart, 191 is the road to take.

Information

There are several different visitors centers in El Yunque. The first noteworthy place where most people stop is **El Portal Visitors Center** (☎ 787-888-1880; www.southernregion.fs.fed .us/caribbean; Hwy 191 Km 4.3; adult/child 4-12/senior/child under 4 $3/1.50/1.50/free; ⏰ 9am-5pm, closed Christmas Day). Built in 1996, El Portal is the key for visitors who want to understand more about El Yunque and tropical rainforests. The facility has interactive exhibits, a 12-minute film in both English and Spanish, a walkway through the forest canopy and a gift shop. Vending machines serve up drinks and snacks, but there's no on-site restaurant just yet. You can also pick up free basic maps and information on the forest. If you don't feel like paying the admission tariff or want to avoid crowds on weekends, head to one of the other visitors centers further up the mountain, where you can pick up brochures and basic maps for no charge.

Located after El Portal, the **Catalina Work Center** (Hwy 191 Km 4.4; ⏰ 8:30am-4:30pm Mon-Fri) is where you can get a camping permit – good for the day it is issued. Rangers hand out maps designating approved camping locations along with the permits.

It's worth enduring the switchbacks and steep road to get to the **Palo Colorado Visitors Center** (Hwy 191 Km 11.8; ⏰ 9am-5pm), which distributes camping permits on weekends. Most of the short and spectacular hiking trails leave from this spot. The picnic area – which includes a series of sheltered concrete platforms hidden in the jungle, overlooking a ravine of rushing water – is hard to match anywhere on the island. The staff here offers first-aid

---

SAFE & RESPONSIBLE HIKING

If you are camping, permits are required. Remember to carry out everything you bring in. Signs throughout the forest are posted in Spanish and English.

■ Watch out for flash floods, particularly in the rainy season. If it starts to rain heavily, immediately head for higher ground.

■ Don't touch any animals. There have been isolated reports of small animals, usually infected with rabies, attacking humans.

■ Stay on the marked paths and don't walk alone if possible. Hike with a buddy.

■ Carry water, a light snack, sunscreen, a map and strong insect repellent, and for longer hikes consider adding a basic first-aid kit and a compass.

■ Wear long pants to shield legs from razor grass and poison oak growing on some trails.

■ Don't drink from streams. River snails produce schisto, a bacteria that causes liver damage.

■ Bring rain gear and wear shoes suitable for rough and wet terrain. Watch out when walking on mossy rocks or climbing near waterfalls and streams.

■ Campers and serious hikers should buy a copy of the waterproof Caribbean National Forest 'topo map' ($10); it's available at visitors centers, or order it before you go from **Trails Illustrated** (☎ 303-670-3457, 800-962-1643; www.trailsillustrated.com; PO Box 4357, Evergreen, CO 80437-4357).

service. There's also a gift shop with maps and the like, and camping permits are issued on weekends.

The **Sierra Palm Visitors Center** is a free visitors center on your way up the mountain. It is not always staffed, but its rest rooms are generally open for tour vans, and there is a picnic area.

Sights & Activities

In addition to short and long hiking trails in El Yunque (see p120), there are a few places directly accessible by road within the forest.

La Coca Falls is the first spectacular natural feature you see as Hwy 191 climbs south toward the forest peaks. There is an 85ft cascade as the stream tumbles from a precipice to the right of the highway onto boulder formations. The gate is open every day from 7am to 6pm.

Less than a half mile further up the mountain, you see the 65ft, Moorish-looking stone **Yokahú Tower**, which was built as a lookout in 1962. This is the first good place for vistas of the islands to the east, but there are better vantage points higher on the mountain. The tower often gets crowded with tour groups. Pass it by unless you have a lot of time and the view to yourself.

The **Baño Grande**, a former swimming hole built during the Depression, lies across Hwy 191 from the Palo Colorado Visitors Center (opposite). A little further along the road, **Baño de Oro** is another former swimming hole that is now a popular spot for photo opportunities. The water hole takes its name from the Río Baño de Oro, which feeds the pool. The name means 'bath of gold' in English, and Spaniards gave the river this name because they mined for gold here in the 16th century. The Baño de Oro Natural Area surrounding the pool is the catchment area for the river and pool. In addition to the short Baño de Oro trail to the pool there are two overgrown trails in the Natural Area, which the National Park Service plans to open in the future.

If you really want to paddle in some water, take the 30-minute walk from Palo Colorado down the mountain to the swimming hole at the base of **La Mina Falls**. Here you'll find a water cascade, quite stunning in its natural beauty. Come early if you want tranquility, because it's popular with cavorting families.

Tours

Most travelers come to the forest with a tour group from San Juan (see p93). In addition, the National Park Service offers guided one-hour hikes from the Palo Colorado Visitors Center through **Forest Adventure Tours** (☎ 787-888-1880; adult/child $5/3; ☒ tours every hr 11:30am-4pm).

Another alternative is to join a hike sponsored by one of the island tour operators. **Eco-Excursion Aquatica** (☎ 787-888-2887) offers a two-hour hike ($45 to $65, depending on size of group) and supplies all the gear (except hiking boots) for a swim, snack and trek. Guides are knowledgeable and eager to talk about the rainforest ecosystem.

You might also connect with one of the park's volunteer guides, who post themselves around the Palo Colorado Visitors Center. Many of these guides are members of local Boy Scout Explorer Post 919. **Jorge Dam** (☎ 787-396-8687), the post's advisor, can arrange hikes in advance. Sometimes he can even come up with accommodations.

Sleeping

Several beautiful inns, B&Bs and guest houses have opened up along the edges of El Yunque – not actually in the forest, but along its fringe. The proximity to the rainforest means lots of loud animal activity: the sound of chirping coquí will send you to sleep, and you'll wake to wild birds whistling. Most places are accessible along the north section of Hwy 191, coming from Río Grande (Luquillo beaches are only a few minutes away). Other accommodations are on the south side, also on Hwy 191. Due to mudslides, south side accommodations must be accessed from the Naguabo entrance to El Yunque. These are good choices if you want to be in close proximity to day trips in and around Fajardo.

Casa Cubuy Ecolodge (☎ 787-874-6221; www .casacubuy.com; Hwy 191 Km 22 from Naguabo; r $90-115; Ⓟ ☒ ☒) Fabulous views across the south side of El Yunque are available from just about every one of the 10 rooms here. Owner Matthew keeps the self-serve bar open and will whip up something fabulous for dinner upon request (breakfast included in room rate). One room on the 1st floor has disabled access. A private trail leads to several well-hidden swimming holes in the rainforest, and Matthew will arrange for hikes to nearby

EAST COAST

HIKING TRAILS OF EL YUNQUE

With more than 23 miles of well-maintained trails, plenty of rugged terrain and warm, wet, windy weather, El Yunque has something for every style of hiker. Come prepared (see the boxed text, p118) and remember there are no water or trash or restroom facilities. Above all, stay on the trails. Getting lost here is as easy as daydreaming.

- La Coca Trail (1.8 miles) – a popular, moderate-to-strenuous hike that will take you a little over an hour each way. The trailhead is just up the road past the falls of the same name – just before the Yokahú Tower – and there is a small parking lot here. It's a fairly benign, low-altitude trail following streams through *tabonuco* forest. La Coca made its mark on El Yunque history when a US college professor disappeared here for 12 days in 1997, claiming after his rescue that he got off the trail and was lost. The Forest Service, which had enlisted a search party of 60 volunteers and aircraft, was hardly amused. If you follow La Coca to its end, you can go left (east) along Carrillo Trail to the eastern part of the forest, or right (west) to La Mina Falls on La Mina Trail (see following).

- Big Tree Trail (0.86 miles) – a short trail of moderate difficulty. It gets its name from the size of the vegetation along the way. The walk takes about a half-hour each way, and it has interpretive signs along its route through *tabonuco* forest before ending at La Mina Falls. All these attractions make this probably the most popular trail in the park. The trailhead is at Km 10.4 on Hwy 191.

- La Mina Trail (0.7 miles) – another popular walk. It leaves from Palo Colorado Visitors Center and heads downhill through *palo colorado* forest to join the Big Tree Trail at the falls. Mostly paved, this is an easy walk down, but a bit of a hike back up.

- Mt Britton Trail (0.8 miles) – if you are short on time and want to feel as if you have really 'summited,' take the 45-minute climb up through the midlevel types of vegetation into the cloud forest that surrounds this peak, which is named after a famous botanist who worked here. This is a continuous climb on paved surfaces to the Mt Britton Tower, built in the 1930s. The trailhead is at the side of Hwy 9938, which veers off Hwy 191 south of Palo Colorado. On weekends the trek up can be slowed by hikers who are physically unprepared but give it their best shot. Take a windbreaker for the rough weather on the summit.

- Mt Britton Spur (0.86 miles) – for the more adventuresome and fit, this connects El Yunque and Mt Britton in an invigorating walk, mostly through the cloud forest. The weather around this area (with the exception being very early in the morning) is generally overcast and rainy, so be prepared.

- El Yunque Trail (2.6 miles) – this is the big enchilada for most visitors and takes you to the top of El Yunque (3496ft, 1049m) in 1½ hours or longer. The trail is mostly paved or maintained gravel as you ascend through cloud forest to the observation deck, which is surrounded by microwave communication towers that transmit to the islands of Culebra and Vieques. If you want a rock scramble from here, take Los Picachos Trail (0.17 miles) to another old observation tower and feel as if you have crested a tropical Everest. Or climb Roca El Yunque, just to the west.

- Tradewinds Trail (3.9 miles) – serious backpackers and campers head west on this trail, although the trailhead is a bit hard to find. Park off the road near the locked gate on Hwy 191 south of Palo Colorado. Walk south on the road about a quarter of a mile until you see the trail leading from the right. Note that the trail is not maintained and can be overgrown; bring clothes to protect your body. With four hours of strenuous trekking, you can reach the forest's highest summit, El Toro (3522ft). This is a good place to pitch camp (but remember to bring your own water from Palo Colorado) before hiking El Toro Trail (2.2 miles), another rugged path that leads through cloud forest and lower-level types of ecosystems along the western border of the forest near Hwy 186. These two trails are part of the National Recreational Trail System.

Taíno petroglyphs. On rainy afternoons, guests can sway away the hours in several hammocks slung around the house.

Río Grande Plantation Eco Resort (☎ 787-887-2779; www.riograndeplantation.com; Hwy 956 Km 4.2, Río Grande; r $100-175, villas $150-300; P ⊠ ⌘) The grounds at this former sugar plantation and mill are immense and picturesque, with a rushing river and tons of birds flying every which way. The sights, smells and sounds of the forest penetrate every corner, and save it from being just another bland option off Hwy 3. Lots of weddings and corporate retreats are booked in the summer, but there's enough room for everyone to spread out. Rooms are large, with big baths, cable TV, minifridges and air-conditioning. Great for kids.

Le Petite Chalet (☎ 787-887-5802; Hwy 186 Km 22.1, Río Grande; r from $75; P ⊠) Perched some 1500ft above sea level, Le Petite Chalet has refreshingly pastoral decor without getting too rustic. The rooms are bright and comfortable with plenty of space, but you never feel too far removed from the surrounding nature. Bird-watchers and visiting biologists favor this retreat. It's a small guest house and fills up fast, especially in the winter months.

Casa Flamboyant (☎ 787-874-6074; Hwy 191 from Naguabo; r $135-175; P ⊠ ⌘) Elegant but relaxed, this very private B&B doesn't accommodate children under 12, but does have several pet dogs roaming the property. Tucked way up high in the mountains, the rooms and pool afford stunning panoramic views. If you tire of gazing into the distance, stroll among the 50 species of native orchids lovingly cultivated on the inn's 25 acres. The main house has three gorgeous rooms with private bathrooms, and there's a private villa set off to one side (accessed across a stone bridge). Guests love to watch storm clouds march past en route to El Yunque while lounging in the heated pool.

Phillips Family Cabins (☎ 787-874-2138; Hwy 191 Km 24.2, from Naguabo; cabins per night $35, longer stays $25; P) This laid-back family-run establishment is a great place to stay if you really want to get as close to nature as possible. Cabins are neat as a pin and eminently comfortable (bedding is provided), but there aren't any amenities to speak of (other than the fresh air, great views and absolute silence, save for rainforest noises).

CAMPING

It's free to camp in the Caribbean National Forest, but don't forget your permit. Camping is prohibited along many of the popular trails surrounding Palo Colorado Visitors Center and El Yunque peak, but you can camp in the wilder parts of the forest, including at its highest peak, El Toro, where it feels as if you have slipped into a primeval forest. Camping is all off-trail, and you must pack everything in and out. There are no water, trash or rest-room facilities on the trails.

Eating

Better bring along a boxed lunch if you want to spend the day in El Yunque! For those who like to cook outdoors, there are picnic tables and grills at Quebrada Grande, Palo Colorado, Palmas de Sierra and Caimitillo. A few kiosks sell snacks and soft drinks around Km 7 on Hwy 191.

Getting There & Away

No public transportation will carry you to El Yunque. If you don't come with a tour group, you can easily get here by car. You can see El Yunque from San Juan even though the mountain forest lies 25 miles to the southeast. Driving from San Juan, there will be signs directing you from Hwy 3 to Hwy 191, but the sign for Hwy 191 is not always visible (heavy winds sometimes knock it down). If you see it, turn right as directed. Otherwise, watch for a large sign announcing 'El Yunque Portal' on the right-hand side of the road. It's at an intersection that also features a big sign for the Westin Río Mar Resort. Turn right at that intersection and go through the village of Palmer (Mameyes in Spanish), keeping your eyes peeled for more signage directing you to Hwy 191 and the Caribbean National Forest – there's a sharp left shortly after turning off the main highway. Just after the road starts to rise abruptly into the mountains, you enter the Caribbean National Forest.

Take note that some highway maps suggest that you can traverse the forest on Hwy 191 (or access El Yunque from the south via this route), but south of the Palo Colorado center, Hwy 191 has been closed by landslides for years. Road maps also suggest that El Yunque can be approached via a network of roads along the western border of the national forest. Don't try it: these roads are rugged, untraveled, unmaintained tracks that dead-end in serious jungle. El Yunque is not immune to thievery, so if you park in a remote area to take a stroll, be sure to lock up and don't leave anything of value in plain sight in the car.

LUQUILLO & AROUND

It is quite entrancing to loll on the white, sandy beaches of Luquillo and watch ponderous, rain-swollen clouds burst open over the mountain tips of El Yunque. Sometimes a short shower will come your way, but more often than not, it's blindingly sunny on the coast, no matter what's going on in the forest. Aside from the fine weather, though, there's little to explain how Luquillo came to be known as the 'Puerto Rican Riviera' because outside of some good beaches and a few pretty shops and resorts, this area doesn't have much in common with St Tropez.

The municipality stretches all the way from the Atlantic Ocean to the edge of the Caribbean National Forest and, without a car, is basically impossible to navigate. The main draw is the long, crescent-shaped public beach of Playa Luquillo, the associated phalanx of food kiosks and the compact urban center about a half mile away facing Playa Azul (Blue Beach). The town has a substantial collection of condo towers and vacation villas that draw a large number of long-term gringo residents in the winter and *sanjuaneros* vacationing in the summer; for the short-term visitor, accommodations are harder to find. Most people visit for the beaches but choose to stay in larger towns with more established nightlife. On the east side of Playa Luquillo are several long, empty beaches usually only used by locals.

Orientation

Hwy 3 will take you to Rte 193 (aka Calle Fernandez Garcia), which is the main artery of Luquillo. It passes right by the Plaza de Recreo, the town's central plaza. Playa Azul is the beach directly in front of the condominium development of the same name. Most of the shops and stores of interest to visitors are on Fernandez Garcia, the parallel street of 14 de Julio, or are alongside Playa Azul.

Information

Economia Laundromat (☎ 787-405-0237; Luquillo Complejo Turistico, Playa Azul; ☺ 8am-6pm Mon-Tue, 8am-noon Wed, 8am-6pm Thu-Fri, 7am-6pm Sat, 7am-4pm Sun)
Luquillo Community Health Center (Calle 14 de Julio)

Beaches

Luquillo traces its name and history to a valorous Taíno *cacique* (chief) and a Spanish settlement in 1797, but nothing of historic value remains in the town, and almost everything you see dates from the mid-20th century or later.

Most of the beaches are irrefutably lovely, although the most famous one – the balneario at **Playa Luquillo** (admission free, parking $2; ☺ 8:30am-5:30pm) – has been criticized recently as overcrowded and often defiled by trash. On quiet days during the middle of the week (except during school vacations) its charm is still apparent. Set on a bay facing northwest, and therefore protected from the easterly trade winds and seas, the public part of this beach makes a mile-long arc to a point of sand shaded by tall coconut palms. The beach itself is a plane of broad, gently sloping white sand that continues its gradual slope below the water. There is a bathhouse, a refreshment stand, a security patrol and well-kept bathrooms.

You do not have to park in the balneario lot if you want to visit the beach. Playa Luquillo extends at least another mile to the west. If you pull off Hwy 3 by the long row of food kiosks, you can drive around to the ocean side of the stalls and park under the palms, just a few steps from the beach and with more cold beer and *pastelillos* (fried dumplings) than you could consume in a year.

Luquillo also has a section known as **Sea Without Barriers** (☎ 787-889-4329), the island's only disabled-accessible beach. Sea Without Barriers has a ramp and other facilities to help anyone with limited mobility get into the water safely.

If the balneario feels too busy (and it does get cheek-to-jowl in high season), head for **Playa Azul**, east around the headland and in the town itself. While the beach is more exposed to the trade winds, seas and dangerous rip tides (people have drowned), Playa Azul is just as broad, white and gently sloping as Luquillo. Snorkeling enthusiasts particularly enjoy these waters, but swim with great caution.

A friendly contingent of surfers hang at the east end of this beach – known as 'La

Pared' (the Wall) – waiting for an offshore breeze to glass off a 3ft break. Scrambling over a stone jetty at the east end of Playa Azul will take you to a strand of beach and bays that stretch over five miles to the **Playa Seven Seas** balneario in Las Croabas (p127). The western section of this undeveloped beach is known as **La Selva**; the eastern end is called **El Convento** and features a beach house that is a retreat for government officials.

Activities

Bob and Susan Roberts have been operating **La Selva Surf Shop** (☎ 787-899-6205; 250 Calle Fernández García) for more than 25 years. This is a well-stocked, friendly place that rents out surfboards and body boards and offers the latest on surf conditions at La Pared, La Selva (further east) and around the Humacao area to the south. Susan is also a great source of local knowledge.

For a guided kayak tour along the coast, check out a host of different day and night options from mobile operations, including **Las Tortugas Adventures** (☎ 787-889-7734) and **Eco-Excursion Aquatica** (☎ 787-888-2887). Prices start at about $50.

The **Berwind Country Club** (☎ 787-876-3056; Hwy 187 Km 4.7, Río Grande; greens fee $70) is open to the public Monday to Friday. The greens fee includes a golf cart.

Westin Río Mar Beach Resort & Country Club (below) is frequented for its two excellent courses: the Greg Norman River Course and the Tom and George Fazio Ocean Course. Nonguests pay $140 for morning tee times and $85 after 1pm.

Hacienda Carabaldi (☎ 787-889-5820; Hwy 992 Km 5.1; adult/child per hr from $20/10), south of town, does trail rides on Paso Fino horses along the Río Mameyes and into the foothills of the rainforest, with time out for swimming and a picnic. Beach rides and simple jaunts around the ranch are also offered.

Sleeping

Midrange accommodations are few and far between at Luquillo, but there is one big resort in the area willing to cater to your every need.

Trinidad Guest House (☎ 787-889-2710; 6A Ocean Drive; d $87; ✷) Built in 1800 for a newly arrived family from Spain, the Trinidad still has a considerable amount of old-world charm. Fronted by big palm trees in a pretty,

outdoor courtyard, the Trinidad has a perfect location for enjoying the best that Luquillo beaches have to offer. There are 10 rooms, six with private bathrooms (small, but pretty) and rates include a breakfast of delicious bread and fresh fruit. There's cable TV in all rooms.

Westin Río Mar Beach Resort & Country Club (☎ 787-888-6000; www.westinriomar.com; 6000 Río Mar Blvd; r $200, d $300-575, ste from $675; P ✷ 🖳 ⛱) North on Hwy 968 off Hwy 3 between Río Grande and Luquillo, this 600-unit high-rise facility sprawls across some 500 acres of former plantation. It's often booked up with conventions, but individual travelers who are able to get in will enjoy the soaring white marble ceilings in the lobby, spacious rooms and huge, kidney-shaped pool shaded by a few palm trees. You can play tennis, go horseback riding, hit the links or bliss out in the resort's award-winning day spa. Rack rates vary considerably; vacation or convention packages usually offer the best deals.

Playa Azul Apartments Realty (☎ 787-889-3425; Hwy 193 Km 1.1; apt per week/month from $400/1000) Located inside the complex of beachfront condos of the same name, this realty agency can rent you a place at any number of facilities, including Sandy Hill condos and the Solimar townhouses. Rentals at Playa Azul tend to be the most affordable, however. Each apartment is different, depending on the taste of the owner, but generally all have air-conditioning, TV and fully equipped kitchens.

CAMPING

For decades Puerto Ricans and adventure travelers have camped with impunity at La Selva and El Convento (opposite). During holidays and on high-season weekends, you'll have plenty of company. Think twice, though, if it looks like you'll be out there alone. Groups of young men have been known to roam the area looking for vulnerable targets. Muggings do occur.

Balneario Luquillo (☎ 787-889-5871, 622-5200; Hwy 3, Playa Luquillo; campsites with power hookup $19; P) There are more than 30 campsites and a bathhouse at this beachside spot, but like many balnearios, the camping area packs sites close together and may be closed during the fall and winter when the islanders stay home.

Eating

Luquillo's famous line of *friquitines* (also known as *quioscos,* or food stalls) along the western edge of Hwy 3 serve all sorts of tasty fried treats and outstanding *comida criolla* dishes (snacks $1 to $2, meals $3 to $9). Some of these kiosks are very run-down, and you can't always be sure that proper hygiene methods are being adhered to. Stick to the ones that look well kept and clean, and attract local business.

Erik's Gyros & Deli (☎ 787-889-0615; 352 Fernández García; sandwiches & combo meals $6-10; ☑ 7am-4pm Mon-Sat) A few blocks south of the main plaza in downtown Luquillo, Erik's has some winning combinations of Puerto Rican and Greek food – who knew feta cheese goes with everything? The gyro sandwiches are fantastic.

Hacienda Carabaldi (☎ 787-889-5820; Hwy 992 Km 5.1; dishes $6-24; ☑ 9am-5pm) Aside from offering first-rate horse rides (see Activities, p123), Carabaldi also has a great restaurant, with panoramic views of the ocean and the rainforest. You can pick from an à la carte menu, and on Sundays there's an all-you-can-eat buffet for $18 per person.

La Exquisita Bakery (☎ 787-633-5554; 1 Calle Jesús Pinero; dishes $1-6; ☑ 6am-9pm Mon-Sat, 8am-8pm Sun) Right on the plaza, this casual bakery serves big hearty sandwiches of all types – perfect for taking to the beach or on a long hike.

Victor's Place (☎ 787-889-5705; 2 Calle Jesús Pinero; mains $10-25; ☑ 11am-10pm Tue-Sun) Once an intimate local hangout, Victor's was recently named one of Puerto Rico's 10 best seafood restaurants. Now try and get seated quickly on a Saturday night! You can feast on great lobster, shrimp, mofongo (mashed plantains) and other house specialties outside on the patio or indoors under fish nets draped from wood-paneled walls.

Sandy's (☎ 787-889-5765; 276 Fernández García; mains $4-15; ☑ 11am-10pm) Sandy's is the most popular restaurant in town. You can buy a burger for $4, or go over the top with jalapeño peppers stuffed with shrimp or lobster for $15.

Lolita's (☎ 787-889-5770; Hwy 3 Km 4.8; mains $6-11; ☑ noon-10pm Tue-Sun) Lolita's is 3 miles east of town on the south side of Hwy 3. The Mexican meals are so popular that the owners have moved into a building twice the original size. A soft taco costs $2.50, and many dinners run under $10. Imported Mexican mariachis provide the music.

Shimas (☎ 787-888-6000; 6000 Río Mar Blvd; dishes $12-28; ☑ 1-10pm) If you have a sushi craving that must be met while in Luquillo, head to Shimas at the Westin Río Mar resort. It serves authentic Japanese food, as well as some Thai and Chinese dishes. There are 12 restaurants and lounges in the Río Mar. Other good eating choices are Ajili Mójili, serving traditional Puerto Rican food, and Cactus Jack's, which has won awards for its innovative Tex-Mex cuisine.

Entertainment

Although you only have two options here (outside of the swankier bars in the Río Mar), Luquillo is far from dull.

El Flamboyán Café (☎ 787-889-2928; Hwy 193 Km 1.2; ☑ 8am-midnight Thu-Tue) This place at the west end of town calls itself a 'cafeteria and game room.' What this means is that the wide-open patio bar has nine busy pool tables, and serves food to the gang that shows up to drink $2 beers. The crowd is mostly local, but everyone is welcome. It offers African drumming, live salsa and other music on weekends.

Brass Cactus (☎ 787-889-5735; Hwy 193 Km 1.3; dishes $8-22; ☑ lunch & dinner) Not at all a prickly place, the Brass Cactus serves big plates of American pub fare with the odd traditional dish thrown in. Children will find lots to eat (burgers, fries, chicken fingers) and the down-home decor (think license plates hanging from the walls) will give them plenty to look at. Around 11pm on weekends the Cactus gets more of a club vibe, with patrons coming in to drink rather than eat. Usually there's live rock music, at least during high season.

Getting There & Away

Públicos (shared taxis) do run from San Juan ($4) to and from the Luquillo plaza, but aside from that, you've got to have your own wheels.

FAJARDO & AROUND

Most travelers heading down the east coast either blow right by Fajardo, or give it a cursory once-over while waiting for a ferry to Culebra or Vieques. But it's a mistake to sell this sprawling municipality short, even though it suffers from heavy traffic and is overly commercialized in parts. Fajardo itself may not have much to catch the eye, but it's

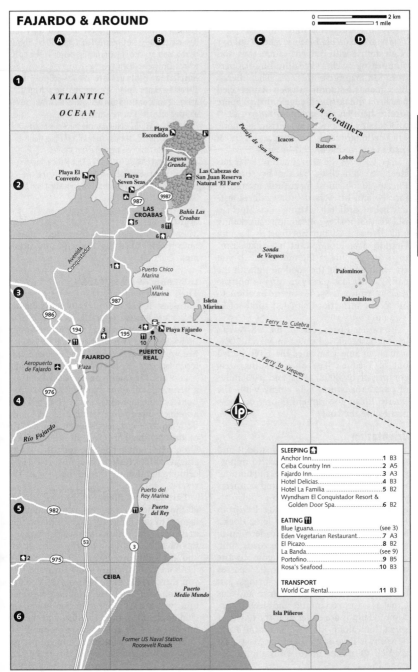

FAJARDO & AROUND

0 ———————— 2 km
0 ———————— 1 mile

ATLANTIC
OCEAN

La Cordillera

Playa
Escondido

Pasaje de San Juan

Icacos
Ratones

Lobos

Laguna
Grande

Playa El
Convento

Playa
Seven Seas

Las Cabezas de
San Juan Reserva
Natural 'El Faro'

987

9987

LAS
CROABAS

5

8

6

Bahía Las
Croabas

Sonda
de Vieques

Palominos

Avenida Conquistador

Puerto Chico
Marina

Villa
Marina

987

Isleta
Marina

Palominitos

986

194

987

3

195

4

1

Playa Fajardo

Ferry to Culebra

7

PUERTO
REAL

10

11

Aeropuerto
de Fajardo

FAJARDO

Plaza

Ferry to Vieques

976

Río Fajardo

982

Puerto del
Rey Marina

Puerto
del Rey

9

53

2

975

3

CEIBA

Puerto
Medio Mundo

Isla Piñeros

6

Former US Naval Station
Roosevelt Roads

SLEEPING
Anchor Inn..**1** B3
Ceiba Country Inn **2** A5
Fajardo Inn.......................................**3** A3
Hotel Delicias...................................**4** B3
Hotel La Familia **5** B2
Wyndham El Conquistador Resort &
   Golden Door Spa...........................**6** B2

EATING
Blue Iguana...................................(see 3)
Eden Vegetarian Restaurant............**7** A3
El Picazo..**8** B2
La Banda......................................(see 9)
Portofino..**9** B5
Rosa's Seafood...............................**10** B3

TRANSPORT
World Car Rental...........................**11** B3

EAST COAST

surrounded by some magnificent nature – both above and below water.

First there's Villa Marina, a beautiful bay often dotted with opulent catamarans and pumped-up yachts. Wealthy day-trippers from San Juan prefer this area. Then there's Las Croabas, a stunning stretch of unspoiled beach on the northern edge of town. Some local fishermen still maintain *nativos* (25ft to 30ft native sloops used for fishing) there. They no longer carry fish, but passengers on picnics and snorkeling adventures.

Las Cabezas de San Juan reserve has steep, crested cliffs, backed by some of Puerto Rico's most beautiful mangrove forests, and off Fajardo's irregular coastline is La Cordillera, a string of archipelago islands that makes for fabulous snorkeling and diving. Last but not least is Laguna Grande, a bioluminescent bay that shimmers and gleams in the moonlight. If you are willing to take the good along with the bad, Fajardo has plenty to offer – not the least of which is a convenient location to hit all the attractions situated south of El Yunque.

Roosevelt Roads, one of the US Navy's largest bases, closed down in March 2004, just about one year after the navy pulled out of Vieques. The once bustling area, comprised of 8000 acres and 100 miles of paved roads, now sits empty while the Puerto Rican government figures out how best to use the land.

Orientation

The city of 38,000 is quite spread out and navigation without a car is next to impossible. Hwy 3 (sometimes bumper to bumper with traffic) divides the city and connects you to other roads leading to popular attractions. Jumping off onto Rte 195 from Hwy 3 will bring you to the ferry docks; follow signs that say 'Embarcadero' until arriving at Rte 987. There the roads split; continuing straight on 195 goes to the docks, while turning left onto 987 passes Villa Marina and eventually brings you to the beach, the nature reserve and Las Croabas. Most restaurants and sleeping accommodations are either near the docks or spread out along Rte 987. Traveling from downtown Fajardo to Las Croabas is just a quick 10-minute drive, assuming there's no traffic.

Information

Fajardo Mayor's Office (☎ 787-863-1400; www .fajardopr.org; ☻ 8am-noon & 1-4:30pm Mon-Fri) There's no real tourism office in town, but the mayor's office does what it can. Call with any questions.

Hospital San Pablo del Este (☎ 787-863-0505; Rte 194 off Ave Conquistador; ☻ 24hr) The largest hospital along the east coast and your best option for treatment for any medical issues that may arise.

Pizz@ Net (☎ 787-860-4230; per 30/60min $3/5; ☻ 11am-11pm) At the marina in Villa Marina, this is a great place to nosh on a pizza and surf the net.

Wash-n-Post (☎ 787-863-1995; Villa Marina shopping center; ☻ 8am-8pm Mon-Sat, 10am-5pm Sun) A one-stop FedEx, Western Union and UPS service that also has fluff and fold.

Sights

There's plenty to see and do around Fajardo, but very little to see and do in the downtown area.

LAS CABEZAS DE SAN JUAN

The full name of this nature reserve on the northeast tip of Puerto Rico is **Las Cabezas de San Juan Reserva Natural 'El Faro'** (☎ 787-722-5882, 860-2560; www.fideicomiso.org; Hwy 987 at Las Croabas; adult/child under 11/senior $7/4/4; ☻ 9am-4pm Wed-Sun; Spanish tours 9:30am, 10am, 10:30am & 2pm; English tour 2pm) It clearly deserves the first part of its title (San Juan Headlands). Here a peninsula of more than 300 acres strikes out from the end of two-lane Hwy 987 like a wedge between the Atlantic and the Sonda de Vieques (Vieques Sound). On the tip of this peninsula – part of Fajardo's Las Croabas neighborhood – you find steep, craggy cliffs crested by a restored 19th-century lighthouse; this is the *faro* of the reserve's title.

Las Cabezas offers glimpses of almost all the island's ecosystems, from mangrove lagoon to dry forest to coconut plantation and coral reef. Visitors will see big iguanas, lots of fiddler crabs, all sorts of insect life and any number of birds.

About 2 miles of trails and boardwalks lead you through the park, but you can't follow them on your own. You must have a guided tour, which lasts more than two hours, including the short tram ride through the dry forest section. Reservations are required.

You can get a glimpse of some of the reserve by simply walking east down the narrow beach from the Playa Seven Seas. Better yet, take a kayak tour (see p128) at sunset, and head into **Laguna Grande** after dark for the green-glowing, underwater 'fireworks' of bioluminescent micro-organisms (see p51). Make sure you go in a kayak or sailboat; engine pollution is slowly killing the very micro-organisms that create the bioluminescence. Check that you're not doing anything to harm the environment before making deals with local boat owners.

Coming from San Juan or Luquillo, you can reach Las Cabezas (as well as the other attractions near Las Croabas) directly and avoid the traffic in Fajardo. Take four-lane Hwy 194 east from Hwy 3. Turn left onto Av Conquistador until it intersects with two-lane Hwy 987. Follow the signs.

PLAYA SEVEN SEAS
Playa Seven Seas (www.parquesnacionalespr.com; admission free, parking $3) is a sheltered, coconut-shaded horseshoe public beach. While it may not be quite as pretty as Playa Luquillo, fear not – it is attractive. The beach, on the southwestern shore of the peninsula of Las Cabezas, gets packed on weekends and during summer; the rest of the time it's tranquil.

For good snorkeling or to get away from it all, follow the beach about a half mile to the northeast along the Las Cabezas property to an area known as **Playa Escondida** (Hidden Beach). The reefs are just offshore. Taking the trail to the west eventually brings you to the nearly empty **Playa El Convento**, with its beach house for government officials.

BAHÍA LAS CROABAS
You find this spot where Hwy 987 ends at a little seaside park rimmed by seafood restaurants and bars looking east across the water to the peaks of Culebra. There is not much of a beach here, but there's a view of the offshore islands and the air blows fresh with the trade winds. The anchorage accommodates the fishermen's co-op and the last half-dozen *nativos*, the 'out-island' sloops that everyone around here once used for fishing and gathering conch or lobster. The fishermen here are friendly, and you can probably strike a deal with one of them for a boat ride (usually about $100 per boat per day).

PUERTO DEL REY
This 750-slip **marina** (☎ 787-860-1000; Hwy 3 Km 51.4) stands behind a breakwater in a cove 2 miles south of Fajardo. It is the largest marina on the island (and perhaps in the Caribbean). You will find a complete marina village here with restaurants, stores, laundry facilities, banking and all manner of boat-hauling and maintenance capabilities. Many yachts stop here to take advantage of the marina's courtesy car and Fajardo's supermarkets when stocking up for a winter in the tropics or the ride back home to the USA. Travelers will find that many of the sailing, diving and fishing charters run from here. It's about 5 miles south of Villa Marina.

Activities
Fajardo is decidedly amphibian – life is as exciting in the water as it is on land. This coastal region is blessed with many tiny islands (not to mention Culebra and Vieques) that provide fabulous opportunities for swimming, snorkeling, diving, fishing or just relaxing on a quiet beach.

BOATING
Almost all sailing trips advertised for travelers on the island sail out of one of the marinas in Fajardo. The operators listed here have been around for a while and know the area well, but there are many more good choices if these are all booked; *Que Pasa* (the island's tourism magazine) updates listings of new charter operators throughout the year. Many will pick you up in San Juan. Advance reservations are recommended for all charter tours.

Erin Go Bragh Charters (☎ 787-860-4401; www.egbc.net; Puerto del Rey Marina) offers ecofriendly sunset trips, dinner trips, daily trips (with BBQ and other lunches provided) and overnight charters to Vieques and Culebra. Captain Bill and his wife Ingrid are a wonderful and knowledgeable team.

Family-run (and very good for families), **Captain Jack's Spread Eagle II** (☎ 888-523-4511, 787-887-8821; www.snorkelpr.com; Dock J in Villa Marina) can do custom trips to any of the offshore islands.

East Island Excursions (☎ 787-860-3434; www.eastwindcats.com; Puerto del Rey Marina) has glass-bottomed catamarans that are in high demand, so book early. All kinds of day trips to La Cordillera islands are offered, and it even does quick runs over to St Thomas. One of the catamarans has a water slide that launches you right into the ocean.

EAST COAST

Traveler (☎ 787-863-2821; Villa Marina) offers daily tours with all-you-can-eat salad bars and snorkeling equipment provided for reasonable prices.

Getaway (☎ 787-860-7327; www.getawaypr.com; Villa Marina) offers day trips with lunch to Icacos, Lobos, Palominos and Palominitos cays. Captain Mingo is a local sailor who knows these waters intimately. His sunset trips are sometimes co-chartered by friendly dolphins; he just seems to know where to find them.

Club Náutico International (☎ 787-860-2400; Hwy 987 Km 1.3, Villa Marina) rents out outboard or sport-fishing boats from this location on the road to Las Croabas. Plan on spending at least $300 a day for the smallest boat, more if you need a captain.

KAYAKING

This is absolutely the most entrancing way to see Fajardo's bioluminescent attractions – and the most environmentally sound as well.

Although technically located in Río Grande, **Eco Xcursion Aquatica** (☎ 787-888-2887; ecoxcursion@libertypr.net; trips $45-65) is a mobile operation with guided flotilla trips to La Cordillera cays for snorkeling and a sunset trip around Las Cabezas and into the bioluminescent Laguna Grande, where microorganisms glow in the dark water.

Yokahú Kayaks (☎ 787-604-7375, 863-5374) provides equipment, and guides are very professional. Children under seven aren't allowed on the night trips, which leave at 7pm and generally last two hours.

Club Náutico International (see Boating, p127) has recently begun offering kayak tours to the bay. Be sure to make it clear that you want the kayak trip and not the power-boat option.

FISHING

Captain Eduardo Alcaide, from **Tropical Fishing Charters** (☎ 787-266-4524; www.tropicalfishing charters.com; Wyndham El Conquistador Resort & Golden Door Spa, 1000 Ave Conquistador), has more than 40 years experience. Prices vary (contact Alcaide for quotes) but expect to pay at least $400.

DIVING

There's no shortage of dive operators in Fajardo. One-tank dives range from $35 to $55, two-tank dives from $70 to $85, and a one-week PADI certification course averages about $200 to $350, depending on the number of people. Trips to St Thomas, Tortola and other Virgin Islands cost about $100 to $150.

Operating since 1963, the **Caribbean School of Aquatics** (☎ 787-728-6606; www.saildiveparty.com; Villa Marina; ☼ 7am-10pm) has NAUI and PADI scuba classes, and Captain Greg Korwek will take you on all-day boat trips to the best spots around La Cordillera and elsewhere.

Run by Carlos Bejar, the PADI-certified **La Casa del Mar Dive Center** (☎ 787-860-3483; www.la casadelmar.net; 1000 Ave Conquistador; ☼ 8am-6pm), inside the Wyndham Conquistador grounds, is great for all levels. The 'Bubblemakers for Kids' appeals to the younger crowd; more experienced divers can take the 'Divemaster' class. There are boat trips to all surrounding islands, including Culebra and Vieques.

Sea Ventures Pro Dive Center (☎ 800-739-3483, 787-863-3483; www.divepuertorico.com; Puerto del Rey; ☼ 8:30am-6pm) is staffed by very experienced professionals offering one-week PADI cer-

---

TOP CORDILLERA DIVES

All of these sights offer excellent snorkeling, too.

Cayo Lobos (30ft) Easily explored caves, tunnels and archways will bring you in close contact with parrotfish. If you do this dive at night, expect to see a lot of eels.

Ralph Point (60ft) Off the coast of Palominos, this dive takes you to where a reef joins a sandy bottom, making coral bowls and mounds.

Big Rock, Little Rock (30ft to 60ft) Also near Palominos, this dive takes you to a fringing reef made of dense stony corals. You may catch sight of an eagle ray.

Spurs (20ft to 70ft) The iron remains of a shipwreck lie in about 70ft of water along the sandy bottom off Palominitos, near a coral reef. It's home to schools of goatfish, lobsters, giant anemones and many more living creatures.

Cayo Diablo (15ft to 50ft) Devil Cay stretches away from the mainland along Cabezas de San Juan. It's a prized spot, with a hard-coral reef that looks like a well-manicured garden. Mind the currents, though – they are strong.

tification courses. For those who just want the basics or already know how to dive, there are multiple trips to Palominos and Icacos Cays daily, and on Sunday there are trips to Vieques and Culebra.

Puerto Rico Diver Supply (☎ 787-863-4300; www .prdiversupply.com; Villa Marina; ☿ 8am-5pm), owned by Kurt Grossen, is a well-stocked diving store offering PADI certification diving classes. There are regular trips to all La Cordillera and surrounding islands, and equipment is included.

Sleeping

Fajardo Inn (☎ 787-860-6000; www.fajardoinn.com; 52 Parcelas Beltrán, Hwy 195; r $90-125; P ☒ ☒) Perched on a hill overlooking the sea (from a distance), this attractive hacienda-style parador is just a few minutes from the ferry dock, in a section of town known as Puerto Real. It's up a slight hill off Hwy 195; follow signs for the inn. Rooms are large and spare, and the whole place exudes a Spanish austerity perfectly in keeping with the colonial decor. The Scenic Inn, an older property on the same grounds, offers rooms with fewer amenities at lower prices ($60 for a double). There are good restaurants, too – see right.

Ceiba Country Inn (☎ 787-885-0471; www.geocities .com/countryinn00735; Hwy 997 Km 2.1; s/d $60/70) A classic mountain retreat, this place has nine units overlooking the Caribbean and the offshore islands. On a clear day St Thomas can be seen on the horizon. Picture a landscaped hillside villa with decks, BBQ grill, continental breakfast and lounge. From San Juan, take Hwy 3 past Fajardo until the road becomes Rte 53. Take exit 5 (Ceiba North) and then make a right onto Rd 975 and go 1 mile. Turn right onto Hwy 977. Half a mile down the road is a sign for Ceiba Country Inn.

Wyndham El Conquistador Resort & Golden Door Spa (☎ 787-863-1000; www.wyndham.com; 1000 Ave Conquistador; r from $300; P ☒ ☒) This 900-unit mega-resort dominates the crest of a hill looking out over its own cove to the Sonda de Vieques, just south of Las Cabezas on Hwy 987. A tram takes you down to the waterfront, and shuttle boats carry guests out to Isla Palominos in La Cordillera. With 12 restaurants, golf, tennis courts, a spa, water sports and a casino, this 'complete destination resort' can entertain you for

weeks. Ask about package deals offering rooms at far below the rack rate.

Anchor Inn (☎ 787-863-7200; frenchman@libertypr .net; Hwy 987 Km 2.7; r from $70; ☒) Fanciful red, black and white decorations lend the Anchor Inn a nautical air. The restaurant on the 1st floor is a popular place with locals (reception in the back), and rooms are clean, airy and comfortable, with cable TV.

Hotel La Familia (☎ 787-863-11930; Hwy 987 Km 4.1; r $78-105) Tucked in a valley that overlooks the golf course at El Conquistador Resort, a mile from the beach, this hotel has expensive views at moderate prices. All 28 rooms have the usual amenities, and there is a small pool with a sundeck. The baby back ribs at the restaurant here are world class.

Hotel Delicias (☎ 787-863-1818; Playa Fajardo Dock; s $75-110; ☒) If you get stuck at the ferry dock overnight and the nearby Fajardo Inn is booked, try here. Right across the street from the terminal, it has 21 rooms with TV and telephone. While highly convenient, it's also a slightly grim place in a grim neighborhood, and the staff can be indifferent to guests. The on-site café is good for a coffee or beer, but not much else.

CAMPING

Playa Seven Seas (☎ 787-863-8180, 622-5200; Hwy 987; campsites per tent $10) A great place to pitch a tent right on the beach in Las Croabas, Playa Seven Seas fills up fast. Make sure you reserve in advance if you plan to come during the summer or holidays. Showers and bathrooms are available; portable toilets are not allowed.

Officials don't hassle people who pitch tents on Playa El Convento, which is reached by the path heading west from Playa Seven Seas. The area is popular so you'll usually find at least one or two tents up at all times; avoid pitching here if there are no other campers. Muggings do occur.

Eating

The most interesting places to eat in Fajardo lie along the road to Las Croabas (Hwy 987), but there are a few choices down near the ferry dock.

Blue Iguana (☎ 787-860-6000; dishes $7-21; ☿ 4-10pm Mon-Thu, 4pm-1am Fri-Sun) The Fajardo Inn has two restaurants, but this one is by far the best, with great Mexican fare in a fun and relaxed setting. In the earlier hours it's a good option for families; later on the pool table and ample bar attracts a drinking crowd. On weekends it's very popular after 10pm.

El Picazo (dishes $2-15) This place is among the open-air bar-restaurants you see when you get to the end of the road at Bahía Las Croabas. Here fried-fish balls cost just $2, and the beer is about the same at happy hour. In the same neighborhood, Restaurant Croabas has grilled fish for $8, and octopus salad for $9. Rocar Seafood has similar prices.

Portofino (☎ 787-860-1000 ext 4330; Puerto del Rey Marina, Hwy 3 Km 51.4; dishes $10-24) Stare at million-dollar yachts in the bay under blissfully cool air-con while enjoying fettucine alfredo, spaghetti carbonara and other delicious pastas.

Rosa's Seafood (☎ 809-863-0213; 536 Tablazo; dishes $14-25; ✆ 11am-10pm Thu-Tue) The jury is out on Rosa's. Some locals say it is still the best deal for great seafood at the docks; others say the prices are too high for what is offered. It is the best option you'll find in this part of town, and the food certainly is tasty and professionally prepared. Is it worth what they charge? Almost, but not quite – however, the convenient location is certainly a plus.

Anchor Inn (☎ 787-863-7200; Hwy 987 Km 2.7; dishes $8-24) This inn has a big dining room specializing in lobster dishes that usually cost about $22. You can go light here with a chef's salad for about $9.

La Banda (☎ 787-860-1000 ext 2443; Puerto del Rey Marina, Hwy 3 Km 51.4; dishes $12-25) Live lobsters are easily transferred from the aquarium to your plate here – with a side trip to the kitchen, of course. If you prefer not to see your food swimming before you eat it, go for the Italian dishes or hearty steaks.

Eden Vegetarian Restaurant (☎ 787-863-7060; 57S Munoz Rivera St; dishes $5; ✆ 11am-5pm) Further back from the beach, closer to downtown Fajardo, Eden's has a wide variety of vegetarian dishes and great *batidos* (smoothies) and juices.

Entertainment

Anchor Inn (☎ 787-863-7200; Hwy 987 Km 2.7) This place gets fired up on weekend nights when salsa, merengue and Latin rock groups perform here.

The casino, bars and restaurants at the Wyndham El Conquistador Resort & Golden Door Spa are actually open to the public; you're perfectly welcome to try your luck at the tables or take in a floor show from the bar no matter where you lay your head later that night.

Blue Iguana (p129) gets busy on weekend nights during high season.

Rocar Seafood (p129) has live music from 7pm to midnight on Saturday, and the liquor store at Villa Marina puts out some tables for dominoes and turns into a popular hangout for locals on weekends. Friday night has live music.

Shopping

The malls are on Hwy 3 just north of town if you need a supermarket, Blockbuster Video, Payless Shoes or Wal-Mart fix.

Getting There & Away

AIR

The small, busy **Aeropuerto de Fajardo** (☎ 787-863-1011; 24hr parking $8.50) lies west of town near the intersection of Hwy 3 and Hwy 976. All aircraft are Islander twins or tri-motor Trilanders.

Isla Nena Air Service (☎ 787-863-4000, 877-812-5144; ✆ 6am-6pm) flies on demand to Vieques (one way/round trip $20/35, eight minutes) and Culebra (one way/round trip $25/45, 15 minutes; one to two flights per day).

Vieques Air Link (☎ 787-863-3020, 860-2290; ✆ 6am-6pm) sends about 10 flights a day to Vieques (one way/round trip $20/36), six to Culebra (round trip $40) and two a day to St Croix (one way/round trip $75/145).

Air Flamenco (☎ 787-801-8256) flights go to Culebra (one way/round trip $25/45) at 7am, noon and 5:45pm. The 3:30pm return flight stops in Fajardo before San Juan.

Air St Thomas (☎ 787-791-4898) does charter flights to St Croix, St Thomas and many other Caribbean islands, with stopovers at Vieques or Culebra on demand.

CAR

If your destination is Fajardo and you are not intent on touring the island clockwise from San Juan, save yourself the aggravating drive on Hwy 3 via Carolina and Luquillo by taking the four-lane expressway drive from San Juan: Hwy 52 to Caguas, then Hwy 30 to Humacao, and finally Hwy 53 north to Fajardo. Two of these roads require paying tolls along the highway; expect to pay about $4.50 total from San Juan to Fajardo.

There's a spacious outdoor parking lot on the right-hand side of the road as you approach the ferry docks. The lot is surrounded by secure fencing and has 24-hour surveillance. It's $5 a day.

Directly across from the public parking lot, the small **World Car Rental** (☎ 787-863-9696; Rte 195 at the docks; per day $28; ⏰ 7:30-11:30am, 1-5pm) offers compact cars at daily rates.

FERRY

The ferries to Vieques and Culebra leave from the **Port Authority terminal** (☎ 787-863-0705, 800-981-2005) for the islands. The terminal is about 1½ miles east of town in the run-down Playa de Fajardo/Puerto Real neighborhood (follow the signs to either). For the ferry schedule for Culebra, see p148; for Vieques, see p161.

The ferry to the US Virgin Islands leaves from the same terminal. **Transportation Services Virgin Islands** (☎ 787-863-0582; www.caribecay .com) operates the high-speed passenger ferry *Caribe Cay* between Fajardo and the ferry terminal at Charlotte Amalie on St Thomas in the US Virgin Islands. This is an excellent alternative to paying steep airfares to visit St Thomas, and this ferry connects with ferries that service the other major US and British Virgin Islands! The ferry takes two hours and runs on Saturdays and Sundays, departing from Fajardo at 8am and St Thomas at

4:30pm. The round-trip adult fare is about $75 (one way is $55). For a round trip, children aged between two and four pay $40; those aged five to 11, pay $60.

PÚBLICO

The **main público stop** (☎ 787-860-1820; www.fajar dopr.org; ⏰ 4am-6pm Mon-Sat) is off the plaza in the old commercial center of town, but you will also find públicos at the ferry terminal and, during summer and weekends, near the seafood restaurants in Las Croabas. Many of the públicos you find at the ferry terminal will take you to and from the Río Piedras section of San Juan for about $6. You can get to Las Croabas for $2; a trip south to Humacao (to catch another público on to Ponce and the south coast) is less than $5. Luquillo is less than a dollar. Palmer (near El Yunque) is $2. If you are coming from San Juan and going to the ferry dock, make sure to tell the driver to go all the way to the port.

TAXI

You can always find taxis at the ferry terminal to take you to Luis Muñoz Marín (LMM) airport in San Juan ($65).

PLAYA NAGUABO & AROUND

Downtown Naguabo is routinely cursed by Puerto Rican drivers for its irritating and impossible to understand one-way road system. There's really so little to see in this town center that you might save yourself the aggravation and give it a pass entirely. Head instead to nearby Playa Húcares (the local name for Playa Naguabo).

Of course, that's a bit of a misnomer as well. Playa Húcares doesn't actually have a beach – the waterfront is a rock seawall overlooking a bay. It does have a dramatic view of Vieques, 10 miles to sea, and Cayo Santiago, closer to the coastline. It's worth visiting to get a look at the brightly painted fishing sloops and the two Victorian mansions standing like sentinels over the sleepy little boardwalk, officially named Malecón Arturo Corsino. One of the mansions, the Castillo Villa del Mar, is on the National Registry of Historic Places (despite the dilapidation and the graffiti) and was once home to a restaurant and art gallery where local painters showed their work. These days it's a run-down old eyesore, but the

---

CAYO SANTIAGO

Home to strange sounds and fabulous sights, Cayo Santiago is a scientific experiment gone wondrously right. Until 1938 it was just one of many pretty but unremarkable islands off Puerto Rico's eastern tip – then a team of scientists from the University of Puerto Rico and Columbia University in New York decided to turn it into a cutting-edge research area. Five hundred Rhesus monkeys were let loose on the peaked, hazy island lying a mile offshore, and today some 1200 primates run rampant on the 39 tropical acres.

Only researchers and scientific personnel are allowed on the island, but visitors can get quite close and eyeball monkeys from their boat. There's fabulous snorkeling around a sunken ship not far from the shore and the isolation is very refreshing.

mansion next to it has been somewhat restored, giving rise to hopes that both structures will eventually be returned to their former state of grace.

On weekends people flock to the line of open-air seafood restaurants just across the street for freshly caught chillo (snapper) and sierra (kingfish). If you follow Hwy 3 a half mile further south, you'll see about 2 miles of thin, tree-lined, vacant beach. Beyond this, the road carries you into the tiny village of **Playa Humacao**. Dilapidated Playa Humacao has one bright spot. There is a pristine balneario and *centro vacacional* (vacation center) at the neighborhood west of the village. **Punta Santiago** has become a bit of a weekend and holiday hotspot, and its bright *friquitines* offer lots of succulent treats like *arroz con jueyes* (rice with crab chunks) and shark nuggets. During the busy season it's fun and upbeat and nowhere near as crowded Luquillo.

Activities

Captain Frank López (☎ 787-850-7881, 316-0441) offers fishing or snorkeling trips and sea

excursions to Cayo Santiago. Prices are negotiable: start your bidding at about $25. Look for La Paseadora boat at Playa Naguabo. The **Palmas del Mar Resort** (below) also offers diving trips to the area.

Palmas Divers (☎ 787-633-7314; Marina de Palmas) will take you to Cayo Santiago and the deeper sites offshore. It's $45 for a one-tank dive.

Golfers can make reservations at either of the two **golf courses** (☎ 787-285-2256) at the Palmas del Mar resort. The greens fee for the 6800yd Reese Jones course is $115, or $70 after 2pm for nonguests; the old course (called 'the Palms') is $105, or $65 after 2pm.

The resort also has 20 **tennis courts** (☎ 787-852-6000), but you will need reservations. Court fees are $24 an hour during the day, or $29 at night.

The **Palmas del Mar Equestrian Center** (☎ 787-852-6000; ◷ Tue-Sun) boards about 40 horses, including hunters and jumpers. One-hour-plus trail rides cost about $40.

Sleeping & Eating

There are several pretty guest houses tucked into the south side of El Yunque that can be reached from Naguabo (see Sleeping, p119). Accommodations in Naguabo are very limited, with the exception of the Palmas del Mar Resort. Yabucoa has more to offer.

Palmas del Mar Resort (☎ 787-852-6000, 800-725-6273; www.palmasdelmar.com; 170 Candelero Dr; r $200-450) This vast resort community lies off Hwy 3 about 5 miles south of the commercial and industrial town of Humacao (not worth a visit unless you need a supermarket). Set on more than 2700 acres of former coconut and sugarcane plantations, Palmas is a world unto itself. The core of this resort consists of privately owned villas and timeshare units built around a marina, beach and golf course. But there is also a casino and two hotels: the Candelero and the Palmas Inn, with more than 120 rooms. Rates start at a relatively low price, and you may do better if you get a golf or tennis package. Inside, try El Chinchorro for fresh seafood, or Chez Daniel for fine French cooking. Très romantique!

Centro Vacacional Punta Santiago (☎ 787-852-1660; Hwy 3 Km 72.4, Playa Humacao; campsites without/with hookups $10/20, r/villas $66/110) This spot has a public balneario and more than 30 cabañas and condo-style duplex cottages in a coconut grove on a pristine beach.

SCENIC DRIVES

Puerto Rico's **Ruta Panorámica** (Scenic Drive) begins in Yabucoa and climbs through coffee country into mountain wilderness via Hwy 182, before threading its way across the tops of the highest peaks (for more on the drive, see p236).

Before rushing out of Yabucoa to the mountains, however, take the time to follow the easy-to-miss **coastal road**, Hwy 901, as it heads southwest toward Patillas. Hwy 901 to Maunabo takes up where the Hwy 53 expressway stops (eventually the toll road will run all the way along the southeast coast to Guayama and join Hwy 52, the San Juan-Ponce Autopista). Go right off the exit ramp at the end of Hwy 53, then turn left on Hwy 901 at the first traffic light and follow this spectacular shoreline drive. Hwy 901 scales mountain cliffs that fall to the sea, in a fashion reminiscent of the roads along Spain's Costa Brava. Almost 20 miles of scenic seaside driving lie ahead as the road becomes Hwy 7760, then Hwy 3. Guest houses, seaside cantinas and campsites are dotted along the way.

There are also more than 40 campsites around Playa Naguabo and Playa Humacao. Make reservations for the campsites through the central San Juan office of the **Recreational Development Company** (☎ 787-853-1660).

A little kiosk with a nice view at the northern end of the dock does great *empanadillas* (dough stuffed with meat or fish) and the whole *malecón* is lined with seafood restaurants. Try the famous *mojito criollo* (rum, mint and lemon) sauce on fresh fish at **Tacominqueo** (☎ 787-643-7168; 🕑 8am-10pm). **Restaurant Vinny** (☎ 787-874-7664; 🕑 8am-10pm) does a bang up lunch for $4; and on the road into town, **Griselle Seafood** (☎ 787-874-1533; at turn on Hwy 3; 🕑 11am-8pm Sun-Tue & Thu, 11am-midnight Fri & Sat) has lobster specials for $20.

Getting There & Away

Coming from San Juan, the easiest way to get to this part of the east coast is to follow Hwy 3 past Fajardo. Exits will soon follow for Naguabo and surrounding towns. Note that the Punta Santiago exit brings you off the highway and into a busy intersection with lots of fast-food restaurants, gas stations and shopping malls. If you are planning on going up into the south side of El Yunque or the Ruta Panorámica (see opposite), gas up here first. Punta Santiago is 10 more minutes down the road by car; follow the signs.

The públicos vans in Playa Naguabo park near the promenade. They go to Naguabo ($1) or Humacao ($2), from where you can move on to the greener pastures of Fajardo, Ponce or San Juan.

The Palmas del Mar Resort will arrange for a minivan to haul you to and from LMM airport in San Juan – about a 40-minute trip in normal traffic. During peak season, the scheduled trip is $27 per person; otherwise it's $75 for one to four people.

The entrance to Palmas is a well-marked road off Hwy 3, a couple of miles south of Humacao. Driving from San Juan, take Hwy 52 south to Caguas and Hwy 30 to Humacao – all expressway, toll-road driving.

YABUCOA & AROUND

If you are traveling south from the Humacao area, take the Hwy 53 toll road to avoid the traffic on Hwy 3. This lightly traveled section of road bisects miles of sugarcane fields and estuary where three mountain rivers meet. The town of Yabucoa lies in the uplands between the mountains and the estuary, perfectly poised to be the processing and distribution point for the coffee grown on the mountain slopes to the north, and the sugarcane raised in the lowlands to the south.

The actual town of Yabucoa has nothing to offer the traveler but traffic jams (don't even think of trying to get through here in a hurry on a Saturday), plus a chance to provision and refuel. The serenity of the adjoining estuary and its bay have been marred by an oil tanker facility called Puerto Yabucoa and a Phillips Oil refinery whose tanks and towers rise from the cane like hissing tombstones.

However, travelers will find a few attractions, including the public beach at Playa Lucía and the lighthouse.

Sights & Activities

The balneario at **Playa Lucía** (parking $2), near the intersection of Hwy 901 and Hwy 9911 in Yabucoa, has great shade under its coconut trees and several little beach-bar/restaurants just off its premises. **El Cocal** is one of the few good surfing spots in the area (ask for directions at the balneario).

Off Hwy 901 along the coast (also see opposite), you can explore the ruins of **Hacienda de Santa Lucía**, an old sugar plantation a mile north of Playa Lucía. Don't expect a haunted mansion; there's only one wall left. **Central Roig** is the still active, old-time sugar hacienda and mill on the same road.

Lovers and solitary types like the view from the base of the **Faro Punta Tuna**, the lighthouse just southeast of Maunabo. From Hwy 901, take Hwy 760 toward the ocean. A path leads down to the extremely secluded **Playa Larga**.

Sleeping

Playa de Emajaguas Guest House (☎ 787-861-6023; Hwy 901 Km 2.5; dm $50/160) As the road descends (westbound) to the beach from the mountains of the Cuchilla de Panduras, you'll find this guest house. The attraction of Edna Huertas' well-used inn is its sense of space: it sits in the middle of a field and orchard like an old plantation house on a rise above a narrow beach. There are seven efficiency apartments, which are like studio apartments with a kitchenette. The popular El Cocal and Sharkey's Beach surf breaks are nearby.

Guest House Lunny Mar (☎ 787-893-8996; Hwy 901; s/d $60/75) A popular surfer hangout just steps from El Cocal, Lunny Mar is a no-frills establishment that's recently undergone a mini-renovation. It's still a bit bare, but the beach proximity more than makes up for it.

Caribe Playa (☎ 787-839-6339, 839-1817; www .caribeplaya.com; Hwy 3 Km 112; r $79-104; 🖳) You will spot this place where Hwy 3 runs along the seashore between Maunabo and Patillas. Tucked right on the shore under a slanting plantation of coconuts, this inn has 29 units, many with beachfront balconies; most rooms have a kitchen sink and fridge, but no stove. There's a restaurant on the premises and a natural pool carved into the rocky coast. Owner George Engels has a collection of parrots and iguanas to keep you company.

Parador Palmas de Lucía (☎ 787-893-4423; www .palmasdelucia.com; cnr Hwy 901 & Hwy 9911; r $90-109; 🖳) This place is on Playa Lucía at the intersection of these two highways in Yabucoa. Here you will find a friendly staff and a new, well-scrubbed hotel. Each of the rooms has all the usual modern conveniences, plus a private balcony with a view of the pool and beach.

Villa de Carmen (☎ 787-839-4711; fax 839-7536; Hwy 3 Km 113; r & ste $50-120; 🖳) A beachfront place with 12 units, all with kitchenettes and laundry service. There are also two pools on the premises, which is a good thing because the beach along the coast between Maunabo and Patillas is narrow and eroded. Thoroughly inspect the room before settling in; some are cleaner than others.

Eating

El Nuevo Horizonte (☎ 787-893-5492; Hwy 901 Km 9.8; dishes $6-22) Just a mile or two west of Coco Mar, the view rarely gets better than it does from this place. This restaurant is perched high on the mountainside overlooking the Caribbean. You can smell the *asopao de langosta* (lobster stew) cooking 200yd before you get here. A cauldron of the stew will set you back about $18 and serves at least two people.

El Mar de la Tranquilidad (☎ 787-839-4870; Hwy 3 Km 118.9; dishes $7-22) Once the road returns to sea level (heading west), look for this establishment, on the seaward side of Hwy 3 west of Villa de Carmen. Beer on the outdoor terrace costs $1.75, and you can get *salmorejo de jueyes* (land crab in tomato sauce) for under $11.

At Playa Lucía in Yabucoa, take time to check out the cheap beer and *empanadillas* at Coco Mar.

Culebra & Vieques

There's no shortage of fabulous beaches and world-class dive and snorkel sites on the island of Puerto Rico, or elsewhere in the Caribbean for that matter. But where do you go when you want that *plus* unique cuisine, environmentally friendly accommodations (of all shapes and sizes, fitting a range of budgets) and laid-back beach towns that eschew the idea of a tourist-driven economy? The Spanish Virgin Islands, of course!

Culebra and Vieques are just a few miles off the coast of Puerto Rico, and are also easily reachable from St Thomas (in the US Virgin Islands). Not too long ago pirates like Bluebeard used the islands' many bays and inlets to play hide-and-seek with Spanish authorities; nowadays the region gets busy with people looking for a break from the rat race. While sporting the same sugary-white sand and temperate waters as the rest of the Caribbean, the Spanish Virgin Islands are remarkably undeveloped. A visit here is your best shot at sharing a 6-mile stretch of sand with wild birds and a few endangered turtles.

Culebra and Vieques owe their wild state to the US Navy and Marine Corps, whose military presence on the islands for the past 100 years or so kept the population low and civilian development limited to small pockets of land. Despite the navy practicing bombardment techniques here, the wildlife has endured. You'll find vast fringing reefs around the islands and mangrove swamps that are nurseries for rare birds and fish. Sea turtles such as the hawksbill lay their eggs on the beaches, and herds of wild horses roam freely. Today, with the US military totally out of both Culebra and Vieques, locals are adjusting to their newfound dependence on tourism. Some developers have moved in, but most residents remain committed to finding a balance between creating jobs and protecting the pristine wildlife.

CULEBRA & VIEQUES

HIGHLIGHTS

- Swim through twinkling waters at Vieques' bioluminescent **Bahía Mosquito** (p155)
- Soak up the rays at **Playa Flamenco** (p142), Culebra's little piece of paradise
- Enjoy the easygoing but hard-drinking nightlife on **Culebra** (p147) and **Vieques** (p160)
- Experience the prime snorkeling and diving in the cays off **Culebra** (p143)
- Bronze yourself alongside sun-worshiping turtles at Culebra's **Playa Zoni** (p143)

- POPULATION: CULEBRA 1418, VIEQUES 9351
- DRINK: HURRICANE

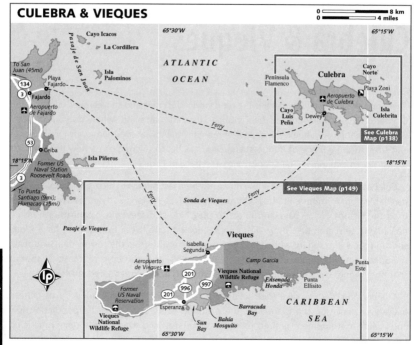

CULEBRA & VIEQUES

HISTORY

Some 500 years ago the islands east of Puerto Rico, including Culebra and Vieques, were disputed territory between the Taínos and the Caribs. Groups from both tribes came and went from the islands according to the season – probably to hunt the turtles nesting here. Vieques had more fertile, flatter land for farming and therefore was the more popular island. The first real settlement came to Culebra during the early 16th century, when Taíno and Carib refugees from Borinquen gathered here and on Vieques to make peace with each other, pool their resources and mount a fierce (but ultimately unsuccessful) campaign to drive the Spaniards from the big island. When Spain conceded Puerto Rico and her territories to the US following the Spanish-American War in 1898, both Culebra and Vieques became municipalities of the Republic of Puerto Rico. Therefore, residents are recognized as US citizens (half of them are ex-pats, in any case).

For most of the 20th century the US Navy and Marine Corps used the islands for target practice and for rehearsing 20th-century military actions carried out on other shores, such as Iwo Jima, the Philippines, Haiti and Kuwait. The navy left Culebra several decades ago to concentrate its activities on Vieques, where it set up a military camp and proceeded to hold practice bombings in nearby waters with alarming regularity. After an errant bomb killed a civilian in 1999, *viequenses* reached their breaking point. A long struggle ensued, but the navy was eventually ejected. Of course, the tracts of pristine land that opened up with the military's departure caught the attention of many developers, including the Puerto Rican government itself, which wants a beefed-up tourism infrastructure on both Culebra and Vieques. Locals are trying hard to bring in new jobs through sustainable tourism that won't destroy the wild land and beaches that make the Spanish Virgin Islands truly special. So far so good – but the battle rages on.

CLIMATE

The famous Caribbean trade winds gently buffet these two islands, but it is still hot, hot,

---

THE JOYS OF ISLAND LIFE

Some important information on the island transport system:

- Ferries go into the open sea: if you're prone to seasickness, a pill is definitely in order. The boats have disabled access.

- If seas are rough, scheduled crossings are suspended; in rainy months you may be stuck at either end for days longer than you had thought. Note that unless it's a national emergency, like a hurricane, the tourism office won't cover your costs if you run out of money.

- When cargo ferries are delayed by bad weather, things like gasoline, perishables and cash in ATMs run out. It's not unheard of for people to arrive the day after a big storm and find that there's no gas for their rental cars and no money to be had until the next cargo ferry comes. Keep that in mind.

- Because the cargo ferries bring over supplies to islanders, the authority does not like to give much-needed space to tourist rental cars. You may find it a hassle to get a reservation (although it's required for a car) and then it may not be honored when you get to the dock. They will bump you if something vital needs to be transported.

- Car-rental agencies do not want you to take their vehicles to the islands for the simple reason that they can't get a tow-truck to you if there's an accident. Nobody will stop you from bringing your rental over, but be aware that most agencies stipulate in the contracts that they won't cover accidents off the mainland. You break it, you buy it. Better to leave your car in the secure lot in Fajardo and rent on the island.

---

hot just about every day of the year. Average temperatures are around 85°F with relatively low humidity. Add the glare from surrounding water and white sand and it feels like 110° in the shade. Rainy season, which doesn't do much to cool things off, is May through November. Hurricane season is August/September through November, with October generally being the wettest month.

PARKS, RESERVES & STATE FORESTS

The Puerto Rico Department of Natural Resources protects more than 2000 acres of land along the Península Flamenco and from Monte Resaca east to the sea. Named the Culebra National Wildlife Refuge (p140), it includes the coastline as well as more than 20 offshore cays. The **US Fish & Wildlife Service** (☎ 787-742-0115; www.fws.gov) administers these lands.

Vieques National Wildlife Refuge (☎ 787-741-2138; www.fws.gov/southeast/vieques), on the eastern and western ends of the island, offers visitors a chance to mountain bike, hike, snorkel and swim on newly opened beaches and pristine land.

DANGERS & ANNOYANCES

Culebra is virtually crime-free, but petty thievery is sadly somewhat common on Vieques, especially around the Sun Bay public beach. Lock hotel rooms and don't bring valuables to the beach. Be careful with cell phones, as thieves have been known to grab them right out of people's hands. Don't leave anything – cigarettes, lighters, sunglasses – in sight in the car and lock the doors, always.

GETTING THERE & AWAY

There's frequent air service from San Juan, Fajardo and St Thomas in the Virgin Islands to both Vieques (p161) and Culebra (p147). Government-run ferries run from Fajardo to Vieques (p161) and Culebra (p148) regularly; and a few operators also connect to St Thomas.

CULEBRA

Most people outside Puerto Rico think only of Vieques when they hear talk of the Spanish Virgin Islands, but the smaller, quieter (and some would say cuter) island of Culebra is actually the preferred tourist destination for locals in the know.

Lying 17 miles off Puerto Rico's east coast, Culebra is geologically more a part of the Virgin Islands (St Thomas is 12 miles

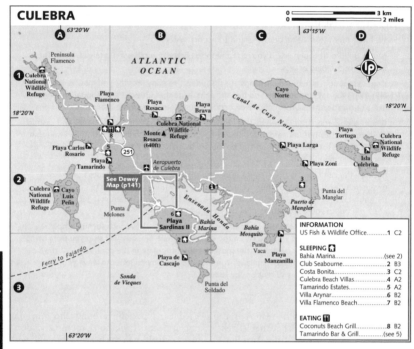

CULEBRA

INFORMATION
US Fish & Wildlife Office...........1 C2

SLEEPING
Bahía Marina............................(see 2)
Club Seabourne.......................2 B3
Costa Bonita.............................3 C2
Culebra Beach Villas.................4 A2
Tamarindo Estates....................5 A2
Villa Arynar..............................6 B2
Villa Flamenco Beach...............7 B2

EATING
Coconuts Beach Grill................8 B2
Tamarindo Bar & Grill............(see 5)

east) than of the 'mainland.' And it looks the part when viewed from an approaching ferry – lush, irregular peaks are fringed by beaches and rugged offshore cays.

Despite its distance, Culebran culture remains strongly Puerto Rican, with a patina of American-style customer service brought in by expatriate entrepreneurs. Several hundred US expats run the bulk of the restaurants, guest houses and tourist services, but that doesn't automatically mean American hours and American attitudes prevail – a restaurant owner may open her doors only when she is in the mood. Don't be surprised when your rental-car guy tells you to just leave his jeep on the street somewhere with the keys in it when you depart, or if your guest house host puts you in charge and heads off to St Croix for a couple of days. Everything is done just a little bit differently – privately built docks, for example, are legally public facilities, and squatters simply build their homes on unpurchased, untitled public land. Only new and uptight gringo immigrants complain, because they haven't yet learned the system.

Beyond the amusing eccentricities of the culture, Culebra's most endearing charms are its beaches and diving sites. Nobody rushes on Culebra (because really, what *is* your hurry?) and nobody cares who you're with. There aren't any specific hotels or restaurants for gay and lesbian couples because they are welcome everywhere.

If your idea of an idyllic vacation is to sprawl on an empty beach, untouched by condo or cabana, and later enjoy a stiff drink at a local shanty bar frequented by everyone from the mayor on down, then you've hit the jackpot.

HISTORY

First hunting grounds for Taíno and Carib tribes, then a pirate stronghold during the days of the Spanish Empire, much of Culebra's 7000 acres has remained essentially the same ever since two-legged creatures took to walking its shores. The US Navy grabbed control of most of the island early in the 20th century and didn't cede its lands back to the locals until 1975. Some modern structures went up on the newly accessible land rather rapidly, but resident expats and native-born *culebrenses* were very quickly able to find a common language and they have continued to work together quite fiercely to hold overdevelopment and commercialization at bay.

ORIENTATION

There's very little you need to know to navigate the island. First, the cheery little dock that welcomes you (if you've come by ferry) fronts a strip of shops that carry all the Culebra essentials: sunscreen, film, hats, bug repellent (something you absolutely do *not* want to be without), bathing suits, beach towels, T-shirts and flip-flops. In the slower season these may be open erratically or not at all. Many also have good tourist information and offer snorkel, kayak and dive trips. A nice food kiosk is the only thing open early in the morning, for those coming in on the 6am ferry from Vieques. The Hotel Kokomo (p145), painted bright yellow, is very hard to miss. Next door is Culebra Vacation Planners (p144); Michael and his friendly staff are a marvelous source of information and can provide lots of insight and suggestions on best beaches for current weather conditions and much, much more. Most local business owners are on hand to greet the ferries. Local cab driver Willy is also usually there, ready to squire visitors to guest houses and then beaches; a public van also does the same trip periodically for $3.

Heading left away from the dock will bring you to Calle Pedro Márquez, usually referred to as the 'main road,' which leads into Dewey, the island's principal settlement. With a map (see p141), all becomes clear very quickly; there are only a few roads leading in and out of Dewey. It is easier to walk than drive in town due to one-way streets and some parking congestion. It would take all of 20 minutes to explore just about every nook and cranny of Dewey on foot. The main road eventually leads out to the single landing strip airport on Rte 251; if you continue past the airport you get to Playa Flamenco. If you take Rte 250 east you'll come to turn-offs for Playa Resaca and Brava, eventually winding up at Playa Zoni. Another road, Calle Fulladoza, heads south to Punta del Soldado. Basic island maps are published by La Loma gift shop (p147), but are also handed out liberally by hotels and car-rental agencies.

Culebrita and Cayo Norte are two popular cays off Culebra that are easily visited; there are about 18 others surrounding the island.

INFORMATION

Few establishments use or have meaningful street addresses on Culebra, so we generally use descriptive addresses here.

Emergency

Culebrenses will tell you repeatedly that if you have an emergency on the island, you will get a much faster and more professional response by calling the island detachment of the Puerto Rican Police than by contacting the municipal police.

Municipal Police (☎ 787-742-0106)
Puerto Rican Police (☎ 787-742-3501)

Media

Culebra Calendar is the island newspaper and has complete listings of upcoming events, jobs, tide tables and articles on important Culebra issues.

Medical Services

Despite its small population, Culebra has good heath services. Some basic toiletries are carried in local shops, but it's wise to bring things like condoms, tampons, saline solution, contact lens supplies and medicine for tummy troubles – not that you are more likely to get sick on Culebra than anywhere else, but you will want something at hand if you do.

Clinic (Map p141; ☎ 787-742-3511) In town on the road to Punta Melones; has drugs and resident doctors. The island also keeps a plane on emergency standby at the airport overnight for medical transport to the main island.
Walgreens (☎ 787-860-1060) With no pharmacy on the island, *culebrenses* call Walgreens in Fajardo. The pharmacy ships drugs to the island on Vieques Air Link flights.

Money

Banco Popular (Map p141; ☎ 787-742-3572; Calle Pedro Márquez; ☽ 8:30am-2:30pm Mon & Wed-Fri)

Post

Post office (Map p141; ☎ 787-742-3862; Calle Pedro Márquez; ☽ 8:30am-4:30pm Mon-Fri, 8:30am-noon Sat) Right in the center of town.

Tourist Information

There are some good websites available. Everybody agrees that Bruce Goble of La

CULEBRA & VIEQUES

Loma gift shop runs the island's best website (www.culebra-island.com); there's also www .culebra.org and www.islaculebra.com.

Tourist office (Map p141; ☎ 787-742-3116, ext 441; Calle William Font; ✆ 8:30am-3:30pm Mon-Fri) Very basic information can be found in this yellow building not too far from the health clinic.

DANGERS & ANNOYANCES

Culebra breeds swarms of mosquitoes, especially during the rainy season (August to November). Some of the daytime species have been known to carry dengue.

Wear your seatbelt and obey local parking laws! Officers love issuing traffic tickets.

SIGHTS
Dewey   Map p141

Depending on the condition of its dirt roads, Dewey (also known as 'Da Town' or 'Pueblo' to locals) is either a simple but pretty island village, or a muddy backwater with lots of puddles to wade through. In either case, there's still plenty of eccentric charm – and eccentrically charming residents – to keep you entertained. Once you get the lay of the land, it's very easy to barhop between the handful of hangouts in town. There's very little to see or do in town besides eat, drink and be merry – check out Entertainment (p147) for more information on that topic.

The little **Museum of Ildefenso** (☎ 787-742-0240; Rte 250; ✆ 8am-noon & 1-3pm) is tucked behind the office of the Department of Natural Resources, and has some historical pictures of the island and lots of Taíno artifacts.

Culebra National Wildlife Refuge   Map p138

More than 2000 acres of Culebra's 7000 acres constitute a national wildlife refuge, which US President Theodore Roosevelt signed into law almost 100 years ago, and which is protected by the Departamento de Recursos Naturales y Ambientales (DRNA; Department of Natural Resources & Environment). Most of this land lies along the Península Flamenco, and from Monte Resaca east to the sea, and includes all of the coastline as well as more than 20 offshore cays, with the exception of Cayo Norte. The **US Fish & Wildlife Service** (☎ 787-742-0115; www.fws.gov; ✆ 7am-4pm Mon-Fri) administers these lands. Monte Resaca, Isla Culebra and Cayo Luis Peña are open to the public from sunrise to sunset daily, and

all have some fairly challenging hikes. Stop by the office on the east side of Ensenada Honda for maps, literature and permission to visit other sections of the refuge.

Here you can also find out what beaches may be closed for turtle nesting or to learn about being a volunteer on an overnight turtle watch. Also check out **CORALations** (☎ 787-742-0115; www.coralations.org), a nonprofit organization that works with Fish & Wildlife to preserve reefs and protect turtle breeding grounds.

Isla Culebrita   Map p138

If you need a reason to rent a kayak or hire a water taxi, Isla Culebrita is it. This small island, just a mile east of Playa Zoni, is part of the wildlife refuge. With its abandoned lighthouse, six beaches, tide pools, reefs and nesting areas for seabirds, Isla Culebrita has changed little in the past 500 years. The north beaches, such as the long crescent of Playa Tortuga, are popular nesting grounds for sea turtles, and you may see these animals swimming near the reefs just offshore. Bring a lot of water, sunscreen, a shirt and a hat if you head for Isla Culebrita, because there is little shade here. See Kayaking (p143) and Boating (p143) for details on renting and hiring boats to reach this island.

Cayo Luis Peña   Map p138

Less visited than Isla Culebrita, Luis Peña is the island of peaks, rocks, forests and coves you'll pass just a few minutes before the ferry lands you at Culebra's dock. This island is another part of the wildlife refuge, and it has a collection of small sheltered beaches. Luis Peña is a short kayak or water-taxi trip from town; it has good beaches and snorkeling all around the island.

BEACHES

The only beach that has amenities is Playa Flamenco, so be sure to bring lots of water and a snack when venturing further afield.

Punta Melones   Map p138

There is only one bathing/snorkeling site you can walk to from town, and this is it. Take the road past the clinic about a half-mile north until you reach a development on the hill to your right. Ahead on your left, you'll see the rocky Melones point, with a navigation light; to the right of the point is a stony beach. If you head down to this beach,

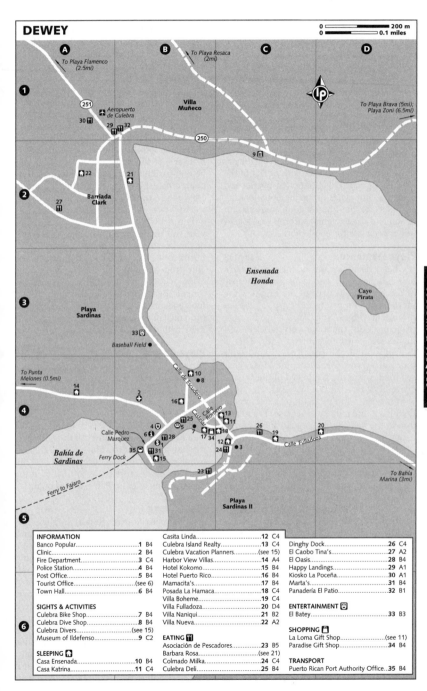

DEWEY

INFORMATION
Banco Popular...................................**1** B4
Clinic..**2** B4
Fire Department..............................**3** C4
Police Station...................................**4** B4
Post Office.......................................**5** B4
Tourist Office...........................(see 6)
Town Hall..**6** B4

SIGHTS & ACTIVITIES
Culebra Bike Shop............................**7** B4
Culebra Dive Shop............................**8** B4
Culebra Divers.........................(see 15)
Museum of Ildefenso.......................**9** C2

SLEEPING 🏠
Casa Ensenada.................................**10** B4
Casa Katrina....................................**11** C4

Casita Linda.....................................**12** C4
Culebra Island Realty.....................**13** C4
Culebra Vacation Planners......(see 15)
Harbor View Villas.........................**14** A4
Hotel Kokomo.................................**15** B4
Hotel Puerto Rico...........................**16** B4
Mamacita's......................................**17** B4
Posada La Hamaca..........................**18** C4
Villa Boheme....................................**19** C4
Villa Fulladoza................................**20** D4
Villa Naniqui....................................**21** B2
Villa Nueva.......................................**22** A2

EATING 🍴
Asociación de Pescadores...............**23** B5
Barbara Rosa............................(see 21)
Colmado Milka................................**24** C4
Culebra Deli.....................................**25** B4

Dinghy Dock....................................**26** C4
El Caobo Tina's................................**27** A2
El Oasis...**28** B4
Happy Landings...............................**29** A1
Kiosko La Poceña............................**30** A1
Marta's...**31** B4
Panadería El Patio...........................**32** B1

ENTERTAINMENT 🎭
El Batey..**33** B3

SHOPPING 🛍
La Loma Gift Shop....................(see 11)
Paradise Gift Shop..........................**34** B4

TRANSPORT
Puerto Rican Port Authority Office...**35** B4

CULEBRA & VIEQUES

you will find great snorkeling at both ends. The point's name comes from the prevalence of a species of melon cactus in this part of the island. It's a good idea to bring shoes you can wear in the water; cacti line the sea floor. There's also not a lot of shade on the beach, so strong sunscreen is imperative.

Playa Tamarindo   Map p138

A little bit beyond Melones, this is a very good snorkeling beach. You can swim here from Melones by heading north along the peninsula; it's also accessible with a car, but the road isn't great. This is an often-overlooked beach; it's not as flashy and fabulous-looking as others are, but it offers a good combination of sun and shade, gentle currents and lots of underwater life for good snorkeling.

Playa Flamenco   Map p138

It's been listed as one of the Caribbean's best beaches, and once you get a glimpse of the horseshoe curve of the bright white sand, lined with palms and cupped between mountain ridges, you'll see why. In normal conditions the water's crystal-clear and there's little surf to contend with. This is the only public beach on the island with toilet and shower facilities, and kiosks that sell food. Camping is allowed in the seaside grove of trees.

When the wind picks up or a storm is in the offing, the currents increase. Pay attention to the flags in the lifeguards' huts – red means use extreme caution.

The beach, which is named for the flamingoes that usually winter in the nearby lagoon, is very close to paradise, and so of course is very popular with Puerto Ricans from the mainland who come over on weekends and holidays to camp and party with a passion. But come on a weekday in any season except summer and you will have Flamenco pretty much to yourself. The snorkeling is not great here, but you can find reefs at either end of the beach to entertain you.

Playa Carlos Rosario   Map p138

If you follow a path west from the parking lot at Playa Flamenco, a 12- to 15-minute hike over the hill will bring you to Playa Carlos Rosario, an antidote to the crowds at Playa Flamenco and one of the best snorkeling areas in Puerto Rico. But don't get confused: Playa Carlos Rosario is not the first beach you'll reach along this path. This first nameless beach is one of the few places in Puerto Rico where you'll see nude or topless bathers taking in the sun in privacy.

To reach Carlos Rosario, head north from this first beach, cross the narrow peninsula, and head down to the sandy basin and shade trees. A barrier reef almost encloses this beach, and you can snorkel on either side of it by swimming through the boat channel – look for the white plastic bottle marker – at the right side of the beach. But be *very* careful: water taxis and local powerboats cruise this channel and the reef, and in 1998 a long-time Culebra resident and diver was struck and killed by a boat.

For really spectacular snorkeling, work your way along the cliffs on the point south of the beach, or head about a quarter mile north to a place called the **Wall**, which has 40ft drop-offs and rich colors. By the way, a lot of local gringos call Carlos Rosario 'Impact Beach' because of all the shelling it took back in the navy days, and you may see ordnance in the water. It could be live; don't mess with it!

Playa Resaca   Map p138

A *resaca* is an undertow and a metaphor for a hangover, so you can probably picture the state of the water on this beach and the way you will feel after climbing up and down 650ft Monte Resaca to reach it. The **US Fish & Wildlife Service** (☎ 787-742-0115) maintains the trail here, and you should call them for permission as well as directions to the trailhead. You'll have to climb the island's highest hill and scramble across rocks to finally hit the beach. Bring a lot of water; it's no picnic.

Playa Brava   Map p138

As the name *brava* (rough) implies, this beach east of Playa Resaca has plenty of surf, so watch yourself. You can just about be sure that there will be no one here to help you if you get pummeled by a wave or sucked out to sea in a rip tide. But it is just this sense of life on the edge that makes Brava attractive.

To get here, travel around to the eastern side of Ensenada Honda. Pass the Km 4 marker and turn left a little way past the cemetery. Follow this road until the pavement ends and you come up against a gate. This is the entrance to a cattle farm, but it is also a public right-of-way, so park your car or bike and head due north on the trail beyond the gate. The second half of the trail leads through a grove of trees that is often rife with butterflies.

Playa Zoni   Map p138
Head to the extreme eastern end of the island and you'll eventually run out of road at Playa Zoni. It's a straightforward 20-minute drive, but the road can be treacherous after heavy rains. It's paved but sometimes large chunks wash away. There's a small parking spot next to the sign alerting you to the fact that endangered turtles cross the beach. Zoni is long and straight, with beautiful Caribbean islands popping up in the distance, but again, it's an isolated place, so use the buddy system when swimming. Some locals think this is a better beach than Flamenco; it doesn't have quite the same soft sand and gentle curves, but it certainly is stunning in its own right and is usually less trammeled. Be careful entering waters for a few days after a storm. Sometimes the heavier currents will have pulled sand away from the shoreline that usually covers rocks; it will eventually wash back in, but until then there's the distinct possibility that you can bark your shins on some very sharp projectiles.

Punta del Soldado   Map p138
This site on the extreme southwestern tip of the island has a rocky beach and terrific snorkeling. To get here, follow the road south across the drawbridge for about 2 miles, passing Club Seabourne and finally scaling a steep hill. Here the pavement stops, so pull over to the side of the road and park. Walk down the dirt road to the beach at the end (about 10 minutes). You will see the reef about 50 yards offshore to the southeast. Locals bring their children to snorkel in the shallow waters here.

ACTIVITIES
Diving & Snorkeling
Culebra has some of Puerto Rico's most amazing dive spots (see boxed text, right). You can rent snorkel gear for about $10 to $12 a day from **Culebra Dive Shop** (☎ 787-742-0566) and **Culebra Divers** (☎ 787-742-0803). Both offer half-day ($25) and full-day ($50) boat and snorkeling trips (see p140 for good snorkeling sites).

TOP CULEBRA DIVES

Cayo Raton (20ft to 50ft) Rat Cay is about 50yd from shore and the reef buzzes with bonnetfish, spotfin butterfly fish, parrotfish, angelfish and sometimes even a peacock flounder.

Whale Rock (30ft to 90ft) Cayo Ballena to the locals, Whale Rock is an arch of black volcanic stone surrounded by bar jacks and yellow tail snappers. Mind the current.

Geniqui (20ft to 50ft) Pronounced henny-key, this site has large tunnels, canyons and the largest saltwater caves that divers can explore in Puerto Rico. Again, mind the current.

Tug Boat (10ft to 30ft) Here's one little tug that didn't make it – coral is beginning to grow on deck. Best to dive in calm weather (May to September).

Amberjack (50ft to 60ft) This is an easy dive that yields good looks at amberjacks, barracuda and angelfish.

The same vendors offer dive instruction and trips. One-/two-tank dives cost around $60/90.

Kayaking
Jim Petersen's **Ocean Safaris** (☎ 787-379-1973) kayak trips have been featured in a number of magazine articles on Culebra – and for good reason. For just $45, you can get instruction and a half-day guided tour to places such as Isla Culebrita or Cayo Luis Peña. Jim also rents out kayaks for $25/40 for a half/full day.

Club Seabourne (p145) has kayak rentals for nonguests.

Sailing Charters
A few hearty sailors don't mind tacking back and forth between the British and US Virgin Islands and Culebra (see the following list). Rates vary depending on destination and number of people.

Captain Francie and Lazy Jack (☎ 787-435-9743)
Flying Fifty (☎ 787-438-5292)
Magnum Force (☎ 340-643-6959)

Boating
Culebra's only glass-bottomed boat, the **Tanama Glass Bottom Boat** (☎ 787-501-0011; trips $25-40) offers some really fantastic two-hour harbor cruises in and around the various reefs, snorkeling trips with equipment included, and other trips upon request. The

boat can generally be found at the Dinghy Dock (see Eating, p146).

The **Ocean View Water Taxi** (☎ 787-360-9807) leaves from Mamacita's (see Sleeping, below) and offers one-hour tours for $25, or fully equipped snorkeling trips to the cays with lunch and kayaks for $45.

To rent your own boat, try **Culebra Boat Rentals** (☎ 787-742-0278; 142 Calle Escudero) at the Casa Ensenada guest house (see Sleeping, opposite).

Fishing
The real fish hawk on the island is **Chris Goldmark** (☎ 787-742-0412; per half-day $200). He can take you out to the flats for some superb bonefishing, or offshore for the big stuff.

Bicycling
With its hills, dirt trails, low-volume traffic and attractions spread miles apart, Culebra is an excellent place to bike for transportation, exercise and sport. Steve Harding's **Culebra Bike Shop** (Map p141; ☎ 787-742-2209; Calle Romero), in the center of town, has serious mountain bikes like Diamondbacks for rent at $15 a day, with discounts if you keep your wheels more than four or five days. **Dick & Cathy** (☎ 787-742-0062) will also rent you wheels. You call them, tell them when and how you are coming in to Culebra, or, if you're already there, where you are staying, and they'll bring your bike to you.

Surfing
The island's not known for great waves, but you can sometimes catch some action at Carlos Rosario, Zoni and Punta Soldado. Culebra Dive Shop (p143) has boogie boards for rent.

SLEEPING
If you're looking for a rental agent, directly across the street from the ferry dock, next to Hotel Kokomo (which it owns), **Culebra Vacation Planners** (Map p141; ☎ 787-742-3112, 866-285-3272; www.culebravacationplanners.com) has some fabulous rental properties spread all across the island. Michael McCarty has excellent information about the best beaches and diving spots, as well as interisland travel. The company can find a one-, two-, three- or more bedroom house or apartment for you to stay in – some are very remote and private, while others are within walking distance of

all Dewey's 'hotspots.' Beyond that, Michael can hook you up with rental cars, trips to nearby islands for snorkeling, diving and all sorts of activities. This is a great resource for families, and travelers with special needs can be sure they'll be taken care of. Most of Michael's properties have disabled access. Rates depend on where you stay – he's got basic rooms for under $100 and mansions with views of the British Virgin Islands for considerably more.

Jim and Cheryl Galasso have run the very professional real-estate and property-management operation, **Culebra Island Realty** (Map p141; ☎ 787-742-0052; www.culebraislandrealty .com; house & apt per week $800-2600), for more than six years. There's a one-week minimum with free dock pick-up.

Dewey
Mamacita's (Map p141; ☎ 787-742-0090; www.ma macitaspr.com; r $85-100; 🕮) Pretty pinks and bright blues abound at this Caribbean-style hotel/restaurant/bar. Rooms are simple but attractive, and some overlook the canal. It's friendly, fun and upbeat, but as a locus of island nightlife (p147), you better love living with music and revelry until at least 11pm if you stay here.

Casita Linda (Map p141; ☎ 787-742-0360; casit alindabeach@cs.com; r for up to 4 people $100) This is indeed a lovely house, even though it can be hard to track down the owners for reservations! Each room is filled with local handicrafts and all have been painstakingly decorated, with beautiful tile work, canal views and a TV.

Villa Boheme (Map p141; ☎ 787-742-3508; www .villaboheme.com; r $95-125; 🕮) The breezy communal patio, lovely bay views, kayak rentals and proximity to town (not to mention the Dinghy Dock restaurant next door) are the highlights of Villa Boheme. Rooms are plain but clean and usually have bunk beds. Some are equipped with kitchenettes for guests who don't care to make use of the shared cooking facilities.

Posada La Hamaca (Map p141; ☎ 787-742-3516; www.posada.com; r $70-90) An attractive building with Spanish architecture right on the canal, La Hamaca pales a bit in comparison to the nearby Mamacita's, but overall it is a good deal. The rooms are simple; some with kitchenettes, while most have private bathrooms.

Casa Ensenada (Map p141; ☎ 787-742-3559; censenada@aol.com; r $90-130; ✖) Jackie Pendergast keeps this B&B just north of town on Ensenada Honda. The inn offers breakfast, separate entrances, air-conditioning, bayside living, a dock and free kayak use. From here you can easily walk into town or to the bars/restaurants north of town.

Harbour View Villas (Map p141; ☎ 787-742-3855; www.harbourviewvillas.com; r $95-175) Owner Druso Daubon offers modified A-frames, sitting on a steep hill overlooking Cayo Luis Peña and the ferry dock. The little villas have French doors opening on to a deck offering some great sea views and refreshing breezes. The place feels pleasantly isolated, but is only about a three-minute walk away from town.

Casa Katrina (Map p141; ☎ 787-742-3565; apt per week $375) Situated in town above the La Loma gift shop are two fully furnished apartments rented out by Bruce and Kathie Goble. They have been on the island for more than 20 years and can really fill you in on local lore. There is a three-day minimum; no children or pets.

Hotel Kokomo (Map p141; ☎ 787-742-0683; r $45-85; ✖) Impossible to miss, Hotel Kokomo is the bright yellow hotel directly across from the ferry dock. New management has given this old building a second lease on life; rooms are still basic, but now they are clean and cheery enough. The cheapest have shared bathrooms.

Hotel Puerto Rico (Map p141; ☎ 787-742-3372; r with fan/air-con $35/45; ✖) Right in the center of town, this hotel is a bit long in the tooth, and it shows. Rooms in the cement structure are none too clean and very simple (no TV), but on the plus side, it is one of the few places around that's Spanish-only.

Barriada Clark

You will find a few private homes that have converted guesthouses or apartments for rent in this residential area in the hills above town, located about 10 minutes outside of Dewey.

Villa Nueva (Map p141; ☎ 787-742-0257; r $50-80; ✖) Welcoming Ernesto Villanueva has four meticulous rooms with private bathrooms for rent. Some rooms have air-con and a private kitchen. There is also a community kitchen as well as a peaceful back porch overlooking the garden.

THE AUTHOR'S CHOICE

Costa Bonita (Map p138; ☎ 787-742-4000; www.costabonitaresort.com; Punta Carenero; r $175-300; P ✖ ☐ ☐) After many pitched battles with local environmentalists, the Costa Bonita resort is finally up and running – but it's a win-win situation. Locals have access to jobs, but they got management to agree to do everything in the most eco-friendly way possible. Costa Bonita recycles, uses 'green' energy, conserves water (and asks guests to do the same) and uses nontoxic and biodegradable materials for building and cleaning. And all without sacrificing comfort or luxury! You'll still have a stellar view, a lovely grotto pool, access to delicious on-site restaurants, and a private boat or plane to pick you up in San Juan, St Thomas, St Croix or any other Caribbean location.

Villa Naniqui (Map p141; ☎ 787-742-3271; cottages $60) These three cottages – Kachi, Kati and Ama – supply a deck at waters' edge overlooking Bahía Honda. Barbara Rosa's bistro (p146) is on the premises and lightweight airplanes buzz by en route to the airport across the street.

South of Dewey

Bahía Marina (Map p138; ☎ 787-742-3112, 866-CULEBRA; r $100-300; ☐) A brand-spanking-new facility with big, beautiful rooms, Bahía Marina's 16 units are highly sought after in the winter months. Built like minicondos, each has one bedroom, two bathrooms and a kitchen/living area with satellite TV and high-speed Internet. There's a full-service bar and restaurant; great for families and large parties, it also has disabled access.

Club Seabourne (Map p138; ☎ 787-742-3169; www.clubseabourne.com; r/villas $165/549; ☐) Club Seabourne ranks near the top of the island's luxury accommodations list. It lies 1½ miles south of the drawbridge (past the Dinghy Dock restaurant) on the Punta del Soldado road. There's a collection of villas (no kitchens) perched on a hillside above a central building with a pool, outdoor bar, library, video lounge and one of the best restaurants on the island (p147).

Villa Fulladoza (Map p141; ☎ 787-742-3576; villa fulladoza@culebra-island.com; apt $55-75) Besides running a book exchange, Villa Fulladoza offers bright rooms in invigorating colors with clean kitchenettes and fans. The shared patio is shaded by several swaying mango trees.

Villa Arynar (Map p138; ☎ 787-742-3145; www .arynar.com; r $90) This attractive B&B offers a view of Ensenada Honda from a hillside south of town. A retired career navy couple, Francette and Bernie Roeder, run this place with spit and polish and are happy to share island secrets with guests. Free snorkeling gear and towels are provided, there's a shared bathroom, and no kids are allowed. It's usually closed in summer.

Playa Flamenco Area

Villa Flamenco Beach (Map p138; ☎ 787-742-0023; studios $100-125, apt $130) Not far from Coconuts Beach Grill on Playa Flamenco, this airy two-story building with four studios and two efficiency apartments is run by Max and Esmerelda Gutiérrez.

Culebra Beach Villas (Map p138; ☎ 787-742-0319; r $125-295) The driveway is off Rte 251 just before arriving at Playa Flamenco, but this three-story condo/hotel is right on the beach. Rooms come equipped with kitchens and cable TV. Some have double beds; others can hold from four to six people in various sleeping combinations.

Tamarindo Estates (Map p138; ☎ 787-742-3343; www.tamarindoestates.com; r $175-210; 🏊) Set on lovely, remote Playa Tamarindo, overlooking Cayo Luis Peña, this 60-acre boutique resort is hard to find because it is on a dirt road that veers west off the road to Playa Flamenco. Tommy and Annie Loving took over the Tamarindo in 2001 and gave the property the gusto that comes from veteran, world-traveling innkeepers. There is also a pool, bar and restaurant (opposite).

EATING

Most restaurants close down in the mid-afternoon (around 2pm or 3pm), ostensibly to prepare for dinner (but probably for a siesta). Things open again around 6pm. Many places only take cash.

Dewey

Mamacita's (Map p141; ☎ 787-742-0090; mains $8-16) Open-air and overlooking a canal, Mamacita's (also see Sleeping, p144) is a laid-back tropical hangout serving healthy breakfasts, hearty lunches and gourmet dinners. It's a place where expats, locals and visitors all mix and mingle, and fun is in the air. Don't forget to say hello to the iguanas that like to sun themselves on the deck. There are some vegetarian options.

El Oasis (Map p141; ☎ 787-742-3175; pizza $8-20) In the center of town, across from the town hall, the Oasis is a popular hangout at night and a great pizza parlor. Enjoy an inexpensive beer with Willy the bartender while waiting for your pie.

Culebra Deli (Map p141; ☎ 787-742-3277; dishes $4-10) In the center of town, this is a hangout for school kids and a place to grab a morning coffee in town. Locals joke about the 'open-air dining' as a lot of patrons eat sitting on the low wall next door. The place has tasty barbecued rotisserie chicken (about $4).

Barriada Clark

Panadería El Patio (Map p141; ☎ 787-742-0374; dishes $3-8) At the end of the airport runway, El Patio offers fresh *pan criollo* (a bit like French bread), fresh coffee and sandwiches.

El Caobo Tina's (Map p141; ☎ 787-742-3235; dishes $4-11) Tina's is north of town in the hillside settlement of Barriada Clark, above the baseball field. This place has excellent and inexpensive *cocina criollo* (traditional Puerto Rican cooking). Tina's is definitely the place to come when you want a lot of food for your dollar. A mound of *arroz con habichuelas* (rice and beans) will cost you $4.

Barbara Rosa (Map p141; ☎ 787-742-3271; dishes $6-11) Barbara Petersen has been a respected chef in Culebra restaurants for years, and in 2002 she opened her own little bistro near the airport. The cuisine features light fare like her much-loved fish and chips (about $11). Locals claim her sub sandwiches ($7) rule.

Kiosko La Poceña (Map p141; ☎ 787-608-7964; Rte 250) Across from the airport, just after you pass the Thrifty Car Rental, sits La Poceña, a down-home kind of kiosk serving up fresh meat, potatoes and pasta.

Happy Landings (Map p141; ☎ 787-742-0135; mains $6-12) Next to Panadería El Patio at the end of the airport runway, this is another popular and economical restaurant with criollo cooking. Try the pork chops ($6).

South of Dewey

Dinghy Dock (Map p141; ☎ 787-742-0581; mains $7-18) Right next to Villa Bohme, across the bridge on the left, the Dinghy Dock is a

CULEBRA & VIEQUES

popular watering hole known for its fresh fish – the owner gets first dibs on whatever the locals bring in from the day's catch. Every Tuesday night, the Silver Truck shows up to sell vegies here. A lot of people come to buy produce and then head into the restaurant, which offers a $7 pasta dinner special.

Club Seabourne (Map p141; ☎ 787-742-3169; mains $18-25) This is the upscale inn (see Sleeping, p145) 1½ miles south of town toward Punta del Soldado. Chef Joan Ricci has the most extensive menu of creative Caribbean cuisine on the island, and it's the only restaurant with a screened porch to keep out the mosquitoes. Travelers swear by the Omaha steaks (about $22). Kevin Haggerty runs a popular happy-hour scene (especially on Friday) at the bar for older island expats who are full of all sorts of inside info.

Playa Flamenco Area

Coconuts Beach Grill (Map p138; sandwiches $5-8) Gaze over the horizon while noshing on all sorts of grilled dishes at Coconuts, a very popular eatery near Flamenco Beach. Try the thick burgers and fries (about $7).

Tamarindo Bar & Grill (Map p138; ☎ 787-742-0345; Tamarindo Estates; mains $14-22; ☽ dinner Thu-Sun) At the boutique resort on the dirt road that takes you to Playa Tamarindo, you can sit on the terrace or take a candlelit table right on the beach. Travelers and locals come here for the sunsets and lobster. We drool for the *camarones con yuccas fritas* (shrimp with French-cut fried yucca, $19).

Self-Catering

Colmado Milka (Map p141; ☎ 787-742-2253; ☽ 7am-6pm Mon-Sat, 7am-noon Sun) Just past Mamacita's is a bridge on your right. Cross it and keep right. The supermarket, the island's second largest (that's not saying much), is there.

Asociación de Pescadores (Map p141; ☎ 787-742-0144; ☽ 7am-4:30pm Mon-Sat, 7am-2pm Sun) Near Colmado Mika, this is a good place to pick up the catch of the day, although it's likely to be frozen to keep it fresh in the heat.

ENTERTAINMENT

El Batey (Map p141; ☎ 787-742-3828) On the road that leads north from town to the airport, El Batey is largely a local place that pulls in just about everybody on the island on weekends, when a DJ cranks the salsa and merengue, and a very mixed and relaxed crowd works

its mojo on the dance floor. El Batey also has the best burgers in town (under $4). If you get a chance to talk to the owner, Digna, ask her about her personal experience as a 'noncombatant' in the so-called Battle of Culebra, which forced the US Navy to retreat from the island in 1975.

Happy Landings (Map p141; ☎ 787-742-0135) At the end of the airstrip, this local favorite also draws a crowd on weekends for salsa. A number of the habitués claim to have made up a drink called the 'Monica': it requires the wearing of a blue dress and the guzzling of an El Presidente beer.

Mamacita's (Map p141; ☎ 787-742-0090) Mamacita's has a lively happy hour and after-dinner scene. On weekends, locals, expats and yacht crews from the harbor favor this place, with its open-air deck and selection of reggae, calypso and buffett. Mamacita's really smokes when *bomba y plena* drummers show up to rock the patio with *bomba* rhythms, as well as salsa and merengue. Everybody dances! See also Eating (p146).

SHOPPING

La Loma Gift Shop (Map p141; ☎ 787-742-3565; Calle Escudero, cnr Calle Romero; ☽ 10am-5pm) Situated in town, Bruce Goble's gift shop has an inventory of all-handcrafted goods that ranges from T-shirts and jewelry to watercolors and jams. Its useful tourist guide costs $1.50.

Paradise Gift Shop (Map p141; ☎ 787-742-3569; Calle Castelar) Head here to obtain an English version of the *San Juan Star*.

A rash of boutique shops has broken out near the dock area and along Calle Pedro Márquez.

GETTING THERE & AWAY
Air

Culebra gets excellent air service from San Juan and Fajardo on the commuter carriers that also serve Vieques: **Isla Nena Air Service** (☎ 787-742-0972; www.islanena.8m.com), **Vieques Air Link** (☎ 787-742-0254; www.vieques-island.com/val) and **Air Flamenco** (☎ 787-742-1040; www.airflamenco.net). There are at least five flights a day to/from San Juan's Isla Grande and Luis Muñoz Marín (LMM) airports, and more flights a day to/from Fajardo. Isla **TILDE** charges $130 round-trip to fly to/from LMM, and Vieques Air Link charges $90 to/from Isla Grande. Fajardo trips are $40 round-trip. Isla **TILDE** offers charter flights to St Thomas ($550); and **Air St Thomas** (☎ 787-791-4898; www.airst thomas.com) does charter flights to St Croix, St Thomas and many other Caribbean islands, with stopovers at Vieques or Culebra on demand.

Ferry

Puerto Rican Port Authority ferries travel between Fajardo and Culebra several times a day. The high-speed passenger ferry takes about an hour. Round-trip passenger fares are $4. The cargo ferry (small/large car $15/19) takes two hours. The authority has also been running a ferry from Culebra to Vieques at 5pm Monday to Friday, but call ahead because it doesn't always go.

To confirm the schedule and to make reservations (required for vehicles), call the **Puerto Rican Port Authority** (Fajardo office ☎ 787-863-0705, car reservations ☎ 800-981-2005; 8-11am & 1-3pm Mon-Fri; Culebra office Map p141; ☎ 787-742-3161; ferry dock, Dewey; 8-11am & 1-3pm Mon-Fri). Note: neither of these offices is great at answering their phones. So it goes.

GETTING AROUND

Most of the island's natural attractions are not near the town, and chances are that your guest house or other rental isn't either. So you will need a ride, by either rental car or taxi.

Biking, kayaking and water taxis are good options for reaching far-flung attractions around the island. See p143 for details.

To/From the Airport

Travelers arriving and departing by air usually pickup or drop off their rental cars in the airport lot. If you have not arranged for a rental car or an airport pickup/dropoff with your guest house proprietor, you'll need one of the three island cabs (see right);

$5 to $7 will get you just about anywhere on the island.

Car/Scooter

Old Culebra hands will tell you this is the way to go, even though car rentals are not cheap during high season. With more than 200 guest rooms and several dozen villas for rent, Culebra's 60 rental cars (mostly Suzuki Samurais) cannot meet the demand during the peak months in winter and summer. Reserve your car (at least for part of your visit) when you book your accommodations, and pick a reliable vendor recommended by your guest house, because some companies have been known to overbook. Those listed have proven reliable in the past. Most also offer scooter service and pickup/drop-off service.

Carlos Jeep (☎ 787-742-3514, 613-7049)
Coral Reef (☎ 787-742-0055)
Dick & Cathy's (☎ 787-742-0062)
Jerry's Jeeps (☎ 787-742-0587)
Thrifty Car Rental/JM Scooter Rentals (☎ 787-742-0521)
Willy's (☎ 787-742-3537)

Taxi

There is taxi service on the island, but the taxis are basically público vans designed to get large parties of people back and forth between the ferry dock and Playa Flamenco (where they will be partying or camping) for a couple of dollars per person. The públicos are not radio-dispatched, so getting a timely pickup has been a problem for many people heading to or from dinner at a restaurant.

Willy (☎ 787-742-3537, 396-0076) generally meets every ferry and also arrives at your door when booked. If he's busy and you're stuck for a ride, try **Romero** (☎ 787-378-0250) or **Kiko's Transportation** (☎ 787-742-2678).

FERRY SCHEDULE

Route	Passenger Ferry	Cargo Ferry
Fajardo to Culebra	9:30am & 3pm Mon-Fri 10am Wed & Fri 9am, 2:30pm & 6:30pm Sat & Sun (schedule varies on holidays)	3:30am, 4pm & 6pm Mon-Fri 10am Wed & Fri
Culebra to Fajardo	6:30am, 11am & 3pm Mon-Fri 1pm Wed & Fri 6:30am, 11am & 4:30pm Sat & Sun	times vary; call ahead

VIEQUES

Twenty-one miles long and 5 miles wide, Vieques lies just 6 miles southeast of Puerto Rico. The name 'Vieques' is a 17th-century Spanish colonial corruption of the Taíno name *bieque* (small island). The Spaniards also called Vieques and Culebra *las islas inútiles* (the useless islands) because they lacked gold and silver. But over the centuries, residents and visitors who share affection for this place have come to call Vieques 'Isla Nena,' a term of endearment meaning 'Little Girl Island.' The name implies that Vieques is the daughter of the sea and Borinquen (the name by which Puerto Rico was originally known).

Until quite recently, people visiting the island would occasionally be startled by the sound of live ordnance coming down from the sky – a loud *whoosh* followed by impact noise that's not soon forgotten. For decades, the US Navy had used a section of land and sea between the two main towns – Isabella Segunda to the north and Esperanza on the Caribbean side – for target practice. But that all ended in May, 2003 when years of protests and resistance from the residents finally forced the navy out.

Now the only sounds you'll hear on Vieques are those from nature: cows lowing into the dusk, coquís making music in the wee hours, small herds of wild horses breaking through the forest underbrush (mind you don't hit one – they do wander onto the roads). Parts of the island are remarkably untamed, having been under navy control for years, and the resulting lack of development is a large part of what makes Vieques so special. Two bioluminescent bays add to the area's tremendous richness, and everywhere beauty abounds.

HISTORY

When Columbus 'discovered' Puerto Rico on his second voyage in 1493, Taíno people were living well and peacefully (save for the occasional skirmish with Carib neighbors) on Vieques. With the expansion of Puerto Rico under Ponce de León, more Taínos fled to the island; Caribs joined them and the

CULEBRA & VIEQUES

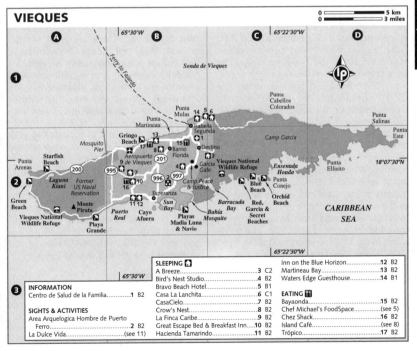

VIEQUES

INFORMATION	
Centro de Salud de la Familia............1 B2	

SIGHTS & ACTIVITIES	
Area Arquelogica Hombre de Puerto	
Ferro..2 B2	
La Dulce Vida...............................(see 11)	

SLEEPING	
A Breeze...3 C2	
Bird's Nest Studio................................4 B2	
Bravo Beach Hotel..............................5 B1	
Casa La Lanchita.................................6 C1	
CasaCielo..7 B2	
Crow's Nest...8 B2	
Great Escape Bed & Breakfast Inn.....10 B2	
La Finca Caribe...................................9 B2	
Hacienda Tamarindo..........................11 B2	

Inn on the Blue Horizon...................12 B2	
Martineau Bay..................................13 B2	
Waters Edge Guesthouse.................14 B1	

EATING	
Bayaonda...15 B2	
Chef Michael's FoodSpace.............(see 5)	
Chez Shack......................................16 B2	
Island Café.....................................(see 8)	
Trópico...17 B2	

two groups mounted a fierce resistance to Spanish occupation. It failed. Spanish soldiers eventually overran the island, killing or enslaving the natives who remained.

Even so, Spanish control over the island remained tentative at best. In succeeding years, both the British and French tried to claim the island as their own. In reality, Vieques remained something of a free port, thriving as a smuggling center.

Sugarcane plantations covered much of Vieques when the island fell to the Americans in 1898 as spoils from the Spanish-American War, but during the first half of the 20th century the cane plantations failed. Vieques lost more than half its population and settled into near dormancy; the remaining locals survived as they always had, by subsistence farming, fishing and smuggling.

Shortly after WWII broke out, the US Navy showed up on Vieques and grabbed about 70% of the island's 33,000 acres to build military bases. More than 50 years of target practice – dropping live bombs on atolls, reefs and deserted sections of land – ensued, even as local ire grew.

Everything changed on the night of April 19, 1999, after *viequense* civilian guard David Sanes Rodriguez was accidentally killed when two 225kg bombs missed their target and exploded near an observation post overlooking the bombing range. The navy suspended exercises for a year as citizens rallied behind organizations like the CRDV (Committee for the Rescue and Development of Vieques), the PIP (independence party) and other protest groups. Persistent protests on the island and a sophisticated media blitz called attention to the navy's occupation and destruction of Vieques. When the navy resumed bombing in the summer of 2000, and again in 2001, massive protests on and off the island led to the arrests of more than 700 protesters, international media attention and support from highly regarded celebrities and politicians in the US. The effort paid off in April 2003, when the navy withdrew from 'La Isla Nena,' leaving behind it tracts of gorgeous coastal land. Puerto Rican, US and international developers are salivating at the prospect of building mega-hotels and more, and many islanders are hoping some construction and investment will bring badly needed jobs.

For the time being, ecotourism, construction, cattle raising, fishing and some light manufacturing (such as the General Electric assembly plant) bring money and jobs to the island.

ORIENTATION

With slightly more than 10,000 people, Vieques is considerably more populated than its sleepy sister island, Culebra. Consequently, it has two towns to Culebra's one. The main settlement, Isabella Segunda (Isabella II), is on the north side where the ferry docks. The small port is dreary, industrial and a bit depressing, especially in the first moments of disembarkation, when cars, trucks and a flood of people crowd the street. Ten minutes later, though, the city will be amazingly quiet and empty. Most people run through Isabella Segunda en route to Esperanza, on the Caribbean side. Esperanza is indisputably prettier, with gorgeous Sun Bay public beach, and it's comprised mostly of English-speaking expat-run businesses. A stroll down the 'strip' or *malecón* (waterfront promenade) will bring you past many attractive and entertaining restaurants and guest houses.

Isabella Segunda, while grittier, has its own highpoints. There are good beaches around town, and the mix between locals and visitors is more apparent. It's gained a (slightly) wider choice of nightlife options in recent years. Both towns, ultimately, are fun and worth visiting. And since they are only separated by a 15-minute drive, there's no reason not to experience each one.

Hwy 200 originates in Isabella Segunda. To get to Esperanza, take either of two routes south over the mountains, Hwys 201/996 or Hwy 997. If you take the latter route, you will pass along the navy fence as you descend from the summits. Nothing has been taken down yet, so the gate for Camp Garcia is clearly visible on your left.

Some of the best bicycling is along Hwys 995, 996 and 201, which wind through the countryside north and west of Esperanza.

INFORMATION

Unless otherwise noted, all of these addresses are in Isabella Segunda. While some actual street addresses exist on Vieques, citizens and businesses rarely use them. Physical addresses are given when possible.

Emergency
Fire (☎ 787-741-2111)
Police (Isabella Segunda only; ☎ 787-741-2020)

Internet Access
Museo de Esperanza (Map p154; ☎ 787-741-8850; Calle Flamboyán 138, Esperanza; per 30min $3; ☺ closes 4pm) This museum allows visitors to use the computer for a fee.

Laundry
Familia Rios (Map p152; ☎ 787-438-1846; Calle Benitez Castaño 1) A few yards up the street from the ferry dock, across the street from the Chinese restaurant, this laundromat can do same-day service or you can use self-serve washers. Change and detergent are available.

Media
Vieques Times (☎ 787-741-8508; www.viequestimes .com; Calle Flamboyán, Esperanza) Published monthly in both English and Spanish; this is no longer the only paper in town (five have opened up in recent years), but it is still one of the best.

Medical Services
Centro de Salud de la Familia (Map p149; ☎ 787-741-0392; Rte 997 Km 0.4; ☺ clinic 7am-3:30pm Mon-Fri, emergency 24hr) Just south of Isabella Segunda on Hwy 997.
Isla Nena Pharmacy (☎ 787-741-1906; Calle Muñoz Rivera; ☺ until 7pm Mon-Fri, until 6pm Sat & Sun) For basic supplies and over-the-counter remedies, Isla Nena's a good bet.

Money
It's a good idea to carry cash on the island (but watch out for petty thieves) because there's only one ATM and lots of places don't take plastic.
Banco Popular (Map p152; ☎ 787-741-2071; Calle Muñoz Rivera; ☺ 8am-3pm Mon-Fri) The only game in town, or on the island, for finances. The ATM does sometimes run dry, especially on Sunday nights.

Post
Post office (Map p152; ☎ 787-741-3891; Calle Muñoz Rivera 97; ☺ 8:30am-4:30pm Mon-Fri, 8am-noon Sat) Across from the Banco Popular, this is the island's only post office. It will take general-delivery letters.

Tourist Information
Good websites include www.enchanted-isle .com or www.vieques-island.com for useful directories of island businesses, services and accommodations.

Puerto Rico Tourism Company (PRTC; Map p152; ☎ 787-741-0800; www.gotopuertorico.com; Calle Carlos LeBrun 449; ☺ 8am-5pm) Friendly and helpful staff is on hand every day to give out maps, brochures and lots of other literature on island life.

SIGHTS
Isabella Segunda   Map p152
This is the town you'll first see when arriving by ferry from Fajardo. A new project is underway to build a prettier dock, which is sorely needed. As the ferry pulls in, the crush of trucks, públicos, jeeps and people is a bit overwhelming. But return to the dock when the ferry isn't loading or unloading and you'll find a town that is exceptionally tranquil by Puerto Rican standards. In fact, you are likely to see more pigeons and stray dogs than people in the town's sun-swept plaza, even though about half of the island's 10,000 residents live in or around Isabella Segunda.

Set on a hillside and overlooking a small cove in the center of the island's northern shore, Isabella Segunda is the oldest settlement on Vieques (1843) and takes its name from the queen who ruled Spain between 1833 and 1868.

With its general serenity, 68ft lighthouse, terraced shops and homes along the waterfront, and colonial fort standing guard on the hillside to the south, Isabella Segunda has a certain aesthetic appeal. A few years ago the town had little to offer travelers except a handful of basic services, but things have changed; today Isabella Segunda boasts some attractive restaurants, more accommodation options and a comparatively lively nightlife.

EL FARO DE PUNTA MULAS
This classic **lighthouse** (☎ 787-741-0060) stands on the hilly point just north of the Isabella Segunda ferry dock. Built in 1896, it was restored in 1992 and contains a small **museum** (admission free), which is open irregularly. Come for the vista and sunset, not the exhibition – a rather paltry collection of photos and artifacts depicting local maritime history, island history and natural history of the coast.

FORTÍN CONDE DE MIRASOL
This small **fort** (☎ 787-741-1717; 471 Calle Magnolia; adult $2; ☺ 10am-4pm Wed-Sun), on the hill

ISABELLA SEGUNDA

0 — 200 m
0 — 0.1 miles

INFORMATION
Banco Popular..............................1 B3
Familia Rios................................2 B2
Post Office..................................3 B3
Puerto Rico Tourism Company........(see 4)
Town Hall...................................4 B2

SIGHTS & ACTIVITIES
El Faro de Punta Mulas.................5 A1
Fortín Conde de Marisol................6 C3
Penny Miller Trail Rides...............(see 9)

SLEEPING
Casa de Amistad..........................7 B2
Ocean View.................................8 B2
Sea Gate Guesthouse....................9 C3

EATING
Café Amistad..............................(see 7)
Café Media Luna.........................10 C3
El Patio Bar and Restaurant..........11 C3
Morales Supermercado..................12 B3
Shawnaa's..................................13 B3
Taverna Español.........................14 B2
Wai Nam...................................(see 8)

DRINKING
Mar Azul...................................15 B2

SHOPPING
Bali Llama.................................16 B3
Centro Commercial.......................17 B3

TRANSPORT
Extreme Scooters.........................18 B1
Puerto Rican Port Authority Office...19 B1
Vieques Air Link.........................20 B3

above Isabella Segunda, is the last Spanish fort constructed in the Americas (1840s). Although never completed, the fort has ramparts and a fully restored central building that houses a history and art museum. This place is definitely worth a stop if you want to see exhibits on the island's 4000-year-old Indian culture or learn about its colonial history under four flags.

Esperanza

Most travelers first see Esperanza through the windows of cars or públicos carrying them south over the island's mountains from the Isabella Segunda ferry dock or the airport, and the vista may disappoint. There's not much to see.

But seen from the deck of an arriving sailboat, Esperanza looks magical. The harbor is deep, clear and well sheltered to the north, east and south (the directions of the prevailing winds) by two tall, lush islands. The white concrete railings of the modern *malecón* rise above the town's narrow beach. And if you arrive at sunset, you will see twinkling lights and hear

music (Paul Simon's *Graceland* is popular) pouring from the cafés and restaurants that line the Calle Flamboyán 'Strip' facing the Caribbean.

Twenty-five years ago, Esperanza was a desolate former sugar port with a population of about 1500. Its residents survived by fishing, cattle raising and subsistence farming. But then a couple of expatriate Americans in search of the *Key Largo*, Bogart-and-Bacall life discovered the town. One of the expats set up a B&B in an old sugar hacienda; the other started a bar and guest house that he called Bananas. Gradually, word spread among independent travelers, and they began to check out this hole-in-the-wall village where prices are cheaper than anywhere else in the Caribbean. The dramatic beaches, snorkeling reefs and one of the world's best phosphorescent bays became additional draws for travelers.

The rest is history. Guest houses and restaurants come and go here, but at any given time Esperanza usually has about 10 inns and an equal number of interesting restaurants up and running.

MUSEO DE ESPERANZA   Map p154

This tiny **museum** (☎ 787-741-8850; www.vcht.com; Calle Flamboyán; ☯ 11am-4pm), on the Strip in Esperanza, is operated by the Vieques Conservation and Historical Trust (founded in 1984 to save the island's bioluminescent bays). The museum contains exhibits on the ecological efforts of the trust, the island's natural history and its early Indian inhabitants. Donations are welcome. Behind the gift shop, the museum runs what is supposedly the smallest aquarium on earth, a series of tanks in which baby sea creatures are displayed for a few weeks before being returned to the ocean. There's also a rotating exhibit on the island's flora and fauna.

AREA ARQUELOGICA HOMBRE
DE PUERTO FERRO   Map p149

You will find this site marked by a sign on Hwy 997, east of Esperanza. About a quarter mile east of the entrance to Sun Bay (Sombé), take the dirt road on your left (it heads inland). Drive for about two minutes until you find the burial site of the Indian known as the 'Hombre de Puerto Ferro,' which is surrounded by a fence. Big boulders identify a grave where a 4000-year-old skeleton (now on exhibit at the Fortín) was exhumed. Little is known about the skeleton, but archaeologists speculate that it is most likely the body of one of Los Arcaicos (the Archaics), Puerto Rico's earliest known inhabitants; this racial group made a sustained migration as well as seasonal pilgrimages to the Caribbean from bases in Florida. Until the discovery of the Hombre de Puerto Ferro, many archaeologists imagined that the Arcaicos had reached Puerto Rico sometime shortly after the birth of Christ; the presence of the remains on Vieques could push that date back nearly two millennia if controversy surrounding the skeleton is resolved. Visitors are welcome to stop by the excavation site, but besides the original boulders, there's not much to see.

BEACHES

There are magical sights to behold on Vieques! With the departure of the navy some new beaches have opened up, but 9000 acres on the eastern half of the island are still closed off while cleanup of ordnance and other explosives takes place. It's a good idea to check with the US Fish & Wildlife Service (☎ 787-741-2138; www.fws.gov) before heading off to explore so you don't wander into any contaminated areas.

Remember, no matter how remote the beach, you never know who's watching. Don't leave your valuables while you swim or snorkel, even on the beach in downtown Esperanza. They'll be gone in a heartbeat. Leave things locked in your hotel, or better yet, a safe.

Playa Esperanza   Map p154

The great thing about this narrow strand is that it is a very short walk from most of the guest houses, restaurants and bars in Esperanza. In addition, there is good snorkeling under the ruins of the government pier, and across the little harbor at **Cayo Afuera** you'll see dramatic antler coral, nurse sharks and, occasionally, manatees.

Sometimes this beach is clean, but hurricanes and fall storms can make it a catch-all for seaweed, beer cans and plastic trash. Playa Esperanza was at its best when the little resort near the east end of the beach was open, with its popular beach bar and cookouts. When that resort went belly up, the beach fell into decay. Rumors say that a 450-acre parador called the Esperanza Beach Club plans to open here. If it does, and the staff cleans the beach, you may discover beach-bum heaven.

Sun Bay   Map p149

This long half-moon-shaped bay, also known as Sombé and Sombé balneario, is less than a half mile east of Esperanza. It's the island's balneario, with all the facilities you have come to expect in Puerto Rico. It's sheltered and popular with families, campers and wild horses. It is also not always staffed, so you can drive in without paying the usual $2. If the gate is locked, take the easy walk east along Playa Esperanza, and then walk across the narrow sand spit to Sombé.

Playas Media Luna & Navio   Map p149

If you continue east on the dirt road that leads you through the public beach at Sombé, you'll enter a forest. Go left at the fork in the road. In a couple of hundred yards, you will see Playa Media Luna, a very protected, quiet beach. If you keep bearing left on this road, you will come to Playa

CULEBRA & VIEQUES

and knows the best spots for beginner, intermediate and expert divers.

There's a dive master on hand at **Martineau Bay** (☎ 787-741-4100; www.martineaubay.com; Hwy 200); he will do tours for nonguests, equipment provided (see Sleeping, p158).

Boating

Captain Richard Barone (☎ 787-741-1980) is your man for a 2½-hour glass-bottom boat ride and snorkeling trip ($25). He also offers a sunset trip and island nature tours, and is a knowledgeable and articulate naturalist.

Run by one of the conservation groups trying to keep the bioluminescent bay in tip-top shape, **Island Adventures** (☎ 787-741-0720; www.biobay.com; Rte 996 Km 4.5) offers 90-minute tours ($23) in an electric boat just about every night, except when there's a full moon (take the trip to learn why!).

If you plan to sail these waters, pick up Bruce Van Sant's *Cruising, Snorkeling & Diving Guide to the Spanish Virgin Islands*. It has good sketch charts of the anchorages, GPS coordinates and lots of local knowledge. It's available at marine retailers or through **Cruising Guide Publications** (☎ 800-330-9542) in Dunedin, Florida.

Kayaking

Golden Heron Kayaks (☎ 787-615-1625; www.golden -heron.com; trips $50-95) offers several different kayak options, one of them being a nearly all-day affair (starting at 1pm and including a starlit-dinner near the bioluminescent bay). Other options are less involved, but no less fascinating and unforgettable; some only feature the bioluminescence, while others include side trips into mangrove forests.

You won't get a guided tour with **Aqua Frenzy Kayaks** (☎ 787-741-0913; per hr/day $10/40), but you can rent a single or a double kayak and keep it overnight. Delivery is available, and staff will give you all the information you need to get into the bay.

Blue Caribe Kayaks (☎ 787-741-2522; http:// enchanted-isle.com/bluecaribe; Calle Flamboyán, Esperanza; $23-30) rents out kayaks to individuals and offers trips through the bioluminescent bay, with a swim stop included. Blue Caribe also does kayak/snorkeling trips in the day around Cayo Afuera. If nobody's in the office ask around for 'Pooch' – check the pier first.

Fishing

Lots of *viequenses* and travelers head for Mosquito Pier, on the northwest end of the island, reached through the former NAF Gate. You can buy gear (lure and line) at Centro Comercial in Isabella Segunda. Plan on catching yellowtail and barracuda.

Call **Caribbean Fly-fishing Company** (☎ 787-741-1337) about scheduling a fly-fishing trip for barracuda, tuna, wahoo and marlin with Captain Franco Gonzalez. Rates are negotiable (cash only).

Horseback Riding

Penny Miller (Map p152; ☎ 787-741-4661; Sea Gate Guesthouse; per hr $40) runs guided trail rides through the mountains or by the ocean, whatever you prefer.

Bicycling

La Dulce Vida (Map p149; ☎ 787-617-2453; Hwy 996; bikes per day $12) is the place to go. The shop is near the Hacienda Tamarindo, on the west side of Esperanza.

In addition to the quiet country rides along Hwys 995, 996 and 201, you will find plenty of good trail riding on the ex-navy land at the west end of the island.

SLEEPING

Vieques is a rural island. You can expect to hear chickens, dogs, cats, cattle and horses making their barnyard noises day and night. Travelers will find guest houses in both of Vieques' main towns, as well as elsewhere.

Just like Culebra, Vieques is an open-minded and tolerant community, and you can safely assume that all tourist accommodations here are gay-friendly. Quite a few of the guest houses and restaurants on the island are owned or staffed by lesbian or gay expats.

If you're looking for a rental agent, Lin Weatherbie runs gay-friendly **Rainbow Realty** (☎ 787-741-4312; www.enchanted-isle.com/rainbow). Both **Beach Chalets** (☎ 787-720-2461) and **Crow's Nest Realty** (☎ 787-741-0033; www.enchanted-isle .com/crows nestrealty) can also help you out. In addition, check the websites listed under Tourist Information (p151). These agents represent a variety of vacation properties ranging from apartments to villas. Expect to pay $675 to $2800 per week.

If you wish to camp, just east of Esperanza you can pitch your tent at **Sun Bay** (Sombé bal-